Searching for Tamsen Donner

American Lives

SERIES EDITOR: Tobias Wolff

SEARCHING FOR
Tamsen Donner

Gabrielle Burton

University of Nebraska Press
Lincoln and London

An earlier version of chapter 47
was first published as
"Ceremony" in *Mediphors:
A Literary Journal of the Health
Professions* 8 (Fall–Winter 1996).
∞
Library of Congress
Cataloging-in-Publication Data

Burton, Gabrielle.
Searching for Tamsen Donner /
Gabrielle Burton.
p.   cm.—(American lives)
Includes bibliographical references.
ISBN 978-0-8032-2285-4 (cloth: alk. paper)
1. Donner, Tamsen, 1801–1847.
2. Donner, Tamsen, 1801–1847—
Correspondence. 3. Donner party.
4. Women pioneers—West (U.S.)—
Biography. 5. Women pioneers—
West (U.S.)—Correspondence.
6. Frontier and pioneer life—Sierra
Nevada (Calif. and Nev.) 7. Overland
journeys to the Pacific. 8. Burton,
Gabrielle—Travel—West (U.S.)
9. Burton, Gabrielle—Family.
10. West (U.S.)—Description and travel.
I. Title.
F868.N5B87 2009   978′.02092—dc22
[B]   2008041074

Set in Quadraat by Bob Reitz.
Designed by Ashley Muehlbauer.

This book is dedicated to
my husband, Roger,

 and

our daughters, Maria, Jennifer,
Ursula, Gabrielle, and Charity,

hardy joyous traveling companions
on the road and in life.

I do not regret nor shall I the fatigue
expense nor embarrassment to which I
have subjected myself. My heart is big
with hope & impatient with desire.

—TAMSEN DONNER, 23, in a letter to
her sister, dated November 1824, written
halfway through her journey from
Massachusetts to North Carolina at a
time when women did not travel alone

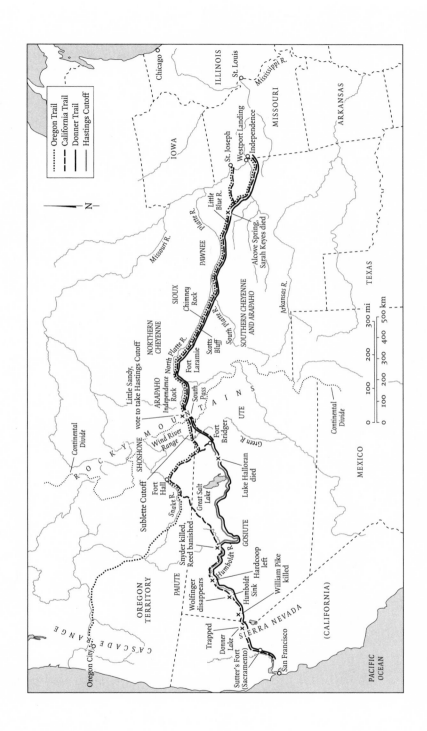

Preface

The story of the Donner Party of 1846 has been told by novelists, poets, filmmakers, and scholars, and it continues to fascinate because it's the American dream turned nightmare. En route to California, Tamsen and her husband, George Donner (the leader of the Donner Party), their five daughters, and eighty other pioneers were trapped by early snows for more than four months in the Sierra Nevadas. Nearly half the party perished, some resorting to cannibalism to survive.

Tamsen Donner sent her daughters out of the mountains with the first two rescue parties and stayed with her dying husband. The final rescue party found George's body wrapped for burial, but Tamsen's body was never found.

In 1972 Tamsen Donner came unexpectedly to our family and took up permanent residence. Over the years I have read widely and deeply on the Donner Party, including the original Patrick Breen diary and many out-of-print books found through rare-book dealers; corresponded with numerous historians, librarians, and genealogists; traveled to cities where Tamsen Donner lived; and retraced the Donners' overland route from Springfield, Illinois, to Donner Pass, California. Through the courtesy of the Huntington Library and the historian Mark McLaughlin, I'm privileged to present in one place for the first time the seventeen extant letters written by Tamsen Donner, seen in their entirety by few outside her immediate descendants.

In the decades since first discovering Tamsen Donner, I've written about numerous other subjects in nonfiction, fiction, and screenplay form. Yet, after every major project, I kept returning to Tamsen.

The story of the Donner Party may be the best known, least substantiated tale of nineteenth-century American overland emigration. There are few primary sources and countless contradictory secondary sources that began appearing soon after the event and continue to the present. The recollections of survivors years later have the strength of personal experience and the weakness of retrospective memory, sometimes confirming another survivor's statement, and just as often disagreeing. Even today, more than 160 years later, scholars and Web wonks argue passionately about the exact place the Donner Party was on a certain date, or the ages of different members. Every detail authenticated, no matter how minor, seems a victory over puzzle and mystery, and it is, advancing knowledge and keeping the past alive and as accurate as we can ascertain. But what we really want to know is *what really happened* in the four months the Party was trapped in the mountains. And that is never going to be known. I wrote an Oregon Trail of words about the Donner Party before realizing that, although I respect historical scholars greatly, I didn't want to write a history of the Donner Party. What I wanted to do was capture Tamsen Donner's spirit.

Stories, like lives, take their own form. For histories and scholarly analyses, please see the Further Reading section at the end of this book. Where possible, I tried to reconcile details believed to be true in 1977 with more recent discoveries, but overall this is a personal narrative, my recollection and interpretation of my young family and myself who found ourselves traveling Tamsen Donner's path more than a century after she had.

1

Roger came home from work one day in 1973 and there, sitting in our driveway, was a cherry red Honda 350 motorcycle. "I just felt I had to know what riding feels like," I said.

Roger apparently shared the feeling. He promptly got on the bike, rode up the hill of our driveway, realized he didn't know how to stop, braked by crashing into a parked car, and shattered his wrist. "Men and their toys," one nurse sniffed. I didn't mention it was my bike.

I was planning to ride it cross-country for the novel I was writing about two women, a real historical heroine and a fictional modern one. Going west, I'd follow the route that Tamsen and George Donner had taken in 1846—Illinois, Kansas, Missouri, Nebraska, Wyoming, Utah, Nevada, Donner Pass in the mountains near Sacramento, California— and riding back east I'd take my modern characters' route, which began in Berkeley, California, paralleled the Donners' route, and ended in Buffalo, New York. The Donner route out was now mostly minor bypassed roads, and I figured that by the time I started home on the modern route, mostly interstates, I'd be a highly proficient rider.

Now on the adventure rating scale, riding a motorcycle cross-country is pretty small potatoes compared to, say, hacking your way through the jungles of Borneo, but add handicap points of being a woman, and 34, and the mother of five children under ten, and your adventure rating shoots right up there. To me, that gorgeous machine was a symbol of possibility, every Schwinn I never rode, California waves unsurfed, and it remained that until I needed it no longer, although it was constantly associated with failure.

"Burton, Roger: PASS. Burton, Gabrielle: FAIL," the police officer called out at the end of the motorcycle riding course we diligently attended three Saturdays running. It was one of those moments that you feel sums up your whole life, **Burton, Gabrielle: Fail**, but it came as a surprise and a shock. Except for the final test, which I knew I had bombed, I thought I had been doing well. Maybe I had been and the drama of the final test blotted it out.

I had ridden my bike up a narrow plank balanced over a small barrel, an absurd test, what were we training for, the circus? The plank teetered and I tottered, my motorcycle shooting off the barrel's side, heading straight for a group of police officers. I had a vivid image of men, their hands crossed in Xs on their crotches, scattering in every direction.

"It's not *fair*," Jennifer, 8, said as I lay on my bed in a funk. "The whole thing was *your* idea."

My sentiments exactly.

Humiliated and discouraged, I eventually dragged myself out of bed, tracked down one of the officers who had taught our class, and arranged for private lessons on Saturdays in an empty office parking lot. He sat amused sipping beer while I made endless figure 8s around rubber pylons until he pronounced me ready to retake the licensing test.

He was a couple of six-packs premature. Internally and externally I was still wobbly and seeing a G.B.FAIL looming in the new officer's eyes, I ashamedly resorted to shameless flirting, only a few eye bats removed from outright solicitation.

"Well," he said, "you never forgot to put on your turn signals and I'm very big on turn signals."

Now licensed, I practiced figure 8s on Saturday mornings in the parking lot alone until I felt I wasn't a death sentence to others or to myself. I discovered that the particular style of motorcycle I had bought was too high slung for me. At stops on the road, my feet unable to plant on the pavement, I struggled on tiptoe to keep 375 pounds aloft, often lost, then struggled to *get* 375 pounds aloft, tears streaming down my beet red face while men in cars sped by yelling snide remarks about liberated ladies. Several times, big hirsute Harley riders stopped to assist me without comment.

I continued to plan my trip to California, closing all escape hatches. I equipped my 350—the smallest of the big bikes or the biggest of the small bikes that could make that kind of trip—with a windshield and fairing for highway winds. I told everyone I knew that I was going and mentioned the trip in a local newspaper article. Three women who read the article, all strangers, called me at odd hours, saying, "Don't go on this trip. You can't with five children." "That's exactly why I must," I said politely. "If I don't have adventures, my daughters won't have adventures," not saying, Butt out of my life, I'm having enough trouble with my own fears without adding yours.

I began lying awake at night, calculating the number of gas stops I'd have to make, ruminating about what powerful machismo turf gas stations can be, that gas stations, tied up with machines, mastery, power, and Vroom Vroom, are where many small-town boys on the road to manhood perform rites of passage: hang out in gangs, puff first cigarettes, and commit first thefts, one or two distracting the attendant while the others grab what they can, flashlights, batteries, candy bars, the item not important, only the deed. Forget the boys; I started thinking about the men who hang around gas stations, a thin environment and time thick on their hands, and my roaring up on my cherry red Honda 350, "Hi, fellas." From hassled at gas stations I progressed fairly quickly to spread-eagled in a remote Western town, and how would Roger ever explain to the children, "Your mother just felt she had to make this trip."

My fear shameful to me, I still wouldn't lower my terms. Several men volunteered to go with me, but in the eyes of the world they'd be my protectors, maybe in my eyes too. I almost went with a woman, finally admitting to myself that I was only considering her because she was a powerful six-footer. The trip, to be done correctly, had to be done alone. It was to be *my* rite of passage. When you're deprived of hanging out at gas stations, the symbols get more elaborate.

Erosion eats away by drips. I don't know when it happened, but at some point, my fears about the trip became greater than my desire to take it. I still worked on the novel, still rode the motorcycle, dropped it, lugged it back up again, but I stopped talking about the trip. Nobody else ever mentioned it again either.

2

The year before I bought the motorcycle, summer 1972, I went to Bread Loaf Writer's Conference in Middlebury, Vermont, nervously bearing a thin sheaf of poems. At age 33, I was away from home alone for the first time since I had married ten years before. My children were 9, 7, 5, 2, and 10 months. I weaned the baby from breastfeeding in order to go.

Many strange things happened on that mountaintop, and this was one of them: One morning, toward the end of the two-week conference, William Lederer, a famous writer and teacher on the Bread Loaf staff, stopped me on the stair and said, "Last night, I dreamed you were going to write a book about people surviving without eating each other."

"What does that mean?" I asked.

"Most people survive by eating each other," he said. "You're going to write a book that shows a better way."

"How do I do that?" I asked.

"How would I know?" he said. "It's your book, not mine."

I had no idea what he was talking about, but he was a mysterious old man—I see now he couldn't have been more than 60—who had mesmerized me with his tales of travel and adventure. He had witnessed the Long March, a massive military retreat of Chinese communists in 1934, and I can still almost stand there with him as day turned to night, watching the never-ending silhouettes of those thousands upon thousands who traversed eight thousand miles of impossible terrain for a year, only one-tenth surviving. He also trafficked in the occult, which, in that rarified atmosphere, gave him an air of spooky prescience. I didn't tell anyone about his dream.

I had gone to Bread Loaf as a contributor in poetry, then came home and signed up to audit two poetry courses at the University of Maryland. I also started writing a short story that began with a mental image of a woman in an unfamiliar room. When I asked myself what she was doing there, I answered that she had just completed a grueling cross-country motorcycle trip with her lover. Motorcycle trip? In one of my poetry classes, I found a cyclist and endlessly pumped him for details.

Many drafts later, I realized I had brought my characters three thousand miles across the country in a physical void, not one blade of grass. I studied state maps and children's geography books.

"Tell me again about coming cross-country," I said one Saturday night to my husband, who had made the trip by car several times. He went slowly, reliving his memories. It grew late; I was tired, bored. "Then we went to this great diner . . . ," Roger said.

I stared at the fluorescent light in the kitchen, his voice droning. "You'd have to go over Donner Pass."

"Mmm?"

"Donner Pass. You know, where they ate each other to survive."

I snapped awake. "What did you say?"

But I had heard what he said.

I got out books on the Donner Party, my first introduction to them. As I read the books, one name kept leaping off the page. **Tamsen Donner.** A remarkable woman born in Massachusetts in 1801, she taught school, wrote poetry, spoke French, botanized, painted watercolors, raised five daughters, and endured personal tragedy and tragedy on a grand scale.

Two of her five daughters were stepdaughters, but still . . . Her five daughters, my five daughters: I don't believe in reincarnation or people calling out from the grave, but was that not something, an amazing coincidence, a link, a bond? It certainly would carry me for many years.

It's known from other pioneer journals that Tamsen Donner kept a journal but, like her body, it was never found. My short story evolved into a novel about two women separated by 130 years, both living in times of social upheaval, both making exterior and interior journeys.

My 1970s modern heroine was a 27-year-old midwestern, Irish Catholic high school history teacher, kicking over the traces, trying to experience the remnants of the "'60s" in Berkeley, California, before the revolution passed her by. She had found Tamsen Donner's lost journal in a rummage shop and was reading it on a spur-of-the-moment cross-country motorcycle trip from Berkeley to Buffalo—nearly a reverse of Tamsen Donner's trip.

The novel, *Nearly Time*, consumed me, turned my sensibility from poetry to fiction, and for better and for worse, took over our family for the next six years. Although the Donner sections were only a tenth of the novel, searching for Tamsen Donner became an integral part of our family life.

We seven traveled to Newburyport, Massachusetts, where she was born and grew up.

We went to Elizabeth City, North Carolina, where she taught school, married, became a mother, and in one terrible three-month period lost her first family: her husband, a son, a daughter.

We spent an entire summer retracing the Donner Party's overland route from Illinois to Donner Pass, California.

We camped, our first time ever in a tent, on Tamsen and George Donner's farm in Springfield, Illinois.

I spent the longest night of my life by myself at the base of the tree where it was believed Tamsen had spent nearly five months in the mountains.

Our kids all became experts on the Oregon and California Trail, dashing off countless school compositions on the subject.

Our dog was named Tamsen.

And all the time, I struggled with how I could be a mother *and* a writer. The women's movement was challenging the notion that being a mother was enough fulfillment for any woman, and I was a card-carrying member, but guilt, depression, and fear were my secret companions. It took years to realize that one reason I was obsessed with Tamsen Donner was that she literally gave up her life to stay with her husband, and I feared that would happen to a deep, authentic part of me and my writing aspirations.

On the strength of that apprentice novel, I got a succession of agents, an invitation to an artists' colony, and encouraging words from editors— but no takers. In 1979 I finally decided the years of raised and dashed hopes were exacting too high a price from my family and me, and it was time to move on. I always said I'd go back to it, but even thinking about it was aversive.

Years passed. I wrote another novel, *Heartbreak Hotel*, that after twenty-eight rejections was finally published and won the Maxwell Perkins Prize and the Great Lakes Colleges Association prize. I wrote numerous articles and essays for newspapers and magazines, often about women trying to balance family and career, finally finding the solution: my children grew up.

In 1996, because I was then living in California attending the American Film Institute, and my husband and adult children badgered me, I went to the Donner Party Sesquicentennial at Donner Pass. *Don't want to be here. Don't want to think about any of this. Rejections. Failure.* By the second day, all the years of research I would have sworn had fled my memory forever were right there. I knew more than the rangers. I seemed to be the only person who had retraced the Donner's route from Springfield to the Sierras. Camped on their Illinois farm. Spent the night at their mountain campsite. Went to Newburyport, to North Carolina, had a dog named . . . I realized with some surprise that I was an expert on the Donner Party. I decided to write a screenplay on Tamsen Donner for my second-year MFA project. I kept this to myself for several days before telling my delighted family, still not sure I wanted to pick that scab again.

Tamsen Donner's great-granddaughter was at the Sesquicentennial—that's how close pioneer history is to us. A chance remark she made led me to seven previously unknown letters written by Tamsen. In the 1930s seven other letters written by Tamsen had been donated by Tamsen's granddaughter to the Huntington Library in Pasadena, California, but as far as the general public knew, only two of her letters existed, both written on the California and Oregon Trail. Tamsen's great-grandaughter and great-grandson had just donated the new batch of letters to the Huntington and they were not yet available to scholars or to the public. By persistence and good fortune, I obtained permission to work with the originals, one of the few outside the family to read them. Because of my previous research, I was able to understand exactly what I was reading and fill in missing parts of Tamsen's earlier life.

Some Chinese believe that when you pass your finger over the signature of a letter, you're close to the person who wrote it. I cannot tell you the thrill it was to hold and read the precious unpublished letters, one held together at the fold lines by white threads, carefully stitched by some loving descendant. And when I read copies of the letters to my husband and grown children, we were all thrilled. I wrote the screenplay, "Country of the Mind," which my daughters' film production company, Five Sisters Productions, optioned.

And so what had started twenty-six years before came full circle. I don't believe good always outs and cream always rises to the top; countless artists' unique contributions have curdled and been lost. But in this case—without getting whoo-whoo about it—I felt Tamsen Donner was speaking directly to me. The letters gave me her voice. Or perhaps it was that when her voice suddenly came across all those years, my earlier painful work had prepared me to hear it.

Before I chanced upon those letters, however, I had already become

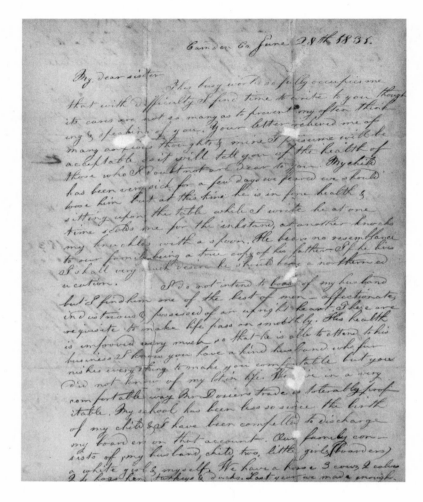

1 & 2. Tamsen's two letters to her sister, the second written on the bottom of the first, dated June 28, 1831, and January 26, 1832. *Reproduced by permission of The Huntington Library, San Marino, California.*

corn, pork, bacon &c. to serve us this year & perhaps a little to spare. This year we have no land as we had no servants of our own, Br Dorcey thought it was unprofitable. We have a fine potato patch & if we could send them to you could give you plenty of sweet potatoes as we shall make several hundred bushels.

I am anxious to go to Ohio but there are some inducements for us to stay that I hardly think we shall leave. This is indeed a delightful country where every thing is produced in such abundance that is necessary for the support of man. Br Dorcey just told me to ask you if you could get potatoes from Boston & says he will send you 20 or 30 bushels if you have room. My husband is ~~Post~~ Post Master you will please to direct so before, & write frequently while he retains the office.

I am truly sorry for Aunt Davis death. The girls are indeed alone, but she has been feeble a long time. My love to them & all other friends

Jan 26th 1832.

My sister I send you these pieces of letters that you may know that I often wrote to you if I did not send.

I have lost that little boy I loved so well. He died the 28 Sept. I have lost my husband who made so large a share of my happiness. He died on the 24 December I prematurely had a daughter which died on the 18th of Nov. I have broken up house keeping & intend to commence school in February. O, my sister weep with me, if you have tears to spare,

Your sister

a writer, and our family, in a little echo of William Lederer's dream, had learned to live together without eating each other. Our lives are shaped by genes, environment, experience, desire, and fluke. When you're young and flailing about and hungry for guidance, a sentence in a book or a conversation can seem so critically important, so *meant* for you, you copy it down and tape it on your wall, though you know you'll never forget it. A latent part of you yearning to be born is wide open at that moment and those words enter. Long ago, a man stopped me on a stair and said that most people eat each other to survive and that I would write a book that showed a different way. Another person—or I at a different time—might have laughed or thought William Lederer's dream simply curious, but I gave his words tremendous significance and, like Robert Frost's diverging roads, that made all the difference. Without my intention or even my notice, Tamsen Donner became entwined, warp and woof, with my struggle to become a . . . A what? Not a mother who wrote; that sounds like a hobby or a sideline. Not a writer who mothered; that also sounds part-time. My husband wasn't a professor who fathered or a father who taught; he just was both. That's what I struggled for, just to be both: a writer and a mother, and vice versa, giving equal weight to both, as men do.

And so, as a writer and a mother, my professional search for Tamsen Donner's history became my family's search, creating part of our family's history, our identity. Of all the countless shards that create a family mosaic, Tamsen Donner is one of our brightest, most precious pieces. With a handful of facts and buckets of myths, we reconstructed/discovered/imagined/invented her. I wouldn't understand why for a long time.

3

Eating each other to survive. Cannibalism is the first and often the last thing most people associate with the Donner Party. To eat human flesh, feed on one's own kind, is a straight shot, an involuntary shudder, to the sensibilities. Three hundred thousand pioneers went overland, yet it's the Donner Party that continues to seize the attention, imagination, and fears, show how slender and malleable the line is between civilized and savage, and ask the unanswerable question: At what point would we cross it?

Eliza Donner Houghton, Tamsen's baby daughter, three years old at the time of the emigration, spent much of her life looking for information about her dead parents, about those months trapped in the mountains. Eliza resolved to stem the tales of horror, the ghastly jokes, the stigma of cannibalism that chased the survivors their whole lives.

Until recently in our culture, alcoholism was a dark family secret; extrapolate from that: what if your parent had been a cannibal? That sounds funny but we only laugh to ward off the terribleness of it. If we today, numbed or shell-shocked from round-the-clock real and grossly contrived assaults on our senses and psyches, still recoil from the thought of cannibalism, imagine the anguish the Donner Party survivors felt, and the titillation of the much less jaded public more than a century and a half ago. Tabloids and their readers, in another form of cannibalism still active today, gobbled and gorged and couldn't get enough of the cautionary campfire tale and vampire story come true. Rumors became fact, became "history," and were passed down from early writers to later ones; even well-intentioned respectable writers passed unknowns on.

Eliza's book, *The Expedition of the Donner Party and Its Tragic Fate*, was published in 1911, when she was 68, and was reissued in 1996 for the Donner Party Sesquicentennial. She was determined to tell the truth. But what was the truth? Even 150 years later at the Sesquicentennial, there were families who said heatedly that none of their ancestors had eaten human flesh.

The linking of cannibalism to the Donner Party is so deep in our shared American cultural memory that recent archaeological digs at Alder Creek, one of the three Donner Party campsites in the Sierra Nevadas, created a stir when they found no human bones. The modern technological methods archaeologists use for historical detective work—cadaver dogs, radar, DNA analysis—can yield results never before possible, but if one reads closely, the researchers don't say cannibalism didn't happen there. While they haven't finished their dig at Alder Creek, they say they didn't find the *physical* evidence they had hoped to find, that they haven't found evidence so far that *confirms* cannibalism.

Maybe they won't ever find physical evidence at Alder Creek where Tamsen and George Donner were, but certainly cannibalism occurred at one, two, or three of the campsites and in the open mountains on escape and rescue attempts. Although some 1847 rescuers, more salvagers than rescuers, were not to be believed, credible rescuers wrote about and testified to seeing evidence at the camps; members of the party admitted or confessed at the time, and agonized their whole lives.

I've always felt that many of the retellings of the Donner Party saga made too much of the cannibalism while simultaneously not really getting it. The idea of cannibalism may be so emotionally laden that you can't even say the word without people automatically layering their own fears and revulsions onto it, but rationally, cannibalism was a terrible yet natural progression for members of the Donner Party in their determination to survive and to keep their families alive.

My own interest in cannibalism flagged pretty fast, but not my interest in Tamsen Donner. For years, not unlike Eliza, I wrote anyone who might tell me anything about her—librarians and historical societies and history buffs around the country—and most of them were kind enough to answer. But even though we're close enough in time to Tamsen Donner to meet her great-granddaughter, it might as well be eons. There are few solid facts about her or other pioneer women. Much of that brief period that forms an integral part of our American identity has dropped into a black hole, leaving us with mute statues of hawk-faced women in poke bonnets in town squares. These statues often seem interchangeable for good reason—they are. The Madonna of the Trail statue in Council Grove, Kansas, is one of twelve identical statues erected by the DAR, Daughters of the American Revolution, in different states.

Tamsen Donner, the stuff of myths, was part of the great American myth: the overland migration that expanded America from the Atlantic to the Pacific. Although the migration lasted only twenty years, the pioneers in their covered wagons on the Oregon and California Trail live deep in our self-image and our dreams. Moving West. "The West is a country of the mind, and so eternal," the poet Archibald MacLeish wrote.

Historian John D. Unruh Jr., in The Plains Across, says that between 1840 and 1860, more than a quarter of a million people emigrated overland to Oregon or California, starting in 1840 with the Joel Walker Party of thirteen people to Oregon. In 1841, the first year wagons went to California, twenty-four people went to Oregon, thirty-four to California. Overland emigration continued until 1860, peaking in 1852 when ten thousand went to Oregon, fifty thousand to California. A blink of activity in time's eye, yet it embodies all that we Americans love to think forms our national character—exploration, quest, adventure, unbridled optimism, romance, heroism, wide-open spaces, bigness, boldness, epic. It also contains other parts we don't claim as readily—sexism, racism, abandonment of the old, theft of land, violent displacement of peoples, murder, and, of course, cannibalism.

Until recently, most pioneer history and mythology was related by white men about white men. Many of the women were on the Oregon Trail against their wills—but not Tamsen Donner. Sitting on the ground in a tent in Independence, Missouri, the "jumping off place," May 11, 1846, she wrote her sister, Betsey, *I am willing to go and have no doubt it will be an advantage to our children and to us.*

In renditions of the Donner Party story, James F. Reed, the Donners' neighbor from Springfield, is almost always the hero, occasionally William Eddy. George Donner, Tamsen's husband, the nominal leader of the Party, is usually portrayed as an amiable man, not quite tough enough for the job. Lewis Keseberg, often described as a taciturn German although he spoke several languages, perhaps the most educated man in the Party, is always the villain.

Writers who get around to heroines usually choose Tamsen, passing down the same myth in variations of subtleness that she represented *womanhood* at its finest, a mother who saves her children and stays with her dying husband at the cost of her own life. She's their heroine and, always convenient for heroines, dies in the end, not staying around to make trouble. (A more complex portrait of Tamsen, published in 1977, is Ruth Whitman's *Tamsen Donner, A Woman's Journey*.)

Although I knew little about her, I was certain that Tamsen did represent womanhood at its finest, but not in the sense that old-time romantics meant. C. F. McGlashan wrote the first substantive book on the Donner Party in 1879, *History of the Donner Party: A Tragedy of the Sierra*, much of it riveting, but my stomach turned at his Victorian descriptions of Tamsen: "O, Land of the Sunset! let the memory of this wife's devotion be ever enshrined in the hearts of your faithful daughters!"

Not in the hearts of *my* daughters. We didn't know Tamsen Donner's story, but it had to be more than suttee. I was going to discover it; I *had* to discover it. She was a genuine heroine, and I needed her. And I was not going to die in the end.

4

1841 was the first year that families went on the Oregon Trail. Before that, when men went off alone into the wilderness, it was only adventure, but when men, women, and children went, they were making a civilization. After that first covered wagon went West in 1841, a few more families went every year, but 1846, the year the Donners went, was "the year of the families," with twelve hundred men, women, and children going in wagons to Oregon, fifteen hundred to California.

1977 turned out to be "the year of the family" for me.

Although I still occasionally rode my motorcycle, I had eliminated the cross-country trip from my talk and my possibilities years before. But my desire to check the historical and modern routes for my novel grew stronger. I wanted geographical details. Atmosphere. A sense of the time it took to get from one place to the other. I still felt compelled to retrace Tamsen Donner's steps.

If I was too chicken to go alone on the motorcycle, all seven of us would have to go in Big Red, our nine-passenger Chevrolet Impala station wagon. I never thought of any other possibility. There *weren't* any other possibilities. Who would take care of the children? If I had gone alone, Roger would have. I couldn't go alone, so everyone had to come with me. But going with my family automatically turned the venture into a different kind of trip and, in my heart, was an admission of personal failure.

Before we started, I made it clear to the children about a hundred times a day that the Oregon Trail trip was a trip for me, my *work* trip. Some things were givens. They couldn't complain. Bickering wasn't allowed. Flexibility was expected. (I was rigid about that.)

Roger and I laid it all out. It'll be hot, you'll get tired, bored. No No No we won't. You will you will you will, and you *still* can't complain.

Throughout the preparations, setting the pattern for every future trip we'd take, we went through a solemn, dead-serious, and perfectly ridiculous ritual: if you want to come on this trip, you have to swear to do all the above, and this, and this, and this. . . . They swore. Maria was 14, Jennifer, 12, Ursula, 10, Gabriella, 7, Charity, 5. Surely Maria, Jennifer, and Ursula knew—though they were smart enough not to mention it—that there wouldn't be any trip if they didn't go, because we'd be home taking care of them.

Another equally obvious fact to any sentient being is that with five children along, no trip was going to be just for me. Desire wears thick glasses, and I was determined to make the trip mine, if only by saying it over and over. Even though they were kids, they were going to be the Perfect Invisible Companions. I had facts buttressing my delusion.

I knew they wanted to go and would monitor/police each other.

They knew Roger and I could and would hold their solemn pledge over their heads.

They knew that we asked a lot of them, but always tried to be fair.

Although Charity at age 5 was still struggling with some of the finer points, all the Burton children were feminists and proud of it. They had marched in the great Women's Liberation marches, had stood up in their classrooms for years against sexism. They thought my work, and my right to work, were both important, and they would do their best to respect that. They knew how much the Donner Party and the novel they had grown up with meant to me; "central to you," Jennifer said years later, "it became central to us." They wanted me to be happy. In a very real way, and I don't mean vicariously or altruistically, my happiness was theirs. They shared my disappointments, saw my unacknowledged depression up close, and definitely preferred sharing my triumphs. Except for the feminist philosophy, directly taught, all the rest of this close identification was unspoken, its unhealthy aspects not yet known. For better and for worse, we were a unit: Roger, the children, I, my work, the Donner Party linked together.

So in the summer of 1977, for less honorable reasons, I started cross-country the way Tamsen Donner had, with my husband and five daughters. We would be gone from July 2 to September 1. A family of seven in a car for two months covering nearly five thousand miles: not very deep down, I was afraid that, in a less dramatic way than the Donners', the trip would be a disaster.

5

Tamsen Eustis Dozier and George Donner reached their common road in Illinois probably in 1838, maybe even early 1839. Courtships moved quicker then. They married May 24, 1839. She was 37, he was "around" 53, give or take a year. Both had already lived full lives.

George's road had wound from his birthplace of North Carolina to Kentucky to Indiana to Illinois to Texas (which was Mexico at that time), back to Illinois. Before he married Tamsen, he had buried two wives and fathered eight children (he had three more with Tamsen). More than a genial patriarch and a prosperous farmer, he deserves his own book, but this isn't it. I think the world of George Donner, but Tamsen Eustis Dozier Donner is my true love.

She was born in Newburyport, Massachusetts, on November 1, 1801, the seventh child, the baby, of William Eustis and Tamesin Wheelwright Eustis. Thomas Jefferson had just been elected the third president of the sixteen states.

She was named after her mother, Tamesin, probably a feminization of Thomas. Until recently, in all the histories, novels, and poems, she's called

Tamsen—even her daughter, Eliza, spelled it that way—and that's how I first met her. The books I later found that recorded vital statistics, the *official* books, recorded different versions: Tamesin, Tamazin, Thomazin, Thomasin. When she married Tully Dozier, her name was recorded in the *Raleigh Register* as Tamozine Eustace, and the person who recorded Tully Dozier's will, as Tully lay dying, wrote: "I give [all my property] to my Beloved wife Tamsan." I had accepted as a given that most women's family names were lost at marriage, but I had considered our first names sacrosanct. It scared me how imprecise the historical records were, how quickly one's name, one's identity, could be lost.

I wouldn't find out for twenty-three years that Tamsen chided and urged her sister Betsey to write much longer letters more frequently; oh, how happy she would be to receive a letter fat with detail addressed to Mrs. *Tamzene* Dozier. This led to the present run of writers calling her Tamzene. But maybe she didn't dot the i in that letter or maybe the dot faded over the years, because in a later letter she very definitely dotted the i in her signature, Tamzine. However, there are inkblots near that dotted i; maybe the dot is really a smear. I folded a photocopy of the letter into its own cunning envelope as she did to see if the inkblots matched up with the letters below, but they didn't. Not that any of the dotted i or no dotted i arguments negated the z. If my feet were to the scientific fire, I'd go for Tamzene—an indenture recently found is clearly signed Tamzene. But she came to our family as Tamsen, and Tamsen she must stay for this book.

It's recorded that, over a fifteen-year period, Tamesin and William Eustis had four daughters and three sons: Tamesin, Molly, John, Elizabeth, William, William, Tamesin. It was a common practice at the time to give the name of a deceased child to a later child, as happened with both William and Tamsen. At the time of Tamsen's emigration to California in 1846, only two of her siblings were still alive: the fourth born, Elizabeth "Betsey" Eustis Poor, nine years older than Tamsen, and the sixth born, William, two years older. Sixteen of the seventeen extant letters by Tamsen were written to Betsey, *my dearest only sister.*

Her road began in Massachusetts, went to Maine, returned to Massachusetts, on to North Carolina, and finally to Illinois to take care of her widowed brother William's children, and to meet George Donner.

January 12, 1840, Tamsen wrote Betsey about her new husband. *I find my husband a kind friend who does all in his power to promote my happiness & I have as fair a prospect for a pleasant old age as anyone. Mr. Donner was born at the south in N. Carolina, at eighteen he went to Kentucky, then to Indianna then to Ill. & a few years ago to Texas. But his movings, he says, are over: he finds no place so much to his mind as this.*

Well, over for a while. Six years later, on March 26, 1846, an advertisement was in the *Sangamo Journal*, Springfield, Illinois:

Westward Ho! For Oregon and California. Who wants to go to California without it costing them anything? As many as eight young men, of good character, who can drive an ox team, will be accommodated by gentlemen who will leave this vicinity about the first of April. Come on Boys. You can have as much land as you want without costing you anything. The Government of California gives large tracts of land to persons who move there. The first suitable persons who apply will be engaged.
—GEORGE DONNER AND OTHERS

The gentlemen got their eight young men, and less than a month later, three family groups and their employees left Springfield together in a little caravan of nine wagons.

George Donner was a hale 60, and Tamsen was 44. Their five daughters were Elitha, 13, Leanna, 11, (both George's daughters by his deceased second wife), Frances, 5, Georgia, 4, and Eliza, 3.

George's brother, Jacob Donner, was in poor health, hoping to spend his last days in sunshine. Until recently, he was thought of as George's older brother, but some historians now believe he was two or more years younger. Jacob's wife, Elizabeth, somewhere between 38 and 45, was the sister of George's deceased second wife—George's sister-in-law twice. (Called Betsy in many books, I refer to her as Elizabeth, so as not to confuse her with Tamsen's sister, Betsey.) They took seven children with them: Solomon Hook, 14, William Hook, 12, (Elizabeth's children by her first husband, divorced), George, 9, Mary, 7, Isaac, [5?], Samuel, [4?], and Lewis, [3?].

Between them, the Donners had six wagons and twenty people.

Their neighbors, the Reeds, had three wagons and twelve people. James Frazier Reed, 45, was a successful furniture maker; his wife, Margret, 32, suffered from migraines that James was certain California would cure. They took Margret Reed's mother, Sarah Keyes, 70, and their four children: Virginia Backenstoe Reed, 13 (Margret's daughter by her first husband, deceased), Martha, 8, James Jr., 5, and Thomas, 3.

Add the Reeds' cook, Eliza, and the eight teamsters, and thirty-two people left Springfield that April 14, 1846. One driver, Hiram Miller, found the wagon train too slow and left the party in July to pack-mule to California. Of the thirty-one others, fourteen died this side of the Sacramento Valley.

In high spirits, the little caravan headed toward the "jumping off place," Independence, Missouri, where they joined a large wagon train bound for California. The expected time of arrival after leaving Independence was four months. If all went well, the Donners would be in California before the leaves changed back home.

I never could have believed we could have traveled so far with so little difficulty, Tamsen Donner wrote to a Springfield friend two months after leaving. *Indeed if I do not experience something far worse than I have yet done, I shall say the trouble is all in getting started.*

6

Due for dinner and to spend our first night on the road at the home of friends in Bloomington, Indiana, July 1, a six-hundred-mile drive away, it was July 2 and we hadn't left Buffalo yet. The night before, Gabriella and Charity lying conked out on the couch, Maria, Jennifer, and Ursula continued working at heart attack pace with Roger and me until 1:00 a.m.; at 5:00 a.m., all seven of us were up and at it again. To be a full day late in leaving seemed a catastrophe, a barometer of the careening lack of control at the center of our lives. Every time the kids slacked their pace or got distracted, Roger and I yelled. Threatened. Carried on. You kids. You want this. You won't do that. We're not gonna. This is impossible . . . In this spirit, we finally got off.

Racing down the highway, we drew close to Columbus, Ohio, where my dearest childhood friend lived. She and her husband, a sweet soft-hearted lawyer who did more pro bono work than paid, were the god-parents of our second daughter, Jennifer. Through college, jobs, marriage, motherhood, no matter how much time elapsed between visits, we were always able to take up exactly where we'd left off—until the late '60s and early '70s when the Vietnam War raged and enemy lines were drawn in America as well. Unless you were there, it's hard to recapture the fierce intensity of that time, not unlike the Civil War in splitting up families and friends. I was there, and it's hard for me to recapture the time's intensity.

And mine. "Don't take yourself so seriously," a college chum chided me at a reunion. I straightened her out. Any ninny could see that you could only stop taking yourself seriously when other people did the job for you. By my grim accounting, the number of people Taking G Seriously was 1, women made only 55 cents for every dollar men made, just try to get a credit card without your husband's signature, judges think raped women ask for it, we're bombing the temples in Cambodia, **these things are all connected!**

During our last visit to my childhood friend in Columbus in the summer of 1970, the Kent State killings were on everybody's mind: May 4, 1970, Allison Krause, Jeffrey Miller, Sandy Scheur, Bill Schroeder, the daisy stuck in the gun barrel, the horror of Vietnam brought home irrevocably. "We are eating our young," Daniel Ellsburg said.

"They asked for it," my friend's husband said, saying what many said then but not anyone I hung out with, and a pall fell on the dinner table. We will never recover from this, I thought. Someone said this, and someone said that, and the evening, forced and funereal, went on. Later that night, my friend and I talked about whether abortion was a woman's choice or automatic murder. She jiggled her rosary beads at me and teased, "I'll pray for you." "Don't you dare!" I hissed.

And now, seven years later, we were on the beltway around Columbus, a day overdue in Bloomington. "We should call so Jenny can say hello," I whispered to Roger. He was noncommittal. "We'll be seeing Maria's godfather in California; it'd be strange to drive right by Jenny's godparents without even calling. It wouldn't be fair for her."

Fair is the stick by which parents of more than one child are driven. "Twenty minutes," I said to my friend on the turnpike phone. "We can stay twenty minutes, do you understand; we're already a day late."

"Twenty minutes," I said as the car drew up to the curb, and she raced out to exclaim at everyone's growth and beauty and obvious character, with special hugs for Jennifer. "Twenty minutes," I said, when she said her husband would be right back, "Sit, sit, he's gone for beer and sandwiches." In exactly twenty minutes we left. "I told you twenty minutes," I said.

A month later, I thought of her husband, flushed, sweating, running into the house with grocery sacks loaded with cold beer, cheeses, and salamis, maybe an extravagant sweet tossed in hastily in the celebratory spirit of the occasion. At the time, I thought only, We will never actually get off on this trip.

(*We will never recover from this.* If you live long enough, and don't polish the little stones in your heart with acid, you learn that old friendships are about much more than concord every moment and that any rift can heal. The four of us never discussed that volatile evening, but more than once in the decades to come, Roger and I were on that same beltway around Columbus, Ohio, made that same call to my old friends without hesitation, stayed for dinner, hey, it's late, let's spend the night, once rolling right into staying the whole weekend.)

We arrived in Bloomington, Indiana, at 10:00 p.m. Dinner was waiting. The next morning, we took everything out of the house and the car, sorted it on the lawn, and repacked it again. Our friend June, an optimistic, adventurous person, was staggered by the number of people and amount of paraphernalia spilling over the sidewalk. "How are you ever going to make this trip?" she whispered. "I don't know," I said seriously, my heart sinking again.

"Ay, yi, yi, yi, we're on our way," the kids started singing "Cuanta Le Gusta" as the car pulled away, a song we often sang when going anywhere. "Almost," I said, but for them movement was proof, and they sang loud and raucously, "We haven't got a dime. But we're goin' and we're gonna have a happy time. What'll we see there. . . ."

"We're going to make a cross-country trip in fifteen-minute legs," I said to Roger, wishing I hadn't called an aunt and uncle I barely knew who lived only a few miles out of the way, wishing two hours later they hadn't been absent in my life. I wasn't the only one touched by my aunt's gracious manner and the elegant breakfast she had prepared. "She gave us all beautiful china plates and silver, even though we were kids," Maria said. "She used real crystal glasses and wasn't worried that we'd break them."

"And when Charity spilled her juice on the tablecloth, she didn't mind at all," Jennifer added. She and Maria, the big sisters, digressed to give Charity some obviously needed pointers on proper behavior. "You have to be very careful before reaching out . . ." "It was just an accident!" Charity said, outraged. "That's what Aunt Melba said," Gabriella said, and with that reminder of my aunt's gentle tones, Maria and Jennifer relented.

"How come you didn't know them, Mom?" Ursula asked, but I just shrugged. I had no idea what real or imagined grievance had caused the estrangement between my mother and her brother, my uncle. In Irish families, those kinds of questions were never asked or answered and a grudge took on its own life independent of cause.

My aunt, an antique collector, sent Maria, Jennifer, Ursula, and me off with authentic poke bonnets—sun bonnets made of calico or cotton— relishing the rightness of their being worn again on the Oregon Trail. Later on at a fort, we found handmade poke bonnets for Gabriella and Charity. We all loved our poke bonnets, and have them still, but after the first day or two we only wore them in the fiercest sun, except for Ursula, who wore hers the rest of the trip, drawing considerable attention: "Well, look at this little pioneer girl! You look just like Laura Ingalls Wilder from the TV show!"

"I thought I looked beautiful," Ursula laughed recently, "but I must have looked exceedingly odd." "In fact, you looked both," I said. We were looking at a photo Roger took of us in our new bonnets, and I remembered looking out at him from under my voluminous pink poke bonnet, feeling shielded, serious of purpose, and slightly foolish.

3. Gabrielle and daughters, four in poke bonnets, in front of the Madonna of the Trail statue in Council Grove, Kansas.

7

The Donners, prosperous solid people, made solid preparations for their trip. Reading groups were common then—it's thought that Tamsen had one at their farmhouse—and in some circles in 1845, the year before the Donners left, Charles Dickens and Margaret Fuller would have given way to John Fremont's *Topographical Report of California and Oregon*. Newspapers, including the Donners's hometown paper, the *Sangamo Journal*, published letters from those who had already emigrated West. And, hot off the press, was Lansford Hastings's book, *The Emigrants' Guide to Oregon and California*, which, along with boosting California, suggested a possible alternative route that would come to be called the Hastings Cutoff.

The fever was on the land. There was a trail to California in plain view. Wagons had done it—you could even improve on the preparations of those who had already gone. It was the last frontier; you'd be in on it from the beginning. To cap it off, many fervently believed that Americans had the *right* to all that land, the *duty* to expand, bring liberty to all: Manifest Destiny.

Tamsen could open a school: an academy for girls where she could educate her daughters and other young women simultaneously. A new land, new ways, promise and possibility, she could expand on all her progressive ideas she had already had success with.

Mr. Greenleaf's prophecy has been verified, she wrote Betsey from North Carolina in 1836, tempering her pride with a little self-mockery. *Fifteen years ago, he said my plan of instruction would one day be found to be superior to the old one. My school is visited by the strangers that pass, & the visitors for miles around, and since the people have become convinced of its excellence, they are as extravagant in their praises as the multitudes [illegible]. If I should only believe what they tell me, I should think that since the days of Solomon none like unto me has arisen. But, somehow, I cannot believe they mean all they say.*

Land was cheap in God's country, a farmer's dream for George. All you had to do was throw the seeds on the ground and reach down and pick the plant. His brother Jacob could live out his years in the perfect climate. No more influenza or malaria to worry about ever again. The Mexicans wouldn't give you any trouble, how could they resist the bolts of sumptuous silks, satins, laces, velvets that Tamsen picked out to help grease land negotations? They chose peace offerings for the Indians too: shiny fishhooks, cheap cotton prints, red and yellow flannels, bright-bordered handkerchiefs, brass finger rings, glass beads, mirrors. In their delight, careful choices, even generosity, it didn't seem to occur to anybody that the Mexicans and the Indians might prefer their status quo to red velvet and gimcracks: Manifest Destiny.

Going overland in a covered wagon was not for the impoverished, unless you could hire on as a teamster. A typical outfit could cost up to $1,500.

The Donners took seventy-five pounds of meat and one hundred fifty pounds of flour for each person. Coffee beans. Sugar. Salt. Corn meal. Tamsen's books for her school and her watercolors and her apparatus for preserving botanical specimens. Medicines and bandages. Clothes with deep hems to allow for growing. Bank notes and silver coins. Horses, oxen, cattle, dogs.

Eliza wrote in her memoir that one wagon had all the things they wouldn't need till California. The second had their food and clothes and all the necessities of camp life. And the third was their family home on wheels.

In biblical lore, seven is an infinite number. For good reason. We had seven sleeping bags, seven foam rubber rolls, seven duffel bags, seven tin cups, seven plastic plates, seven sets of silverware, and seven zipper vinyl envelopes containing seven journals, seven ballpoint pens, seven sets of colored pencils. We had seven chapsticks with each person's name taped on, and separate bags containing seven raincoats, seven jackets, seven bathing suits, seven pairs of hiking boots, seven pairs of sandals. We also had a borrowed canvas tent so humongous we told people we had borrowed it from Ringling Brothers, a borrowed Coleman stove, a clever wire contraption to make toast around the campfire, dozens of matches dipped in paraffin for rainproofing, rubber bands for the braids, syringes for the snakebite antidote, a guitar, a harmonica, a camera, addressed envelopes and checks for the house payments, flour for thickening stews around the campfire, sanitary napkins, and a bag of beef jerky that, in a small panic, Roger and I had made the night before we left. These and septuple other items rode in the car with us and on top of the car in a large canvas container zippered on three sides that, until the first rain, we assumed was waterproof. The zipper didn't break until Nebraska, where we were able to get it repaired for only a little more than the bag had cost. Frequently, we mailed things home, but with the children collecting souvenir pamphlets fivefold, the tumor on top of the car grew.

8

Tamsen Donner had the 1840s, a decade of unrest, change, and turbulence, and I had the years that people call the '60s, although they started deep into that decade and spilled over into the next. The '60s started for me Easter Sunday, 1967. Maria, 3, Jennifer, 2, and Ursula, 5 months, dressed in brand-new Easter clothes, carrying their Easter baskets, Roger in suit and tie, and I, in hat, gloves, and heels, were walking—strolling—down Connecticut Avenue in Washington DC, singing a local version of "Easter Parade." "On the Avenue, Connecticut Avenue, the photographers will snap us . . ." Indeed, a TV photographer did snap us for the evening news: the quintessential American family.

We wandered over to Dupont Circle where a scruffy man was speaking to a scruffy crowd about the Vietnam War. And just like that, I had an epiphany: **The war is wrong.** "We have to join these people," I said to Roger. A little appalled, certainly without enthusiasm, Roger took Maria's and Jennifer's hands, I pushed Ursula in the stroller, and we hooked onto the tail end of the ragtag group waving their placards to process back down Connecticut Avenue, this time getting dirty looks or angry horn honks. I was nervous but never more certain of anything in my whole life.

Hippies were all the rage—in both senses of the word. I knew I couldn't be a hippy because I was old, 28, a traditional housewife with three small children. On my 30th birthday, I sobbed that my life was over. Roger and a male colleague staying with us, both in their 40s, guffawed, but I knew then, and know today, that it would have been, had I kept on the same trajectory.

I stayed in the antiwar movement, driving alone into DC from the suburbs to attend meetings while Roger watched the children. Many of the meetings seemed much too radical to share with him. I'd sit there silently, scared really, while people shouted, "We've got to kill the pigs!" Oh, that's just rhetoric, I'd think, they don't really mean that. "Burn the buildings down!" I don't want to do that, is that really necessary, what do I know, I've been duped about everything, every day Buddhist monks are immolating themselves.

On the weekends I played bridge, gave and went to dinner parties. I kept index cards with handwritten notes: Basil has an affinity for tomato. Mel, Cream with coffee. When I poured Mel's coffee, I lifted the cream bowl without hesitancy. "How did you know that?" Mel asked, flattered, and I smiled my Mona Lisa enigmatic smile, which conveyed that every fact about Mel was worth remembering.

Now at dinner parties, I blurted out, "The war is wrong!"

Mel or another of Roger's colleagues finally broke the silence. "Gabrielle, I don't think you understand the domino theory . . ."

"It's wrong; I know it's wrong; we have to stand up . . ." I tried to override the droning lecture, my emotional reactions though gut certain petering out, until I turned beseechingly to Roger, "Tell him what I mean, Roger," enormously grateful when Roger "translated" for me.

At the dinner parties I was ten years younger than anyone else, a BA from a small women's Catholic college in Michigan that valued social justice more than scholarship in a roomful of Ivy League PhDs. At the antiwar meetings, I seemed much older than anyone else, too over-the-hill and out of date to have a voice—"Don't trust anyone over 30," was the prevailing mantra.

I secretly kept my eye on the burgeoning women's liberation movement. One afternoon in '69, shortly after that tearful 30th birthday, I closed the kitchen door, and in an act of both desperation and bravery, called the Washington DC women's liberation movement headquarters. Speaking quietly so I wouldn't be overheard, I asked to be put on the mailing list. I hoped they'd put their newsletter in a brown wrapper.

And I kept caring, caring, caring for our children. Sometimes I felt like small adorable chicks were pecking me to death.

I always said I wanted to marry and have many children. Like many other things I said, it was an unexamined belief. I never thought beyond the declaration, what it meant, what the practicalities would be, what would happen after I achieved my goal. I was simply going to marry and pop those babies right out, end of story. I had an arranged marriage; I met Roger and carefully arranged it. Maria was born nine and a half months after our wedding, her four sisters within the next eight years. Some shallow-thinking people thought we kept trying for a boy, but I kept having babies because I believed with every fiber of my sixteen years of Catholic education that being a mother was what a woman was supposed to do—my *reason* for being—my destiny—my fate—and of course, my choice. It was heretical and selfish to think: Is this all there is? What if my daughters found out I thought being a mother was not enough? They'd be scarred forever.

I had been carefully taught to examine my conscience but not my situation. My method of dealing with unease was to deny it or take a nap. Roger, puzzled and pained over my daytime sleeping and nighttime tears, suggested I go back to school or, even more impossible, get a job, not having a clue that I couldn't even consider such things because I was a full-time wife and mother—my purpose, my destiny, et cetera—not to mention the damage to his ego if he wasn't the sole breadwinner. Until the women's liberation movement came along, I pretended complete contentment to the outside world; Mary and Joseph couldn't have done better. I had achieved my aspiration and if I found it lacking, that was my failing as a woman, a *real* woman. I certainly wasn't going to blab it around.

I may have learned about paradox from Jesuits who specialize in it, but I didn't recognize mine: insisting to others and myself that I only wanted one thing—to be a wife and mother—while yearning for something else—anything else—I couldn't take steps in a new direction, because they would lead me away from what I thought I was supposed to want. You might think that a good example of screwed-up Catholic thinking, and you'd be right.

In early 1970, right after the birth of my fourth daughter, Gabriella (christened Gabrielle but called this throughout her childhood), I attended my first public women's liberation meeting, a lecture given at a local public high school. It was a last-ditch attempt to save my daughters' lives. I knew my life was irretrievably beyond my control. When I got there, I found the women's movement had come in time for me. I wasn't a malcontent or an unnatural woman, or if I was, there were hundreds of thousands of us. And we were all filled with bottled-up rage, which uncorked with a joyous blast.

The First Wave feminists in the 1800s were called Suffragists, popularly trivialized into Suffragettes, and we members of the Second Wave of the women's liberation movement proudly called ourselves "women liberationists," railing when men used the trivializing "women libbers." Women liberationists. Quite a moniker, when so many women today are afraid to say the *f* word (feminist).

It was a glorious time to be living in Washington DC. My "sisters," our daughters, Roger, and I marched shoulder to shoulder down Pennsylvania Avenue in huge women's liberation parades past all the great monuments to freedom. In the massive antiwar protests, Roger and I held up our children to put lighted candles on the White House fence. We knew, as the Donners did, that we were part of history as it was happening.

The marches continued, but with a different tone after the invasion of Cambodia and the students at Kent State were killed by National Guardsmen. The Watergate lies eroded trust in government. The innocent belief of the women's movement—that we would just point out the injustices and they'd be righted by fair people—knocked hard into reality and recalcitrance. We moved to Buffalo, New York, in the summer of 1974, the day Richard Nixon resigned in disgrace from the presidency. The heady years of naïve hope were over.

But before all that happened, for just a flash in time, it seemed as if the women's liberation movement, the civil rights movement, the antiwar movement, gay liberation, free speech, the sexual revolution, and the ecological movement had coalesced into one giant movement, its spirit tremendous excitement, deep hope, and an unlimited sense of possibility. The world was bursting at the seams, exploding, everything being looked at with fresh eyes, rules and roles up for grabs. Every week, my consciousness-raising group met for six hours to talk about how we got where we were and where we wanted to go. *Six hours*: we wouldn't have dreamed of missing it; it was our lifeline. If it were a good meeting, we all went home and had a big fight with our husbands.

I started writing an article about why Roger should share the housework and, like its subject, it grew. Every week the women in my group asked, "How's your article going?" "Fine," I said, even when it hit 160 pages, unable to say even to myself that it appeared to be a book: it was simply too preposterous for a housewife in the suburbs to write a book. Then one week, I hesitantly confessed, "I think it's a book." Sadie, our leader in those leaderless times, the woman I admired most, said, "You're the *perfect* one to write a book!" An imprimatur tossed off with such certainty and belief, it gave me permission to claim the mantle.

I finished *I'm Running Away but I'm Not Allowed to Cross the Street*, the first book to be edited, printed, collated, bound, and published by the first feminist publishing house, KNOW, Inc., in Pittsburgh. I became a public speaker, carrying the word of women's liberation to such eager audiences as the "Friday Evening Baptist Potluck Get-together" and the local Kiwanis Club. I sewed peace symbols, flowers, and rainbows on my daughters' jeans, brushed their (and my) waist-length hair, and examined sexism in their textbooks. Round the clock my kids and I belted out the lyrics to the Beatles, Hair, Janis Joplin, Carole King, James Taylor, Helen Reddy, I am woman, hear me roar, I am invincible . . . I wrote poetry. I ran as a delegate for Shirley Chisholm, the first black woman to run for president, and Roger and I went to Miami to work for her at the Democratic Convention.

And then I went to Bread Loaf.

During those seachange two weeks on Bread Loaf Mountain in Vermont, I had been told I had many things to learn, but I could be a serious writer. I was proud of *I'm Running Away but I'm Not Allowed to Cross the Street*, and amazed that I had done it, but because it was a light take on a serious subject, I didn't consider it "serious writing." I even subtitled it "A Primer of Women's Liberation."

A serious writer. I had never been a serious anything.

For many years, I thought of my life as BB and AB: Before Bread Loaf and After Bread Loaf.

And in the AB part, someplace in all those inchoate discontents and yearnings roiling inside me: **Most people eat each other to survive.** I grew up in that kind of family and was determined not to replicate it. **You're going to write a book that tells a different way.** If I did that, it would mean I was going to succeed, had succeeded. I could be a perfect mother, so there, and I would be a writer too.

9 Illinois

Missouri, Kansas, Nebraska, Wyoming, Utah, Nevada, California is the route of the California branch of the Oregon Trail, but our official retracing began, as did Tamsen Donner's trip, from her home in Springfield, Illinois.

Buffalo, N.Y.
June, 1977
The Weiland Family
Rte. 1, Clearlake Township
Springfield, Illinois 62701

Dear Weiland Family,

In my research for a novel on Tamsen Donner, I read in a book (*Wheels West* by Homer Croy) that your farm was once owned by George and Tamsen Donner. In July, my family (husband and five daughters) and I will be retracing the old Donner Trail to Donner Pass. We should be in Springfield around the 3rd of July, and it would give me great pleasure to see the farm the Donners originally set out from.

I hope that we may call on you.

Sincerely,
Gabrielle Burton

A handwritten letter on the bottom of my letter came back:

Dear Sir,

There has been lots of people come to see the place they started from but it is not there anymore. It stood on a hill. You could see where the house was and the well and the road that left the house.

But the state has done away with all of that. They put a road through and took all of that. They took the whole hill. It would be in the middle of the road now. It is route 72.

They just opened it in November last year. The hill is gone and it is all level there now so there isn't any thing left of that place. Sorry.

Leonhard Weiland

You are welcome to come if you want to see. It don't look like a farm any more.

Within a mile of the Weilands' at high noon on July 4th, I visualized our showing up a day late in the middle of their old-fashioned 4th of July family celebration, worse yet, in the middle of a rare day of rest from farmwork.

We loitered down the road, eating sandwiches in the car so as not to compound our bad timing by arriving ravenous at lunchtime. That morning, as we were leaving Bloomington, June had run out to the car with two beers to go with the sandwiches she had packed us, "for your 4th of July picnic," she said. Driving in killing heat for hours, passing through every town too early or too late for parades, our 4th of July going fast on us, Roger and I split a lukewarm beer for Yankee Doodle, the last drop not down when Roger said, "The Weilands are probably Methodist teetotalers." We crunched peppermint till each of the kids okayed our breaths.

Breathing green, feeling shy and intrusive and ridiculous carrying my large reel-to-reel tape recorder, we made our way to the house through bokking chickens, quacking ducks, scattering geese, and assorted droppings. "This is a real farm," I told the children.

Mrs. Weiland asked us in to sit on the narrow, screened-in front porch, long enough for a swing, several chairs, a small table, and a refrigerator. I sat on the swing; Mrs. Weiland took a chair; her grandniece Cindy, age 13, Roger, and our kids positioned themselves around the porch. I set up the tape recorder, borrowed from Roger's lab, trying to appear casual, efficient, and professional. If Mrs. Weiland felt awkward about the machine, I was too consumed with feeling like an imposter on the brink of being unmasked to notice. I had brought the tape recorder because that's what real writers did. I thought I'd record my impressions so I wouldn't forget them. It hadn't occurred to me to prepare a list of questions; I had no idea what to ask her.

"What's that?" Cindy asked.

"What's what?" I asked.

She pointed to the tape recorder.

Not one Burton kid cracked a facial expression, but I could feel their incredulity as I demonstrated.

"You like sody?" Mrs. Weiland asked the children. She turned to Cindy, "Get the children some sody."

Sody, soda, or pop, we didn't drink it at our house; it was a big deal for our kids. They took off running after Cindy into the house.

I mentioned Homer Croy's book, *Wheels West*, with its lengthy footnote quoting Mrs. Weiland's father-in-law. She had never seen Croy's book, which surprised me—hadn't he sent her father-in-law a copy? Roger went out to the car to get the book.

Mrs. Weiland and I sat stiffly and waited. "My father-in-law was a

German immigrant," she said. "He came to the U.S. in 1897 when he was 18 and to this farm in 1905. He went to Wisconsin first, and he was in the Spanish-American War. He went to Cuba."

To capture her father-in-law's German accent, Croy had written his words in Brer Rabbit dialect, every word misspelled. Mrs. Weiland silently read the lengthy quote, looked up, and said, "Now there's one thing wrong here. He don't talk like that." She pointed to one of the numerous 'dats' (Croy's rendering of the speaker's *that*). "*Dat*. He never said that. He never used those kinds of words. He had an accent, but not that much. He talked better than that. He talked just about like we do. You could tell he was German."

The screen door opened and a man stood there, smiling my Grampa Joe's crinkly eyed sweet smile. "How do you do? Leonhard's my name."

"These are those people from New York," Mrs. Weiland said.

"Hello, Gabrielle is my name." I shook Leonhard Weiland's hand. "I'm a woman."

"Yeh, I could tell that," he said.

We all laughed. My mumble about his letter addressing me "Dear Sir" trailed off into nothing.

Leonhard Weiland laughed easily and often; Mrs. Weiland was reserved and reticent. Not good at small talk myself, she and I went at it in blurts. He was Leonhard right off; it took some time to get around to calling her Mabel. "M-A-B-L-E when I was a kid and that looked too fat. That L-E looked like a fat name to me, so I changed it to E-L."

Both of them 72 years old, they had raised six boys, none biologically theirs, and now were raising Cindy, whom they had brought home at birth from the hospital. "She's harder than all the boys put together," Mabel said a half dozen times.

The children were in and out—the screen door banging a wince through me each time—listening to the conversation, drinking sody, Ursula sketching Leonhard in her journal. "You've certainly got my nose there," he said to her, his eyes twinkling as he examined her drawing while Ursula beamed. Roger and I drank beer, drenching our peppermint breaths. On the first round, Leonhard brought two beers, one for Roger and one for him, and he asked me if I wanted one too. I did. After that, he always brought three. The heat was intense, though much more tolerable on the porch than it had been in the car. If it were like this in Illinois, how were we ever going to stand it out West? The children switched to ice cream, and we drank more beer. Every time I took another beer, Mabel's lips tightened—Leonhard seemed amused—and I hoped she chalked off my swilling as a New York aberration rather than a personal character failing.

Even if I were going down the tubes in her eyes as a bad woman, a worse mother, I was determined to match Leonhard and Roger, was not going to have this turn into an Ernest Hemingway afternoon of drinks, tales, and male bonding with Mabel and me gradually withdrawing until we found ourselves in the kitchen, might as well do the dishes as long as we're here. It was my story after all, I kept reminding myself, we were there because of me. Often when I asked Leonhard a question he gave the answer to Roger. I felt he was only old-fashioned, not deeply sexist. But then, he had my beloved grandfather's sweet crinkly smile.

Deep swift racist comments moved in and out of the conversation. Although Leonhard expressed biases more graphically than Mabel, his "niggers" snuck up with a chuckle while her "colored people" hung harshly in the air. Three miles away, Lincoln was turning over in his grave, and I was cringing on the front porch, uneasy and awkward about challenging people who were giving us so much hospitality. Now and then, in an accent strange to my ears, I made a little speech about America. My blurted attempts to sow religious guilt or shame—"Now I assume you're Christians . . ."—came out of left field. I often struggled with this conflict: wanting to simply hear what people thought versus wanting to change what people thought. The writer versus the Catholic missionary I once had been: natural enemies.

Outside the sun went higher, a dog barked incessantly as Cindy set off firecrackers. Mabel grew more relaxed, and I shuffled through feelings like a deck of cards: vigilance of my Donner Party turf, nervousness that the children would misbehave or get hurt, uncertainty as to how long we should stay, frustration that the conversation kept breaking into one on one, Leonhard and Roger doing a stereo to Mabel and me—Please god, let the tape be picking him up—and sheer pleasure and awe at being where I was.

"You want to walk around?" Leonhard asked.

"You sure you have time?" I asked. All afternoon, I was nervous about taking their time; clearly they had a lot of work to do—he had just come in from baling hay; she had a sinkful of dishes, dinner to prepare, who knew what else.

"I'll take time," he said, and we rounded up the children.

At the edge of Highway 72, he pointed to where the line from the Donners' fence had been. The year before, Bicentennial Year, with the whole country in an orgy of heritage remembering, Illinois Interstate 72 had cut through Tamsen and George Donner's original farm site, leveling the hill where their house had stood. "There was a hill, a good-sized hill," Leonhard said, "and right up on top is where they lived. You could see where the house had set, there was a well. You could see the road they left from very plainly.

"You'd thought they'd put a marker or something there, but they never would. They moved the proposed site for a golf course, but couldn't move it for this. They know'd it was there. They could see it. I tried to tell them, but it didn't do no good. I didn't want them to go through there at all. I offered five thousand dollars to go around me but they wouldn't do it. So I went to the lawyer and he told me there was nothing I could do. He said they'd take it. Regardless. After I'm gone, there's nobody going to remember that place."

Roger took a picture of me standing exactly where Leonhard said the Donner farmhouse had been: I'm standing on the flat, grassy strip between lanes in the middle of Highway 72.

"Nobody'll know where it was at. You know that? Nobody'll know. I used to show people. But I can't show you nothing. It ain't there no more. I know about where it was at. I showed you close as I could. I bet I didn't miss it two feet either way. It's hard for you to picture in mind the hill the way it was."

I stood there trying to burn the spot and its identifying surroundings into my head, wanting to tell Leonhard, I'll remember, I'll pass it on for you. But it was just a place in the middle of a highway, farmland on either side. If I came back here, I knew I could never find it.

10

I didn't want to leave the Weilands' house and dawdled as long as I could, not realizing that an Easterner's tolerance for dawdling was probably much lower than a Midwesterner's. "People don't have time to visit anymore," Leonhard said twice, but I was many months away before I heard him. "With the horse and buggy, we never traveled so fast, but had more time to get together. Now you don't have time to go see your neighbor."

After getting extensive directions to the nearest campground, unsuccessfully trying to telephone for space, all of us using the bathroom, and each Weiland signing each Burton's journal—"Now I want you to come back in fifty years to see me, you promise?" Leonhard said to Charity, who promised—my hand was pushing the screen door open to leave, when Leonhard said, "Hey. If you wanta throw out back there, if you find a place there that suits you, you can park out there. I mean there's everything there that you got out at Riverside Park Campground. I don't know anything they've got we haven't. You've got water, bathroom if the kids have to go—we'll leave the door open for you. You're welcome to if you want. If it suits you, you're welcome."

Does Bethlehem suit the pope? To spend our very first night on our own on Tamsen and George Donner's land: I was ecstatic.

We all seven put up the immense blue and yellow tent with its tangle of ropes and awnings and myriad stakes—the first time we had done it. Except for Roger, the rest of us had never put up *any* tent before. We dumped eight by ten feet of canvas out on the ground and tried to force it into a tent shape. "No, no, it goes *here*." "Well, what's *this* thing?" "Doggonit I told you to hold it till I said." "Gabriella and Charity, what are you doing inside there? Come out of there this second." "Wait a minute, are you saying we got this whole thing up inside out and it *matters*? . . ." It took us two hours. They must have rolled inside the house.

Then we took Cindy with us into Springfield, 13 years old and her first time to see Lincoln's house and tomb. In the car, she said to us, "November 16, 1976, I got some teeth out."

Maria got me aside and let me know she was mad that I'd asked Cindy; now we had a "guest" and they wouldn't be able to say what they really thought about everything they'd seen, that the farm was dirty and stinky and messy and they were bored and sweaty and hot and Cindy had never seen a tape recorder, wasn't that strange?

"Think of it as an educational experience," I said, and she relented, a good sport until I said we were spending the evening at the farm. Here I had told them that Springfield, Illinois, Lincoln's home, would probably have a wonderful 4th of July, there hadn't been any parade and now I was saying we weren't going to a real fireworks display, we were going to hang around the farm while people set off firecrackers, she *hated* firecrackers, they hurt her ears. ("Dad may come to the rescue," she wrote in her journal, "but it's *Mom's trip*, we have to do everything her way, she sure knows how to ruin a good time." But I didn't see that until years later when I asked her if she could share her journal, and we both got a good laugh out of it.)

Dad didn't come to the rescue. We sat outside in the hot dark night, talking, drinking beer, the children lighting sparklers we had bought in town. The Weilands went to bed fairly early, so we did pile the kids into the car, following the lights in the sky and the noises until we found the organized fireworks display, but I could have sat outside in the yard with the Weilands forever. There were so many layers to my pleasure. The Weilands, Springfield, Illinois, Abraham Lincoln, the 4th of July, middle America, patriots and pioneers and kids drawing their names with sparklers, hot night, cold beer, firecrackers and country smells all mixing into our incredible piece of good fortune to be sitting there on Tamsen and George Donner's farm heading west talking about the Reeds facing east on a 4th of July 131 years earlier at Fort Laramie, Wyoming.

America turned 70 that 4th of July, 1846, and James Reed's daughter, Virginia, 14, described it in her memoir, *Across the Plains with the Donner Party*, published forty-five years later. "Camp was pitched earlier than usual, and we prepared a grand dinner. Some of my father's friends in Springfield had given him a bottle of good old brandy, which he agreed to drink at a certain hour of this day looking to the east, while his friends in Illinois were to drink a toast to his success from a companion bottle with their faces turned west, the difference in time being carefully estimated; and at the hour agreed upon, the health of our friends in Springfield was drunk with great enthusiasm." I read Virginia's description aloud to the Weilands and we all marveled.

Years later, I read the more spontaneous letter that Virginia had written to her cousin a week after that July 4, 1846. It's in *Unfortunate Emigrants*, Donner Party narratives edited by Kristin Johnson, published 1996, and it shows how history gets tidied up. "[S]everel of the gentemen in Springfield gave Paw a botel of licker and said it shouden be opend till the 4 day of July and paw was to look to the east and drink it and they was to look to the West an drink it at 12 o clock paw treted the compiany and we all had some lemminade."

Leonhard's father had bought his farm in 1905, coming along looking for a better life fifty-eight years after the Donners had left looking for the same. Leonhard and Mabel met on a blind date in 1923, married in '26, and moved out there in '28, one year before the Depression, nearly fifty years before.

They talked a lot about Ma Black, a woman old when they were young, long dead now, who had owned the Donner hill; Leonhard thought she was George Donner's granddaughter.

"My father always wanted to buy that piece of land," he said, "but by the terms of the will Ma Black couldn't sell it."

"She'd been left that farm for her lifetime and the lifetime of the heirs of her body," Mabel said several times.

Leonhard bought it after she died.

He didn't have his glasses, so Roger read him our copy of George Donner's ad:

GOOD FARM FOR SALE

The subscriber offers for sale his farm lying two and one half miles east of Springfield on the state road leading to Mechanicsburg containing 240 acres of land, about 80 acres under good improvement, an orchard with bearing trees . . .

"That orchard's gone now. I know where that orchard is. We used to get apples out of there all the time," Leonhard said. "They used to have a nice orchard up there, oh, about five or six acres up there. They used to have a summer apple there—oh, it was good eating. When we were kids we used to go there and steal 'em. 'Course kids don't think it was stealing, Ma Black'd look out the window and say, 'Go on and get your apples.' She didn't care; she was nice, I'll tell you."

There is on said farm a good house with two brick chimneys, a first rate well of water. There is also an 80 acre lot of good timber facing the above land. Anyone wishing to buy will call on the subscriber living on the farm.

—GEORGE DONNER

George Donner didn't sell that farm until a week or two before they left. When he went to California, none of the six grown children, five daughters and one son, from his first marriage went with him. Eliza wrote that her father provided them all with land, and also left land for the children of his second marriage, Elitha and Leanna, if they should decide to come back. I didn't know who Ma Black was or where she fit in. It didn't really matter to me.

All that mattered was that Tamsen and George Donner had lived there together for seven years; three daughters, Frances, Georgia, and Eliza, had been born there, two stepdaughters, Elitha and Leanna, raised there; the trip to California and a new life planned there. On April 14, 1846, George Donner said, "Chain up, Boys! Chain up!" for the first time to the men hitching the oxen to the covered wagons, and the Donners started down the road for the last time to travel three miles to Springfield to meet the Reeds, say good-bye to family and friends, and leave the next morning for California. On that piece of land is where the Donner saga had begun, and Leonhard Weiland had known ever since he was a boy that that made it a special place.

"You really going right through the Donner Pass when you go?" he asked.

And when we nodded, "Then you'll have something you've done," he said. "You've started where they started from."

When Leonhard had asked if we'd like to spend the night, I'd said, "We don't want to wake you up in the morning; we're going to get off very early."

"You won't get up too early for us," he said.

All the next morning, Cindy came out to our tent bearing presents. Fresh eggs for breakfast, tomatoes, cucumbers, green peppers. Two milk glass containers that they used to pack cottage cheese in in the 1930s when they were dairy farming—"People are coming around now buying them up for antiques," Mabel said. A tiny amber glass root beer mug, also old. Drawing paper for the children. A bulletin from their church, Third Presbyterian. A color photo of Cindy, Mabel, and Leonhard in his Shriner's hat. We signed our names in Cindy's Bible.

It took us four hours to eat, strike the tent, and pack the car. Redfaced, snapping, and sweating, we got off at 11:30.

Roger and I couldn't get over the Weilands taking us in when we had nothing to give back to them, their extraordinary generosity, the closeup look at farm life. Maria felt it was a little too close up look. She thought the Weilands were nice, but she was allergic to the animals and the manure and the mess. "The whole thing was a good learning experience," she said, "but I'm glad it's over. I don't ever want to live on a farm again!" "They shouldn't have put the highway through," Jennifer said, and all her sisters echoed her indignation.

Homer Croy had the right neighborhood but the wrong farm, Kristin Johnson, the Donner Party historian, told me in 2008. It's true the Weilands lived on a farm that George and Tamsen had once lived on—that's where we spent the night. They sold that farm March 13, 1841, Johnson said, to George's son, William, for the sum of "one (and natural love and affection) dollars." They moved to George's father's farm one and a quarter miles away. That's the farm the advertisement I read to the Weilands was for, the farm George Donner sold in March 1846, the farm they left to go West.

Does it really matter? Yes, it is important for scholars and historians to get the details right. And yet, on that first Donner farm in 1976, for Leonhard Weiland and me, the Donners' spirit was still resident.

11 Missouri

All through May and June, I had written authors, museum curators, genealogists, and librarians. "A trip like this will probably be wonderful in retrospect," I said to Roger as we walked to the mailbox to mail a fresh stack of letters. "What I can't fathom is the doing of it." He laughed but I wasn't joking. I particularly wanted to talk with authors of books on the Donner Party to ask their advice on good trail books and routes, since the material I had was contradictory or confusing.

Buffalo, N.Y.
June 17, 1977
Postmaster
Maryville, Missouri 64468

Dear Postmaster,

Recently, a letter I wrote to Homer Croy, author of <u>Wheels West</u>, was returned to me stamped "Deceased." Although I never met Mr. Croy, I have read his book enough times to feel a sense of personal loss.

I wonder if any of Mr. Croy's family still live in Maryville? In July, my husband, five daughters, and I will be retracing the old Donner Trail to California (in connection with a novel on Tamsen Donner that I'm writing), and we'll be passing close to Maryville. If any of the Croy family still live there, I would appreciate having the opportunity to contact them.

25 June, 1977

Dear Sir:

Your letter addressed to the Postmaster here was given me for reply—the reason being that Homer Croy was a close friend of mine, and I have a rather "complete" collection of his works, all autographed by him.

Homer always looked me up when he came here, and I took him around to meet "Characters"—and he made mental notes of them, with the thought of putting them in a book later. If you should stop here, I will discuss some of them with you.

Hope you make out well with your book. I went back to the place where the Donner Party left on their trip West—as I recall, near Springfield, Illinois. I have many hobbies, and also a successful career as a Realtor and farmer—will be "70" my next birthday. Postponed a trip this summer to England, due to an accident of Mrs. Hooper's—(Reunion of 8th Air Force which I was in in WWII)—maybe later. Regards,

Tom Hooper

Before I had a chance to answer Tom Hooper's letter, he telephoned. He was as surprised by my gender as I was by the call, but we both recovered quickly. He had thought of something else about Homer Croy I might be intrigued by. I was much more intrigued by a stranger in Missouri tracking down my phone number, eager to talk with me.

Tom Hooper's stationery was printed with an oval photograph of him with a saying underneath, "Ask Tom, He Probably Knows." As we drove around Maryville looking for his house, we all managed to say, "Ask Tom, He Probably Knows," until we were shouting it in response to anything anyone opened her mouth to say. The rest of the trip and after, that saying would pop out of the blue as a total non sequiteur response to somebody's question—becoming part of our family language that every family has, unique shorthand that's never quite as hilarious or interesting to someone who hasn't shared the original experience.

We'd say Hoop-er, but he said it closer to Hup-per. We all enjoyed saying Hup-per a few dozen times too. It sounded funny to us, the essence of midwestern—in a way, a different language. As the accents and expressions changed from state to state, they conveyed a sense of movement: ground covered, ground changing. We imitated them half in mockery—these people talk funny because they don't talk like us—half in acknowledgment—here we're the strangers who talk funny. Many of the expressions were rural—in Indiana, a man said, "This ground's so dry you can't raise an umbrella"—and thus automatically funny to urban people totally out of their realm. Crossing paths with various mountain men, Indians, and Mexicans, the emigrants probably parroted their accents and expressions too, the strange sounds tangible evidence of a shift: new language, a signal of entrance onto new land. Tamsen Donner, a poet—probably with a unique accent herself, eastern, southern, midwestern strains all mixing in as she went from Massachusetts to Maine to North Carolina to Illinois—surely rolled the new sounds off her tongue and ear for the sheer pleasure of it.

Tom Hooper had had several successful careers and it didn't take long to see why. A man of multiple interests, he maintained a clear focus. Barely inside the house, he was asking me if, what, and where I had published. Apparently satisfied with my credentials, he left Roger and the children to Mrs. Hooper in the living room and whipped me out to the kitchen. "I have a hearing problem, and we can talk more quietly out here." When I pulled the chair out to sit at the kitchen table, he said, "You better bring your machine."

"Forgot my machine," I mumbled in the direction of Roger, Mrs. Hooper, and the children, and hoofed it back to the kitchen. I was there because Hooper had said, "Stop by." It seemed an opportunity—for what I had no idea, nor did I know what his interest in me was. As if I did this sort of thing every day, I found an outlet down by the baseboard almost behind the refrigerator, tested out his voice level, adjusted buttons, and, feeling nervous, mystified, and goofy, sat up straight in my chair winging it while he talked about some of the local "characters" he used to take Homer Croy to meet, "a doctor down here in a little bit of a town, the best authority in the entire world on giants. He's listed not in *Who's Who* but in *Who Knows What About What*. This is even harder to get into than it is in *Who's Who*."

"I didn't graduate from college myself, but I put my wife and daughter through," Hooper said proudly. He was a liberal arts college of one with a great intellectual curiosity. One of his many hobbies was lecturing at service clubs like the Tuesday Men's Forum where he might talk about Homer Croy, or his collection of antique hand tools, or his collection of Civil War books: "I have seven hundred; I've read four hundred of them." He was presently working up a World War II talk, and also had a talk on Samuel Pepys with whom he felt a strong affinity. "I've already tried it and it goes over good. You know of Samuel Pepys? Samuel Pepys and I were born on the same day. February 23. I was born in 1908, he was born in 1632. I have kept a diary since 1921. He kept a diary, a masterful diary. Now more parallel business. I write shorthand. Samuel Pepys wrote a different style—but I can read it."

He paused and said, "I felt the parallelism of your five daughters and the five daughters of this lady [Tamsen Donner]."

"There are many parallels between her life and mine," I said portentously.

He nodded in rapport and said, "Samuel Pepys wore a red vest. I have been known to do that too. Samuel Pepys went to sleep in church. I have done it. Same birthday, same diary keeping, both write shorthand. The preacher and I just laugh about this. The reincarnation of this screwball."

Mostly he talked about Homer Croy, and without warning he said, "If you should decide you want to collaborate on a book on Homer Croy, I'd be glad to work with you." Before I found his book, *Wheels West*, in the library, I had never heard of Homer Croy who, Hooper told me, had written more than thirty books, several made into movies, had traveled widely, made and lost fortunes, and was a renowned practical joker. Dale Carnegie had dedicated his book *How to Win Friends and Influence People* to Homer Croy "who doesn't need to read it," Carnegie said inside.

"Homer said he couldn't write a book about Dale Carnegie because he'd have to tell the truth," Hooper said.

"What was the truth?" I asked.

"Dale Carnegie was quite a lady chaser," Hooper said.

He showed me nearly every domestic and foreign edition of Croy's books, paperbacks, hardbacks, original manuscripts; he wanted to own them all because he was a collector, but he was not an indiscriminate admirer. "He wrote a lot of them that bombed out, you know."

Five years already invested in a book that seemed destined to be endless, for a moment I toyed with the idea of a book about Croy, a concrete project with a beginning, middle, and end, as a way out of my dilemma. I thanked Hooper and said I couldn't, and he reserved the possibility that I might change my mind.

I didn't tell him that my only interest in Croy lay in his connection to the Donner Party, and the more Hooper told me about Croy's other books and joke postcards, the less interest I had. Tom Hooper's connection to Homer Croy—now that was interesting. What also fascinated me was the way the printed word rippled out in unknown circles: Homer Croy was responsible for my sitting there talking with Tom Hooper as earlier Croy had been for my meeting Leonhard Weiland on the old Donner farm in Springfield, Illinois.

While we talked in the kitchen, organ music and laughter wafted in from the living room. "Mrs. Hooper teaches fourth grade," Ursula said. "I hope my new teacher will be that much fun." Home from the hospital only two weeks for a broken pelvis, Mrs. Hooper had baked a cake for our visit. ("She knew we were coming and she baked a cake, baked a cake . . . " the kids sang in the car for a hundred miles or so.) After she served us iced tea and the best lemon cake I ever tasted, before or since, Tom Hooper stamped envelopes for each of the children with his extensive collection of rubber stamps, one of which was **Ask Tom, He Probably Knows**.

Everything speeded up at the end; Hooper got nervous for reasons unclear to me; after taking photos indoors and outdoors, Polaroid and regular, he raced off to the car to get the children pencils; there was a lightning trip just for Roger and me back inside the house down to the basement to see his collection of cast iron seats, antique farm implements, brass and nickel harness, thirty-five hundred books, two wagon wheels from the Pony Express so beautifully finished covetousness leapt in me; he ran all around the basement from one thing to another, "Come here, come here," and we darted between the washing machine and the dryer over to a dim board of hardware tools to see one that nobody else had one like; "Come on," we ran behind the water heater to something else, he was red-faced and sweating; I was afraid he was going to have a heart attack; I began heading toward the stairs, "Thank you so much . . . " "But I haven't shown you the . . . " and we were off again. Outside he ran back in to get me a Civil War pamphlet he had published; he autographed it for me and also gave me a card showing Homer Croy in front of a billboard he'd made up to advertise one of his books.

As fast as his agitation had come, it left. As we drove away, he was sitting on the porch with Mrs. Hooper waving casually as if he had all the time in the world. Initially I thought the children had made him nervous—not their behavior, which was perfect, but their sheer numbers. Maybe he had assumed we were staying a day or two, had planned to show us the old Croy place and "characters" of interest and was disconcerted when we were suddenly leaving. Maybe he was just hungry, as we had arrived before 5:00 p.m. and it was now past 7:00 p.m.

First the Weilands, and now the Hoopers: Roger and I were amazed by the warm welcomes, not realizing for years that our amazement said as much about us as it did about them. Although the Weilands were only tangentially connected to the Donners and the Hoopers not even that, both made me feel I was on the right track. That they accepted me as a writer and took my quest seriously also made me feel legitimate: a real writer.

12

When I say that our children had been perfect at the Weilands and the Hoopers, that's not an exaggeration. Behind closed doors, they horsed around, cut up, vied for attention, fought, yelled, but out in public, they were *expected* to be perfect. From the time they were tiny, I had taught them that perfect behavior was the price of admission to the adult world. I often prefaced our entrance into a nice restaurant or theater or museum with the following: "In our culture, people don't really like children. If you want to go in here, you can't act like a child."

Before I got into the women's movement, the children were both extensions and reflections of me: the *mother*. By the time I finally started working on an identity of my own, their public behavior was almost hopelessly impeccable.

When we had guests for dinner, they were always included, expected to listen to the conversation, wait their turn to ask questions or contribute comments, and clear the dishes after. The Burton children in their clever disguise of adults in little kid suits were often praised by real adults, not only for their manners but also for their conversational skills, which often meant a conversational skill not everyone knows: active listening.

Once, after they were grown and I had discovered with some astonishment in therapy that I had a few control issues, I lamented not having let them act like children more frequently in public—just act up sometimes because they were tired, hungry, bored, just *because they were kids*. When I told Gabriella this, she said, "Well, it wasn't as if we didn't go to playgrounds and run and scream with kids in the neighborhood." "I asked too much of you," I said, and without agreeing or disagreeing, she said simply, "We saw worlds we would never have seen."

Near the Hoopers and Maryville, Missouri, which was right on the Oregon Trail, was a state park on the Lewis and Clark Trail. We spent the night on the edge of a small lake called Big Lake, talked about Sacajawea, the Shoshone Indian woman who had guided Lewis and Clark, and tried to see what they had seen. The physical setting still beautiful, the lake was polluted with motorboat oil, the ground layered with hundreds of metal tabs from pop and beer cans, cigarette butts, broken beer bottles.

After I told Charity, "I'm sorry, honey, you can't bring them along with us as pets," she and Gabriella stuffed their pockets full of tiny inch-long peeper frogs that later made their escape inside our tent and, with high-pitched peeps and tiny poings, hopped on us all night long. It got funny after a while. Every time a little poing made someone jump, Ursula begged, "Don't move! You'll squash them." "I think I'm going to make frog legs for breakfast," Roger said, getting a simultaneous "Dadddddd!" from the three oldest, Gabriella and Charity continuing to lie *very* still, riding out the peeps and poings, until they realized nobody was mad at them. "Ping-_Pong_!" Charity said, cracking up Gabriella and herself, with Roger and me squeezing hands in amusement over their obvious relief. The peeping chorus performed most of the long night.

I finally figured out that the sponge rubber pads under our sleeping bags were making my eyes tear copiously, swollen nearly shut in the morning. Jennifer lost Roger's set of car keys, and Roger flipped. We had two sets of keys in case anything happened, but nothing was supposed to happen this early on the trip. We spent an hour taking everything off of and out of the car well, finally finding the keys underneath the car by the front wheel. It poured rain. We threw the tent and all our paraphernalia into the back of the car and sat squinched up in the first and second seats, the car steaming, the wet canvas reeking, waiting for the rain to lessen so we could repack the top. After two hours, we just drove away.

The Donners by this point, almost a month out, nearly to Independence, Missouri, would have had their routine down, their whole act in shape. We, four days out, had a few bugs to iron out. It took us hours to unload, hours to load; the lock on the back door was broken; the air conditioner was broken; the heat was killing us: we were like the clown car in the circus.

13

We headed for Independence, Missouri, which—with St. Joseph, Missouri, in 1846, and later other towns along the Missouri River, Westport, and Council Bluffs, Iowa—was a "jumping off place" for the pioneers. They came from all over to Independence, spending days or weeks buying supplies, repairing wagons, shoeing animals, attending meetings, and hooking up with others to "jump off" as soon as the prairie grasses freshened, so the animals could feed freely.

The night before they left Independence, Tamsen wrote her sister Betsey, back in Newburyport, Massachusetts.

Independence, Mo, May 11th, 1846

My dear sister,

I commenced writing to you some months ago but the letter was laid aside to be finished the next day & was never touched. A nice sheet of pink letter paper was taken out & has got so much soiled that it cannot be written upon & now in the midst of preparation for starting across the mountains I am seated on the grass in the midst of the tent to say a few words to my dearest only sister. One would suppose that I loved her but little or I should have not neglected her so long, but I have heard from you by Mr. Greenleaf & every month have intended to write. My three daughters are round me, one at my side trying to sew, Georgeanna fixing herself up in an old indiarubber cap, & Eliza Poor knocking on my paper asking me ever so many questions. They often talk to me of Aunty Poor. I can give you no idea of the hurry of this place at this time. It is supposed there will be 7000 [sic, probably meaning 700] wagons start from this place, this season. We go to California, to the bay of Francisco. It is a four months trip. We have three waggons furnished with food & clothing &c. drawn by three yoke of oxen each. We take cows along & milk them & have some butter though not as much as we would like. I am willing to go & have no doubt it will be an advantage to our children & to us. I came here last evening & start tomorrow morning on the long journey. Wm's family was well when I left Springfield a month ago. He will write to you soon as he finds another home. He says he has received no answer to his two last letters, is about to start to Wisconsin as he considers Illinois unhealthy.

Farewell my sister, you shall hear from me as soon as I have an opportunity, Love to Mr. Poor, the children & all friends. Farewell

T.E. Donner

This widely published letter was one of the two letters I knew about at the time of our cross-country trip. Of the seventeen letters now known, it's the sixteenth.

The first time I read this letter, shortly after I had begun the research for the Donner portion of my novel, I secretly felt let down. Already deep into the women's movement, I found the letter's tone too simple, inadequate somehow for the heroine I was seeking, inadequate for my expectations, vague as they were. Now I know that that *nice sheet of pink paper* was what I was running away from, but then, an expert in denial, I was able to almost instantly deny my disappointment. I didn't have to mention that pink paper to anyone, not even myself. I read the letter many times over many years, and luckily a time came when I began to really *see* Tamsen Donner sitting there on the ground in the middle of a tent the night before a momentous undertaking, the noise and colors and confusion of a country fair swirling around her, and right plunk on top of her, her three little girls, Frances, 5, Georgia, 4, Eliza, 3, sewing, knocking the paper, clowning in an oil cloth cap, "Look at me, Momma. Look," everybody clambering on her and pestering her when she was trying to write her *dearest only sister*. At some point, the letter, its writer, came to seem so good-natured, so patient, as to be a model of good humor. Best of all, she was having her cake and eating it too.

After that pink paper and wealth of domestic detail, I was exhilarated by the single sentence slipped into the middle, *I am willing to go and have no doubt it will be an advantage to our children and to us*. Tamsen Donner was not being taken on the trail against her will, and she wanted her sister to know that.

And that signature, *T.E. Donner*, formal for us now, masculine, but a sister's signature then. I grew to love that *T.E. Donner*, Tamsen Eustis Donner, her birth name providing her middle initial. Since joining the women's movement, I had begun using my birth name for my middle initial also. My daughters kept their names when they married—"My husband and I both kept our names," they told people who commented— which pleased me, although I would never have dreamed of keeping my "maiden" name. As girls in my generation, we practiced both our penmanship and our fantasies by writing out possible married names, Mrs. Tom Sabo, Mrs. James Mullen; at my wedding reception, one of my friends whispered in my ear her approval of my choice of husband and my new status: "Mrs. *Doctor* Burton!"

Tamsen's other letter written on the trail was signed *Mrs George Donner*. I gave her the benefit of her times on that one, but as Bob Dylan and I knew, the times were a changing: any letter addressed to Mrs. Roger Burton in the 1970s, I scrawled across the front, "Deceased. Return to Sender."

14

There are many parallels between her life and mine. I told Tom Hooper that, and for years, I was always saying or thinking that, as if there was some mystical tie between Tamsen Donner and me. But, other than the five daughters, what were the parallels? She was a dedicated schoolteacher; after teaching one year, I had peeled down the highway June 1, yelling, "School's out!" and cashed in my teacher's retirement. I hemmed and mended my children's clothes and once even made slipcovers, but I certainly didn't knit stockings or make leather vests from scratch. I wasn't an Easterner, fluent in French, a watercolorist, a skilled amateur botanist, a member of the German Prairie Christian Church . . . Two of her five daughters were stepdaughters—even that wasn't a direct parallel.

After a lifetime of male protagonists in history and fiction, women liberationists in the late 1960s and early 1970s wanted our founding mothers, to retrieve our history, or as some said then, herstory, <u>her</u> story. That Tamsen Donner was a woman was not only important to me but a necessary requirement. She came to me at a time when I was most hungry for heroines and role models, and I welcomed her with open arms. But there were other strong, brave women in the Donner Party; I felt no such affinity or parallels with them.

Margret Reed, 32, though not in good health, tried to walk out over the mountains. Her husband banished, her personal fortunes dramatically reversed, she kept her family together and alive. In the starkest of circumstances, she prepared a Christmas celebration for her children.

Peggy Breen, mother of seven, sometimes stereotyped as a shrew, kept her entire family alive with her remarkable strength, determination, and focus.

Margret Reed, Peggy Breen, Elizabeth Graves, Levinah Murphy, all valiant women, may have shared some of the same qualities that drew me to Tamsen, but Margret had migraines, Peggy was Irish and certainly not lace-curtain Irish—the distinctions between that and shanty Irish learned at my mother's knee, not that I ever paid attention to such things—Elizabeth and Levinah both seemed old and matronly, though Elizabeth was Tamsen's age, Levinah mine . . . Whatever the reasons, their names didn't leap off the page.

My previous heroes had been Tom Dooley, the handsome Catholic doctor who ran away from a cushy life in St. Louis to practice "jungle medicine" in Asia, and a character from a novel by Miles Connolly, Mr. Blue, a passionate Catholic wildly in love with life, who teetered on the edge of tall buildings, tying twenty-dollar bills to balloons and gleefully releasing them. Highly romantic characters who both defied convention colorfully while having deep contemplative sides, but still quite a distance from Tamsen Donner.

Yet I never wondered once why she inspired me, why I was immediately drawn to such a disturbing, remote character.

From the hill of years I stand on now, the reasons seem quite clear.

I thought her a tragic heroine, the adjective as important as the noun. She had suffered tragedy and triumphed over it, which to me translated to depth and hope, both of which I desperately wanted to have. She had been marked by life and I had a few marks too. When I was 19, a man told me I had the most tragic face he had ever seen, and I thought it was a compliment. I also thought he could see into my soul.

She seemed restless, seemed to want *more*.

Until the invisible well-oiled gates of the Institution of Marriage slid soundlessly shut, I always wanted *more*, whatever and wherever it was. My mother always wanted out of Michigan and, although I made it a principle not to identify with her in anything, I wanted out of Michigan too. Lakes and evergreens were fine in their place, but it wasn't my place, I had a big-city lights and excitement soul. Throughout high school and college I repeatedly and unconsciously doodled I *must escape* in the margins of books—in my French book, *Je doit escape*, accent over the *e*. I wanted to escape from a small town and an unhappy family, but it was deeper and wider than that.

Tamsen was adventurous, cheerfully taking an arduous trip at age 17, 18, or 19 from Newburyport to Maine for a teaching job, sailing at age 23 from Boston to North Carolina for another teaching position. Happy in North Carolina with her first family, she writes Betsey, *I'm eager to go to Ohio, but this country has so many inducements I doubt that we will*. Happy here; wondering what's there. Forty-four years old with five children, she picked up stakes and went West.

Drawn to adventure: you either are that way or you aren't, and the one can't explain it to the other.

Being an adventurous girl in a small town at a small Catholic school in the '50s was a guaranteed C in Conduct. Boldness and pluck were admirable in martyrs but qualities to be tamed, curbed, routed out of girls. Even in college, my senior adviser told me about once a month, "Time will temper your youthful impetuousness." She meant it for my own good, but it still strikes me as a curse.

I found socially acceptable ways to combine adventure with escape, most dramatically when I needed to do secret, self-imposed penance for losing my virginity, an offense of such magnitude it still seemed nearly unforgivable a year after it had happened. I could have done volunteer work in Lansing, Michigan, but I spent my senior year in college writing letters around the world offering to bathe lepers or whatever was needed. Mother Teresa, before she was Mother Teresa, said I could come to India, but for a minimum of three years because of the language difficulty. Inordinately penitent, consumed with guilt and remorse, but no flagellant, I knew three years of service was excessive. By my higher math, one year was sufficient—I was still *almost* a virgin. The bishop of Bermuda telephoned me—this was *long distance* then, and my mother handed me the phone with awe—overselling his case with promises of frequent breaks at the beach, pink sand, turquoise sea . . . Hey, I'm not going on a vacation. A simple blue airmail form came from Barbados, then British West Indies: "We can't pay you, we need you, please come." Perfect. And off I went, after getting a local businessman to donate my airfare, excited, scared, feeling like a rat because everyone thought the sinner was a saint. I tried mightily to deflect canonization—"I'm going to be a lay missionary," I said. "That's someone who lays missionaries"—but I couldn't publicly confess. Virginity was maniacally important for a Catholic girl in the '50s, and "losing" it was not something you bandied about, especially if you wanted to make a good catch. If my parents, after paying for four years for the first college graduate in the family ever, wondered why I didn't get a job, they kept it to themselves, only expressing pride. After ten months in Barbados, faith shaken, sins almost forgotten, I fled back to Lansing for my brother's wedding. My uncle from Washington DC walked in, an alcoholic, salty, pugnacious Irishman thrice married to the same woman now living alone in a small apartment, and my new escape hatch combined with adventure clanged open. Three days later I showed up on his doorstep and lucky for me he opened the door.

Probably the most important factor in my attraction to Tamsen Donner at that point in my life: she had adventure but also had many children. Or perhaps more correctly, she had adventure in spite of having many children. She satisfied convention while defying it.

In retrospect, the fact that little was known about Tamsen was perfect.

She was almost tabula rasa. I could reject all the virtues men had written on her, and search for her. I could write myself on her, make her up, give myself permission to be adventurous. She was a blank page I could write my own story on.

I wasn't the only one who wrote my values and beliefs on Tamsen Donner. Most male writers called her a heroine without knowing any more about her than I did, without examining her actions closely. They presented her as the Perfect All-Giving Wife: she stayed with her husband till death did they part, wasn't that wonderful? Well, yes. *Till death do we part*: romantic, solemn words that still resonate deeply within us today, no matter the divorce rate. That the vow cost her her life too, didn't that just make her more admirable? Hold on here. I started to wonder how many men have secretly thought suttee an appropriate custom.

Jessy Quinn Thornton, who had traveled with the Donners until the turnoff to Oregon, started the ball rolling in his book, *Oregon and California in 1848*. According to him and his unidentified informants, Tamsen had a fearful battle convincing George to let her stay with him, "'Life, accompanied with the reflection that I had thus left you, would possess for me more than the bitterness of death; and death would be sweet with the thought in my last moments, that I had assuaged one pang of yours in your passage to eternity. No! no! this once, dear husband, I will disobey you! No! no! no!' she continued, sobbing convulsively."

Tamsen would have convulsed all right. With her quick temper she was ever trying to tame, she would have lambasted Thornton. Only ten years before, when her recently widowed brother, William, had written, asking her to come to Illinois, she blistered up the page telling Betsey:

[William] *says he would be not only very much disappointed but also very much hurt if a new school or a new place of abode kept me from him. Query. Did Wm ever invite me to his house on a visit? Would he now but from self interest. And will he think the favor was conferred by me or by himself when I leave a school worth $500 a year to take care of & educate his children. You* *say he says "he will take care of me." I am greatly obliged to his lordship & to gratify you both I will allow him to take care of me so long as I am necessary to him. But——I am abundantly able at present to take care of myself & to supply every necessary and unnecessary want.*

Does this sound like a woman who'd say, "No! no! this once, dear husband, I will disobey you! No! no! no!" and then burst into convulsive sobs?

Tamsen Donner stayed to help her husband die. To be with someone when he or she is dying, to help that person die, is certainly worthy of admiration. But few writers pursued the rest of the equation: who would help their children live? Eliza wrote that she told them, "God will take care of you." God was busy someplace else. Elitha, 14, was married off in less than two months—"Donner Party Survivors Find Romance at Fort," the museum exhibit said—and 13-year-old Leanna lived off and on with Elitha and her new husband. The three little girls, Frances, Georgia, and Eliza, wandered around Sutter's Fort, their eyes on the mountains, saying, "If Mother would only come." They wore rags, the dresses made of fine material Tamsen had sent with them stolen by a woman who thought they wouldn't know the difference. Finally parceled out months later, the five sisters would not be reunited for fourteen years, in October 1861, at Eliza's wedding.

Tamsen's choice: to let her husband die alone or to let her children live alone. Or put another way: to help her husband die or to help her children live.

And in some space between those terrible life-and-death choices that weren't choices at all, what about *her* life? What about the *woman*, the self, in that mother and wife? That may be a modern question that wouldn't have occurred to her, but it certainly was a question of my time.

More than a few women in the turbulent 1960s and 1970s left both their husbands *and* their children; there were despairing moments when that possibility crossed my mind. If I'd had fewer children, if they had been older, more self-sufficient, if Roger and I had extended family nearby, I might have been one of those runaway women, feeling escape was the only alternative to madness or suicide. Years after it had happened, I became close friends with a "runaway wife," who had left five children behind. I never doubted that she had seen no other recourse; I'm not sure there was any other recourse. She reconciled with her children, who showed no more ill effects than others whose unhappy mothers had stayed home. Still, more than once, I have breathed a prayer of thanks and relief that I didn't run away.

I was drawn to Tamsen, haunted by her, and it took me a long time to understand that the question I was asking was, how could I honor my responsibilities to Roger and to my daughters without its costing me my life? That was my obsession with Tamsen Donner, which I kept calling "many parallels between her life and mine." What I was asking was not how did she do it but should she have done it? Did she make the correct choice? Were there only two choices?

This I believed: Tamsen picked her husband over her children, but she always intended to survive. This great love story or story of great honor was not a suicide story or child abandonment story. I had to believe it then to preserve my heroine and my hope for my own life and my daughters'. I still believe it today.

15 Independence, Missouri, the "Jumping Off" Place

I can give you no idea of the hurry of this place at this time, Tamsen wrote Betsey. We walked around Independence, Missouri, looking at old houses and restored areas, trying to see the town through Tamsen's eyes. Independence now bustled in such a thoroughly modern way that I found it difficult to imagine the kind of colorful chaotic bustle that she had seen, so vividly described by Bernard DeVoto in *The Year of Decision: 1846.* The congested riverfront, steamboats docking, passengers streaming down the gangplanks, the crash and bang of every conceivable kind of cargo being unloaded.

The spring of 1846 had been the wettest in years, DeVoto said. Mud was everyplace, and the "sidewalk" planks were sinking into mud. They walked along just like us, I said to the children, Tamsen probably holding Frances's and Georgia's hands as I held Ursula's and Gabriella's, George holding Elitha and Leanna's hands as Roger held Maria's and Jennifer's, Eliza riding on George's shoulders as Charity rode on Roger's. But where we saw gift shops and tourists, DeVoto says they would have seen Indians with painted faces wearing blankets, Mexicans in serapes speaking Spanish, grizzled mountain men in buckskin, bullwhackers, trappers, soldiers, gamblers, missionaries, drunkards.

Hawkers would be selling everything imaginable. They'd pass blacksmiths, iron ringing, sparks flying. Bewildered emigrants moving from shop to shop, completing their preparations, exchanging information and rumors in a variety of accents.

"I hear two thousand Mormons are on the move, every man with his finger on the trigger."

"Well, wouldn't you do a little killing if your relatives were killed and you'd been burned out?"

"You a Mormon? We don't want any fanatics in Oregon."

"I'm a Presbyterian and I'm going to California!"

"I hear five thousand Mormons are on the warpath, out there just looking for a slaughter."

"Rivers full of salmon in Oregon."

"There's more land in California, you damned fool."

"I got family in Oregon."

"Didya hear? Ten thousand bloodthirsty Mormons only a week behind us."

Mormons, widely considered dangerous radicals, were being driven West from their towns, and many emigrants of 1846 feared possible retaliation. There's no mention of this fear in the accounts of the Donner Party survivors, although for a while they traveled with Lilburn Boggs, the ex-governor of Missouri who had signed the executive order calling for the expulsion or extermination of Mormons. Levinah Murphy, who with her large clan was part of the Donner Party, was also thought to be a Mormon. Besides vengeful Mormons and angry Mexicans, the other big fear of the trail was Indians. But except for a few costly raids on their cattle by Indians late in their journey, none of the three fears materialized for the Donner Party.

You can imagine, I said, that in the muddy roads, wagons and herds would be in traffic jams, tempers flaring. Maybe James Reed's outsize family wagon, driven by his teamster Milt Elliott, sideswiped smaller wagons, planting the seed of resentment against James Reed. Reed himself on his thoroughbred mare, Glaucus, might have passed the walking Donners, his daughter Virginia prancing by on her beloved pony, Billy, that, a few unimaginable months down the road, would be left in the desert.

Charles Stanton, a young merchant from Chicago who would become a tragic hero, made arrangements in Independence to travel with George and Tamsen. Irish immigrants Patrick and Peggy Breen and their seven stairstep kids from Iowa were there too. They joined the Donner Party later on. Those long months trapped in the mountains, Patrick Breen kept a journal that wasn't lost.

When the Donners and Reeds found out that Captain "Owl" Russell's train had left Independence a week before, they decided to easily catch up with their nine wagons and apply for permission to join his company. Former governor Boggs of Missouri was with Russell. And Daniel Boone's grandson.

We have the best of people in our company, Tamsen wrote. *Some too that are not so good.*

I pondered that *not so good* many times—who did Tamsen mean? Most likely she meant various drivers and herdsmen—drifters, who hooked on as hired help and drank and gambled their wages away. Respectable and well off, she wasn't a snob. Here, in Springfield, Illinois, she had written Betsey eight years before, *many of our Eastern people think they will come & bear rule, setting a pattern of good manners & fine living—they really appear ridiculous & it makes me sorry for them. Bring up your children with enlarged ideas & teach them better sense than to say 'We are the people.'*

The Donners and the Reeds, upstanding, well-off, native-born Americans, would readily be welcomed into Captain Russell's company. Others might be told the company was too unwieldy to accept any more: maybe it was or maybe the applicants weren't the "right kind" of traveling companions. The Irish Catholic Breens traveled by themselves for quite a while, but we don't know why. Breen may have applied to a company and been brushed off—an early version of No

Irish Need Apply. If that had happened and Paddy Breen was anything like the Irish I knew, that would be a direct invitation. The companies didn't travel in a straight line anyway, but spread out widthwise, so the Breens or anyone else could camp where they pleased. That's why they came to America.

The prairie grasses freshened, the Donners left Independence, on May 12, 1846, expecting to be in California in early September. Eliza Donner Houghton wrote in her book that as their wagons pulled out of town, an agent from the American Tract Society handed each child and adult a Bible and tracts to distribute among the heathens.

We visited replicas of early log cabins staffed by people in old-fashioned clothes; educational for the children, but not resonating in any way with the Donners. And then, someplace on our walk around town, I picked up a tourist brochure that mentioned that James Bridger, the famous trapper and mountain man, was buried in Kansas City, Missouri.

16 Kansas City, Missouri, and Kansas City, Kansas

Even today when I think of the Oregon Trail trip, the first thing I think of is the graves. For the two thousand miles of the California branch of the trail, Merrill Mattes, in *The Great Platte River Road* conservatively estimates the number of deaths at twenty thousand, or an average of ten graves to a mile, nearly one a block. But I didn't know that when we started out.

Our first grave was James Bridger's. I didn't even know he was buried in Kansas City, Missouri, until I chanced upon the information in that brochure. I didn't expect him there. Bridger belonged out in Fort Bridger, Wyoming, where his path and the Donner Party's crossed in 1846 when he advised them to take the fateful Hastings' Cutoff. By the time we found the cemetery, it was locked for the day.

Not even suppertime in midsummer, and locked. There's something sad and infuriating about locking a cemetery, as if there's no longer a place to be free from precautions, vigilance, and vandalism. Something humorous, too, since the more usual fears people associate with cemeteries can't be locked out. Ghosts might wisp through, but the iron gates posed more problem for us. Roger drove slowly around the enormous cemetery as we scouted, in a manner Jim Bridger would have been proud of, first for someone with a key and, failing that, the best place for us to break in.

It's either the Irish or the Catholic in me, but I don't recall ever being uncomfortable with cemeteries, open caskets, or death. At 5, I was allowed to stay hours each day with my Grampa Joe in the funeral home; for three days I cried, hugged him, cried some more, and periodically someone took me next door to the A&W root beer stand for a hot dog. My grandmother and mother always took me to the cemetery to set out the plants on the birthdays and anniversaries of relatives I'd never known. Later just Momma and I set them out on Gramma's anniversaries. My dad went at the crack of dawn to the city market to buy the plants—always geraniums—drove us, and raked the plot. If my brother went in those years I've forgotten it, but after our parents and sister died and I had long moved away, he became and remains the faithful caretaker of the family graves in our hometown. To this day when I see geraniums at somebody's house, my first thought is that they're on their way to the cemetery.

When I was 14 and leading Frank Roznowski around by the heart, he taught me to drive in the cemetery. Only 15 himself, Frank had a special license to drive his blind father to work. (I never wondered why Frank's mother didn't drive, the same way I never wondered why my own mother didn't.) Frequent access to a stick shift Plymouth gave Frank considerable status and power among the ninth-grade boys who, in order to get rides, tool around town, or cruise for girls at Sully's Drive-In, had to do what he wanted. Frank wanted to do what I wanted and I, growing up in Lansing, Michigan, where cars were king, was burning to drive. The boys sat in the backseat, feeling envy and resentment—that I, a girl, by unfair use of biology, was acquiring a skill rightfully theirs—along with a scorn for Frank's eagerness to be duped that they couldn't show, and resignation over the whole matter as, day after day, we all headed to the cemetery. "Good thing they're all dead; she'd kill them for sure," they muttered and mumbled, and each time I stalled, they groaned and piled out and pushed till the motor turned over and I immediately stalled again.

I remember standing at many grave sites. I didn't have so many relatives, but somebody was always dying. You went to the funeral home for the visit and the rosary, to the church for the funeral, and after that to the cemetery, in the big, black cars if you were family or feeding into the line behind in private cars. Everybody got a little flag for their antenna, and people watched you drive by, men on the sidewalk taking off their hats. You moved right along in town, but at the cemetery the line slowly snaked around the dirt roads at about the same pace but much smoother than I would later drive Frank's car. At the grave site there was always a little milling and regrouping and then the service would begin. I remember the flowers, the turned-up dirt, the words—they lowered the body with everyone present in those years—I remember being sad, but not scared.

Of course, nobody I knew would have been caught dead in a cemetery after dark.

My children hadn't had as much or as varied experience with cemeteries. They would learn to drive at school on simulators with Roger supervising their actual road practice, which white-knuckled me. We lived in a city far from our birthplaces where we didn't know many people well enough to take significant part in their lives, let alone accompany their bodies to the cemetery. But we had poked through lots of graveyards on Sunday afternoons just for the history and quiet of it.

It certainly never occurred to me to let Bridger's grave go. To miss it in Kansas City, the official start of our retracing the California and Oregon Trail, would be a sloppy beginning at best, maybe a bad omen. That I hadn't even known his grave was there was a little too close a reminder of how inadequate I felt my preparations for this trip were.

Eagle-eyed Maria spotted an official-looking sign inside the cemetery, jumped out of the car, and read excitedly: "If you're locked in, go to the east gate to get out." We drove to the east gate, found a man who didn't care if we wanted out or in, found the grave before dark, read and reread the text, and photographed it. I felt exultant.

James Bridger
1804 1881
Hunter, trapper, fur trader, and guide.
First white man to see Great Salt Lake, 1824;
the South Pass, 1827; Yellowstone Lake and
Geysers, 1830. Founder Fort Bridger, 1843

Bridger's grave popping up out of place like that, our finding out in time and not a thousand miles down the road, and overcoming the obstacle of the locked gate, bode well for the trip, and we took off in high spirits.

The three cities of Independence and Kansas City, Missouri, and Kansas City, Kansas, merge one into the other. At Kansas City, Missouri, after finding Bridger's grave and eating supper, there was a sudden fierce thunderstorm that exhilarated and comforted the children; "I feel so safe riding in the car," Maria said. "Me too, me too," her sisters agreed happily, while Roger and I, unnerved by the lack of visibility and flash flood potential, told them, "No, we are not going to play the radio, even if that would make your experience 'perfect.'"

In the car, we dug out and struggled into our seven brand-new identical khaki-green army-surplus rubber rain ponchos to dash through the downpour to find a motel. "We look like fruitcakes," Maria said, an accurate statement, and wouldn't get out of the car, but Jennifer, the family scout, led her sisters happily through the puddles. That motel was full, and so was the next. By the time the storm stopped, the car smelled like wet rubber and so much adrenaline had surged through us, we decided to drive on for a while.

We crossed the Missouri River into and out of Kansas City, Kansas, around 9:00 p.m. The land was suddenly flat—prairie, cornfields, Dorothy Gale's Kansas—the way I expected Kansas to be. We were nearly the only car on US 56 and, about twenty miles down, outside of Gardiner, there was a Kansas historical marker and wagon ruts. *Wagon ruts.* I read the marker aloud:

OREGON AND SANTA FE TRAILS

At this point, US 56 is identical with these famous trails which from the Missouri River followed the same general route. Near here they branched, the words "Road To Oregon" on a rough board pointing out the northern fork. So simple a sign, one writer observed, never before announced so long a journey. Here a second sign pointed southwest along the Santa Fe Trail. Of its 750 miles, two thirds lay in Kansas. As early as 1821, pack trains hazarded this route between the Missouri and Spanish frontiers. By 1825 it had become a commercial wagon road. From 1840 to 1870, 1,000's of travelers plodded the 2,000 tortuous miles of the Oregon Trail, recording with fearful monotony the new graves along the way. Down the Santa Fe Trail went troops bound for the Mexican War of 1846–1847. Over these two roads branching here into the wilderness traveled explorers, traders, missionaries, soldiers, Forty-niners, and emigrants: the pioneers who brought civilization to the Western half of the United States.

We all stared silently at the wagon ruts. *The Road to Oregon. Down the Santa Fe Trail. The Mexican War.* I was looking at history. Except for the telephone poles—everything still, the sky streaked blue-gray casting our family and the trees into silhouette, the flat land stretching to the horizon—it was easy to see how it would have looked then.

Ursula, 10, wanted to pitch our tent there and hear the trains all night long. The vote was five to two for a motel. Ursula was disappointed; I, the other Yes, was somewhat relieved. The ground was wet from the recent rainstorm; there were mosquitoes; no one wanted to unpack the top of the car to get the tent; we had a long day coming up.

In the wagon ruts, there were two Pepsi cans and a paper cup. I picked them up, found a trash can; we got back in the car and, exercising an option the pioneers didn't have, drove West till we found a Vacancy sign.

17 Kansas

The next day started with blue skies. We drove up and down lush green and rolling hills—Dorothy would never have gone to Oz had she seen this part of Kansas. We stopped on a dime at every one of those roadside markers you usually speed by and, if it in any way concerned the Oregon Trail, read it as carefully as if it were a personal message left for us. And eventually there was one: the first marker that made reference to the Donner Party.

> ### ALCOVE SPRINGS AND THE OREGON TRAIL
> Six miles northwest is Alcove Springs, named in 1846 by appreciative travelers on the Oregon Trail. The Donner Party, most of whom later froze or starved in the Sierras, buried its first member, Sarah Keyes, near the Springs in 1846.

The Donner Party's first death. Technically they weren't the Donner Party yet; that wouldn't form until out at Little Sandy, Wyoming, nearly to James Bridger's fort. At Alcove Springs, Kansas, they were still part of Captain "Owl" Russell's large wagon train. But Sarah Keyes had set out in April from Springfield, Illinois, with the Reeds and the Donners and would forever be part of the roster.

We drove six miles northwest, then went up to a new tract house to ask directions. I was embarrassed, felt silly, Hello there, we're looking for a grave of someone who died 130 years ago, but Roger wasn't, or Jennifer hopping out with him, or Ursula hastily putting on her poke bonnet, and the woman who answered the door was eager to help. It used to be a little park, she said, but now it was closed down. She hadn't been there in years; it was just really interesting to meet people who came all the way from Buffalo, New York, to see it. And look at this little pioneer girl! You look just like Laura Ingalls Wilder from the TV show! She gave us country directions, pointing in the general direction, a turn here and there, a dirt road. It was difficult to find, she said, though we were quite close.

Roger, whose brain is the original Mapquest, quickly found the first turn, and another, and the dirt road. We sailed down that dirt road, excitement mounting. The day itself made me giddy, high summer, dust rising off a curving country road, sun shimmering on aspen leaves, sun motes, sun spots everywhere, everything hazy and golden and caught: it was summer that was caught, a day out of time and Mark Twain, and we moving through it a million miles from nowhere with no responsibilities, on a lark, an adventure, a mission. Adding to the sense of timelessness, there were no people, no other cars, and after some time it came to us, no sign of a grave either. We stopped at a farmhouse to ask again. This woman was not tickled that we had come all the way from Buffalo, New York, she didn't know anything about any grave, she didn't have time to talk to us, and she clearly had never seen Laura Ingalls Wilder on TV. I got out our books and went over it all; she listened grudgingly, uncomfortably, suddenly pointed toward the barn. "Ask there if you want," she said, and shut the door.

Barking German shepherds and Labrador retrievers surrounded us. Bunched tightly, we took it slow and easy out to the doorway of the barn. "Hello," I said to a man working four feet from us. He appeared

4. Sarah Keyes's gravestone in Alcove Springs, Kansas. You can see the stone from the road.

not to notice seven people surrounded by barking dogs. I cleared my throat, "Pardon us, sir." In slow motion, he came over. He cut me off midline: "There isn't any park anymore; vandals, hoodlums trashed the place. Bums." I tried to express regret and respect; it seemed fairly obvious that we weren't bums on a beer blast. His eyes stayed narrow. "I don't know where the grave is," he said. "If you go there, it's private property; you'll be trespassing." We thanked him and carefully made our way back to the car. We figured it had to be close.

And it was. You could see the single stone from the road if you were looking hard enough.

It was just beyond the barbed-wire fence we held up for each other and crawled under. It wasn't the original stone that John Denton chiseled words on; that deteriorated or was stolen by vandals; the DAR, Daughters of the American Revolution, provided this one. It wasn't even the original spot—Sarah Keyes's bones were probably under the new road built by the Corps of Engineers around 1965, local preservationist R. O. Klotz of Blue Rapids thought; others think the grave was on the bluff overlooking the Big Blue—but it was close. How moved I was reading the stone on the heat-still day. Not by the words, which are traditional and sentimental—

God in his love and charity has called in this beautiful valley a pioneer mother. May 29, 1846

—but that someone cared enough to mark the spot so that we and others who cared could come along and know that it really had happened: the members of the Donner Party were not just characters in old books, they were actual people who had stood, milling and regrouping, on the ground where we now stood, looking at some of the same trees, passing by the Reeds and murmuring the kind of words that comfort and don't comfort. Only a fraction ago in the spectrum of time, they were <u>here</u>. I had the most elemental proof of life: a grave.

Sarah Keyes was in her seventies, "older than your grandparents," I told the children. She was an invalid. Two sons had to carry her from the Springfield, Illinois, house and place her in the wagon. Her sons tried to dissuade her, her granddaughter Virginia wrote; but if there were hushed family conferences, grown children gathering to whisper "You won't believe what Mother's got in her head," if there were realistic concerns and reservations, Sarah Keyes's wishes were ultimately deferred to. Why did she undertake such an arduous trip? Some books say she hoped to see another son, an emigré of '45, coming back on the road. Virginia wrote that she would not be parted from her only daughter, Margret. That might strike some as strange in our time, but in the nineteenth century, mothers and daughters had not been turned into enemies, were cohorts in travail, comforts and inspirations to one another, which I believed was the natural order of things—though I'd rarely had it with my own mother—and exactly the kind of relationship I expected to have with my daughters. I wouldn't consider—*allow*—any other kind of relationship and never doubted that if they were going overland, they'd want me on the trip too.

James Reed, Margret's husband, built a special wagon to make his mother-in-law as comfortable as possible with a raised platform for her bed, spring seats, and a tiny sheet metal stove vented through the top. Dubbed the Pioneer Palace by later writers, it was a wagon so relatively grand that many have thought it caused resentment along the trail, becoming a variable contributing to James Reed's banishment from the train. Later on, it had to be abandoned, but on a fine April morning, cached wagons and banishment undreamed of, her sons cross-linked their arms and carried their mother out of the house, placing her in the gleaming wagon on a large feather bed and propping her up with pillows. They implored her to reconsider. They knew and she knew that it was the last time they would see each other. "I can now see our little caravan of ten or twelve wagons as we drove out of old Springfield," Virginia wrote, "my little black-eyed sister Patty sitting upon the bed, holding up the wagon cover so that Grandma might have a last look at her old home."

Springfield, Illinois, to Alcove Springs, Kansas: 470 miles. If there

5. James Frazier Reed's initials carved into rock: JFR 26 May 1846, Alcove Springs, Kansas.

was a son traveling back, they never met; she had less than six weeks with her daughter.

That May day, their first death, had to be sad, but Sarah Keyes was old, and her time, perhaps hastened a bit, was near. Although death was always a hazard of emigration, no one would dream that it was rushing down on so many in that crowd of mourners. "It seemed hard to bury her in the wilderness and travel on," Virginia wrote later, "but her death here, before our troubles began, was providential, and nowhere on the whole road could we have found so beautiful a resting place." All the emigrants turned out to assist at the funeral: a coffin was made from a cottonwood tree; a minister said words; a young Englishman, John Denton, chiseled Sarah Keyes Born In Virginia and her dates on a large, gray stone. She was buried under a shady oak, the stone placed, wild flowers planted. Not ten months away, 28-year-old John Denton would freeze to death alone in the snow with no one to mark his passing or bury his body. But on May 26, 1846, there was still time for ceremony, and Sarah Keyes, surrounded by family, friends, and members of the company paying their respects, was laid to rest by the Big Blue River.

Through a grove, over an old wooden-beam bridge that had been torched in the middle, down the dry creek bed, we also found the Spring where James Frazier Reed had carved his name—the last three lower-case letters, *eed*, now worn away—into stone: "Here it is!" Jennifer yelled exultantly, beating Maria by a hair, their excited sisters close on their heels, and we all gathered around, taking turns tracing the letters with our fingers, JFR 26 May 1846

Other names were there, too, at Alcove Springs—Bruce and Jim and Duke—as well as beer cans and condoms, forerunners of the trashing of pioneer sites we'd see across the country. It made all my daughters mad—"How can they do that?" Ursula said. "It's so disrespectful," Jennifer said. I felt proud of their caring and connection to things larger than themselves, but for me that day, the life of the Donner Party was so tangible, so palpable, no punk kid detritus could touch it.

18 Nebraska

Driving a small right angle in the northeastern corner of Kansas, we headed up to Nebraska on Route 77. Nebraska was just a slide in my mind from all that corn to a cornball state, a place of farms, hicks, squares, out of it. We had visitors from there once, schoolteachers, one wore a corsage, talked with a nasal twang or maybe it was a flat, expressionless tone, you recognized it right away; the airline lost her luggage, I rolled my eyes internally—it figured, right? for a person from Nebraska.

In Lincoln, a waitress in Johnson's Cafe said, "You're from New York, eh? I met some people from New York. They'd never heard animals. They came out to my farm and tape recorded sounds. Pigs and cows and chickens. I couldn't believe it. They were really from the sticks."

We had cut up to Lincoln to visit Roger's relatives, had tried to call them from Kansas to say we were earlier than the date mentioned in our letter, called a half dozen times from Johnson's Cafe to say, "We're here!"—but they weren't. We drove to their house, walked all around it, not a sign of them. Roger said they wouldn't mind if we put our tent up in their back yard. I wasn't so sure; he had only seen this second cousin once in thirty years. "It'll be fine," he said, dumping the stake bag out.

We were now able to get our blue and yellow tent up in just a little over an hour. Everyone was to give her or his all was the rule. At home, we shared the housework, the philosophy being that the house was there for all of us, we had all made the mess, so it was everyone's responsibility to clean it. Everyone agreeable to a distribution of chores, the actual doing demanded constant vigilance on my part. I cared the most, partly because I'd end up being stuck doing whatever was undone, but mostly because I had daughters. If they saw me as genetically endowed to do housework, what kind of model was that for them and their future relationships? Better they saw a virago, who once slammed her fist so hard on the table she had to leave the room to nurse her hand in secret. My ferocity was reinforced by some feminist friends with sons who were allowing male privilege to claim its own. You couldn't afford to let daughters slide an inch if they were to have a shot at equality.

Putting up the tent, there were too many watchdogs to permit extensive malingering. Roger was always unflagging and unstinting; Maria, Jennifer, and Ursula, without a great love for the task, usually gave quite a bit—unless Maria was making a late appearance or early exit to write in her journal—the three of them in an unspoken competition over who was the best helper. Gabriella and Charity carried stakes and hooked ropes and puttered around while I, after showily driving several stakes, would try to disappear over a hot Coleman stove. I hated cooking out, but not nearly as much as setting up the tent.

Periodically I glanced up to see that the next-door neighbors were still standing to the side of a window watching us. I imagined a husband and wife arguing: "You go over." "I don't want to go over." "*Somebody* has to go over." "If you feel that way, *you* go over."

A screen door banged. A woman walked reluctantly toward us. She had a dachshund on a leash. She cleared her throat. We smiled. "May I help you?" she asked. "We're almost done," Ursula said cheerfully.

"Why are you putting it up here?" she asked. "We're the Eastern cousins," Roger said. Visibly relieved, she offered us lemonade and the use of their bathroom. The dog's name was Useless or Worthless, we never did get it straight. The Nebraska cousins would be home late the next day.

We woke up to rain, went downtown to eat, then went to the Capitol to track down a picture of Roger's grandfather who had been a state senator in the early 1900s before moving to California. Afterward we went to the historical society to see pioneer exhibits. When we came home, the Shumans were there; they had a feeling we might come early, they said, so they had come home early. They moved Roger and me into the house, and fixed the children sleeping places in a small trailer in back. We stayed two more nights. They fed us continually, helped us make repairs, and as experienced campers, helped us repack everything, laughing at our jokes but not our preparations. "Stay as long as you like," they said. "We're so happy to see family."

I was grateful: not many people take you in when you're seven. (Just when meeting five children, a dishearteningly common refrain was: "Don't bother telling me their names, I can't remember them.") Now I sat at the table each day crowded with cousins and food, touched by the warmth and smiling faces, but as the days went on—the air conditioner being fixed, a zipper for the canvas top found, someone to sew it found, a day trip to the farm where Roger's mother had been born, now a working pig farm, old pictures of his distant relatives, cousins' children performing, our children performing—I grew simultaneously tense with fear that I'd lose the trip, started thinking of DeVoto's description of the Donner Party waiting by the Weber River for Hastings to come back, "the season shortening, a richer purple in the mountain shadows, frost creeping farther down by night on the peaks." We had barely begun the official route, the route ahead still nebulous, Sarah Keyes's grave at Alcove Springs filling my head, and already, in attention more than miles, we were deviating. "[N]ever take no cutoffs and hury along as fast as you can," Virginia Reed wrote three months after her rescue.

When the pioneers left their homes, relatives, and friends, they were saying good-bye forever. Unexpectedly, on a quantumly different scale, the Shumans' treatment of us caught a resonance of the pioneers' farewells. Our last morning out in the driveway, as cousins came and went, tucking in a fresh batch of cookies, tightening a strap, going over the directions one last time, I felt that this was our miniversion of the Donners' and Reeds' bittersweet leave-taking in Springfield, Illinois, our kin bidding us farewell and safe journey. "Good-bye, take care," they called again as we drove down the street, feeling nurtured, feeling that we were not only on our way, we were also on our own. That dog's confused name came along with us the rest of the trip. Even today, years later, if someone says, "That's useless," anyone in hearing will answer, "No, it's worthless." And vice versa.

From Lincoln, we took Route 34 to Grand Island, Route 30 west to Ogallala, and Route 26 across Nebraska to Wyoming, small bypassed roads that basically parallel Interstate 80 and, from Fort Kearny on to Fort Laramie, parallel the Platte River, the great highway across Nebraska for the Oregon, California, and Utah pioneers. There wasn't only one Oregon Trail. As emigration increased, the wagons spread out so that in some places the trail might be a mile wide. What must the Indians have thought watching scores of wagons go by, and then hundreds, and then thousands, so many covered wagons rolling down the Great Platte River Road in Nebraska that some called it the Great White Topped Road.

I grew to love Nebraska. The plains. Many people think that the plains are where you make time, but it's where we started slowing down, getting a sense of pioneer time and distance covered. The covered wagons generally made ten to fifteen miles a day, twenty with effort, and although we hadn't slowed down that much yet, there'd be days to come when we wouldn't make much more in our big red station wagon. That every day we took longer to cover less ground seemed humorous and exactly right. My urgency disappeared: we were actually on the Oregon Trail. I had never thought we'd make it. Even after we started,

I was afraid that the summer would go and we'd find we had piddled the trip away in side trips to snake farms and Stucky shops, that the trip had never been a business trip at all but was always and exclusively a family vacation, which, on some unspoken level, would reveal that I was not a writer at all but always and exclusively a mother.

We eased into pioneer rhythms and a certain trip rhythm. Life becomes greatly simplified in a car. Each day, we drove further away from whatever we had left undone or done badly. We had a new start, and after a while Roger and I forgot what we had forgotten. Contained, complete in ourselves, the trip was our existence and our reprieve.

19

Only a week out that already felt timeless, things were shaking down into a kind of routine. If we had stayed in a motel, we got up and repacked the car; if we had tented, we broke camp and repacked the car: the chore of repacking the car omnipresent and onerous. Once at a motel, too tired to face the unpacking, we slept in our underwear. At campgrounds, Roger always got up early and eager. At the last possible moment, I'd lumber out, the immediate signal for whichever kids were still lolling to get up too. The same pattern pretty much repeated at motels. Roger's growing annoyance/anger at my reluctance to get up was visible but unvoiced, so I was able to not notice it.

For breakfast we usually bought a half gallon of milk and ate corn flakes out of our tin cups. Then the children walked around wherever we were while Roger and I found a restaurant for coffee. For lunch and often for supper we bought picnics out of grocery stores—I told the children they could choose whatever they wanted within our budget, then got mad if they contemplated junk food. We had all agreed that the trip would be a "Health Food Trip," not only to improve our nutrition but also for economic reasons—every time a family our size stopped for Tastee Freeze, there went another five bucks. Sometimes we found small-town cafes and split the day's specials. In restaurants, everybody economized, especially 7-year-old Gabriella, who studied the menu endlessly, her little brow puckered in deep concentration, her eyes carefully scanning the page, while we waited and the waitress came and left several times. We knew she was reading—at age 4 she had read a newspaper ad over Roger's shoulder, "Why Be Bald?" and after we recovered from our surprise, Roger, who was losing his hair, said, "Was she trying to tell me something?" Finally Gabriella looked up and announced, "I'll get the pork chop special, because that comes with cole slaw, applesauce, hash browned potatoes, *and* green beans. It's a better buy than the Salisbury steak. I'll share the cole slaw." Maria and Jennifer exchanged a look. Amused or envious, they never pointed out that she, almost the smallest child, had again picked a larger item than even Roger had, more expensive than theirs combined, or that they hated cole slaw. The children could order a drink or a dessert; they always chose the dessert, drinking water with their meals. To this day, Maria, Jennifer, Ursula, and Charity don't drink pop. Only Gabriella, after she was grown up, answered the siren call of soft drinks—too much close menu reading.

Our station wagon had three rows of seats and a flat storage space over the car well behind the third row. Using a complicated system that they kept track of, the children rotated their seating daily. We already had a family system called First Turn that simplified countless other decisions.

First Turn had begun years before when we had a half dozen brown plastic drinking glasses and one pink plastic glass that both Maria and Jennifer always wanted. Roger or I got the idea of assigning them First Turn days to have the pink glass. When people brought presents or there was a special treat, First Turn chose first. As our family grew, so did the system until we were seven, and each of us had one day a week to be First Turn. Maria was Monday, Jennifer Tuesday, Ursula

Wednesday, Gabriella Thursday, Charity Friday, Roger Saturday, and I had Sunday. From getting the first crack at something coveted, First Turn subtly evolved to include chores. When we got our dog Tamsen, First Turn did potty patrol. First Turn thought up the supper menu and cooked it on her or his day and chose the book to read aloud while the other six did the dishes. It might be Garcia Marquez's *One Hundred Years of Solitude* or *Winnie the Pooh* and, just as no negative comments were allowed about a supper—"This is the best meal we have tonight"—any piece of reading could be picked without comment. Our children grew up to form a family business and they use the First Turn system today. Without particular intention, our little First Turn system was grassroots training for a '60s ideal: the cooperative system.

Each day in the car, First Turn child had the coveted front seat between Roger and me, the other four often sitting together in the second seat, rotating the window seats. Sometimes one would crawl over and stretch out in the third seat, but not regularly because each disliked smelling the exhaust fumes drifting in from the open back window. "There aren't any exhaust fumes coming in there," I said, fully believing this until they convinced me years later that they had barely escaped brain damage. "A Car Is Not a Bed" was a family maxim; in other words, if you expected to be as comfortable in a car as in a bed, you were bound to be disappointed.

Maria, Jennifer, or Ursula also rotated sitting next to Gabriella and Charity, helping them with whatever they needed that day from braiding their hair to spelling words for their journal entries. All five took daily shifts being responsible for the water jug—reaching over the seat, pulling it up, pouring cupfuls as many times as requested without grousing, knowing that for the next four days they'd be served.

The front seat child was supposed to be the navigator, following the maps, but that often broke down with Roger taking up the slack. More popular was the other role of the front seat child, the accountant, even Charity with some aid, keeping the day's accounts, totaling up every cent spent in a small spiral notebook, announcing at day's end if we were within or over our budget. If we were over, we had to pull back the next day. The budget was an arbitrary figure I had chosen before we left, not based on any reality, except my belief that it would be obscene to spend over that amount. Maria and Jennifer were such ferocious watchdog accountants that in one town Roger and I found ourselves in the humiliating circumstance of guiltily bolting down a piece of apple pie with our coffee and not reporting it to the accountant. (He bolted it, I encouraged him.)

Once we reached California, land of dreams, the children aspired to be on the *Gong Show*; they practiced audition songs daily: "Five singular sensations, every little step we take . . . " They also frequently wrote in their journals or drew pictures in them, especially Ursula, who had a talent and liking for art. They collected, sorted, and swapped postcards, freebie brochures, bird feathers, wildflowers, and other oddments for scrapbooks they planned to make back home. Unknown to us, they also collected a ton of rocks that made the trip back home with us. Roger almost always drove, so I could look, absorb, tape, and concentrate. Once or twice he had Maria drive, much to her and her sisters' ecstasy. I tape recorded scenery, impressions, details. Sometimes Roger recorded more extensive descriptions of scenery. He knew about different kinds of baling, irrigation, and silos and could tell wheat from alfalfa, whereas I was more of the school of What's that yellow stuff? Roger was also the photographer, taking black-and-white photographs of anything I asked him to, and as a result, suffered the photographer's fate of absence from all the photos.

I read aloud frequently. In addition to books on the Donner Party, I had found a remarkable book in Lincoln, *The Oregon Trail Revisited* by Gregory Franzwa, a detailed guide in tenths of miles on how to find the Oregon Trail today (the California Trail splits at Fort Hall, Wyoming, the Donner Trail at Little Sandy, Wyoming). It's curious that I so strongly felt we were ill prepared, because I also had photocopies of pertinent trail information from other books, regular and topographical maps, AAA camping and tourist guides, and folders for each state. Maybe that feeling had more to do with just the idea of the difficulties of bringing a large family on a long trip, and the camping, than with the actual trip preparations. First thing in the morning, I read about what was coming up that day. When we went into a new state, I read about its history, geography, and economy, excruciatingly boring stuff that Roger found interesting, I might find useful or necessary for describing my modern characters' routes, and we both agreed should be inflicted upon the children. We sang any song connected with any state, "Back home again / In In-dee-ann-aaaaa," and considered whether nearby sights were interesting enough for a detour from the Oregon Trail.

In the '80s, '90s, and early 2000s a spate of books with new theories and new routes were published, but in '77, I tried to thread my way through the thicket of older books with their contradictory information. If we were heading to a Donner-related site, I'd read all the versions of the stories I had, which might be wildly disparate, or just as bad, copycat versions of each other, then make a guess on which version seemed most logical or possible. The "little caravan of ten or twelve wagons leaving Springfield, Illinois," that Virginia Reed wrote about in her memoir was actually nine. She wrote that her grandmother was 75, yet the dates that John Denton was to have carved on the stone made Sarah Keyes 70. Similar discrepancies filled the sources on the Donner Party, one writer handing them on to the next until frequent repetition lent them the appearance of fact. Many of them were minor except to historians and a nervous writer who, confronted constantly with the paucity of certain historical knowledge, considered every fact recovered, tiny or not, a triumph and a comfort.

In the afternoon, I'd read the descriptions of all the upcoming campgrounds; we'd narrow it down to two or three and vote. Often before we got there, I'd desperately try to think of a reason we should stay in a motel to avoid the arduous unpacking and packing. In theory, camping and cooking out had seemed wholesome ideas that suited our limited budget, but in practice, I quickly found them exhausting and unrewarding. Feeling that was weak and citified and a bad example for the children, I tried to be a good sport or, failing that, not to openly complain and sabotage the whole attempt. Roger was the only one really committed to camping and tried several times without total success to reproduce his vivid boyhood memories of Spam cooking on the open fire. The children, probably trying to juggle cues from both of us, moved from enthusiasm to resignation and back again.

He travels fastest who travels alone, Kipling said, and I can vouch for the corollary. The practical details of traveling with five children, bathroom stops, camping spots, grocery stores, laundromats, exiting anyplace, this one carsick, that one restless, can we go swimming today, I've got a knock knock joke, are endless. ("I got one," Ursula said. "Knock knock." "Who's there?" "Oregon." "Oregon who?" Ursula could barely contain herself, "Oregonna eat that or can I have it?" She collapsed. "I got one, I got one," Charity said, "Oregon." "We just did that." "No, this is different. Oregon." "Oregon who?" "Oregon TRAIL!") Many details the children took care of themselves, the older looking after the younger, but there were still a million more. I did many of them on automatic, trying to keep the Tamsen Donner part of my mind active and segmented. What I was looking for was so vague, tenuous, and fragile I had to look off to the side of it, not scare it away before I saw it clearly, whatever it was. I couldn't explain this to the children; didn't even have enough confidence in my right to have this experience and these feelings to articulate it.

A good deal of the time I left the children to themselves or to Roger, unless I was reading aloud. They were often expected to entertain themselves. And to stay alert. We didn't want them to sleep their way across the country. We were in and out of the car a lot, so there was considerable diversion and stimulation. They had long attention spans, partly developed from years of frequent one-hour visits to art galleries where we told them, "Look carefully at every painting and afterward you can pick a postcard of your favorite picture." This resulted in one intensely attentive hour in the gallery and two much more intense hours in the gallery gift shop picking the postcard. When they quarreled, I turned some attention to helping them resolve it, but if they didn't work it out within what I considered a reasonable amount of time, either Roger or I swiftly put the quarrelers on silence. **Go on silence.** And they did. Years later, genuinely baffled, Roger asked them, "Why did you do that, go on silence?" "Because you told us to," they said. If they simmered and seethed then, I didn't hear it, or I disregarded it. And then they'd forget the argument—although one or more might carefully record in her journal that *she* had been right—and be back to spotting cows or seeing which truck drivers would return their peace signs. Mostly they didn't balk or resist our control. They had intellectual interest in the Oregon Trail and the Donner Party; they felt happy and lucky to be on a trip. "We were *in* on every part of it," Jennifer said. "We had a vote and a strong voice—if not a controlling one," she laughed. "That was a heady experience for kids." I knew they were extraordinary kids and told them so frequently. When they stopped being extraordinary, I came on like gangbusters. Although I didn't understand it at the time, I was trying to block out 130 years of modernization, my family, a big red station wagon, and my fears and self-doubts as a writer attempting to understand and portray a real woman accurately. I was trying to create a separate identity as a person and as a writer within a huge family while still being the mother of that family. In some ways I was like the tour leader and in other ways like an individual traveler who mistakenly got booked on a group plan.

20

The writer Sheila Ballantyne said, "We create the family because we need it and then we're always trying not to have it swallow us up." Tell it, sister. I wanted to be *with* the family, *in* the family, yet I wanted to have my separate identity, I wanted us to stay separate together. I wanted to be Mom to five people and only five people; I didn't want to be Mom to the world. To the world, I wanted to be a writer.

I tried for years to separate being a writer from being a mother, but they marched along in tandem, enhancing and robbing, feeding and starving each other. There were times I was a better writer than a mother and vice versa, but only moments, never months or years. It always seemed an unwinnable tug of war—the writer/mother mother/writer was always guilty/always guilty. And then one day the tension eased, the children's needs no longer threatening to swallow mine. I was 33 when I began writing a novel, 47 when I published one (not the same novel): fourteen years of limping and galloping writing and family.

Roger and I changed tack every twelve minutes, trying to keep seven lives afloat at the expense of none; in fact, it was at the expense of all, each of us going down a few times, sometimes needing CPR, but no one drowning. The all-time endless problem was child care. Before the women's movement, I'd occasionally said I might try doing something outside the house if a perfect babysitter turned up. After joining the movement, I realized that Mary Poppins was not going to knock on my door any day soon. Adopting the truck accident philosophy—if I were hit by a truck and hospitalized, we would find a babysitter—I found an au pair working for my neighbor, willing to take Gabriella and Charity, preschool age, to my neighbor's house three hours each morning. I was terrified that after I had made all this commotion, I'd sit down to write and nothing would happen. Something wonderful happened. Pages began to fill. After a while, that three hours acted just the way people said marijuana cigarettes would: I WANTED MORE.

As au pairs go, the au pair went. Memorable babysitters followed.

Evelyn was from Guyana. I taught her the prevailing '60s philosophy: "We shouldn't be possessive of our children, they belong to everyone," which I fervently believed until the day Charity was crying and Evelyn took her out of my arms to console her. I took her back, Evelyn reached out, and we had a tug of war as ferocious as Solomon's mothers until I won. Still, Evelyn was extremely competent until my trip to Bread Loaf Writer's Conference coincided with the government's notice that her visa was up. She fell apart, so distraught she called Roger and told him she wasn't functioning. He worked ten minutes from home and rushed up to find a police officer who had retrieved Gabriella from the middle of the nearby street. At Bread Loaf I received an urgent message to call Roger. I said, "Honey. If you had been on a business trip and this had happened, I would have figured out something." Roger figured out something. Evelyn disappeared into the Washington DC underground, maybe there still, I never tried to find her. This very minute I can feel my 33-year-old self on the outdoor pay phone at Bread Loaf, listening to Roger, genuinely sympathetic, fully confident that he could handle the situation, the mountains in the distance, my life changing, opening up undreamed-of possibilities: I never thought of going home for one second.

BB and AB. Before Bread Loaf and After Bread Loaf.

Zoila from Central America saw me as the head mother, but during dinner, she hawked oysters across the kitchen table into the wastebasket, a habit not only disgusting but so worrisome we took her for a TB x-ray. She didn't have TB, and when I told her the hawking bothered me, she tried without total success to restrain herself. She may not have understood me, her supreme achievement in learning English a phrase from Sesame Street, "You are a cucumber." I would be telling her something important, and she'd beam me a big smile and say in heavily accented English, "You are a cu-cumber." It drove me crazy. When she left—on a materialistic variation of my "All children belong to everyone"—she took all my good jewelry with her, including the engraved gold women's symbol necklace given to me by the women who worked on my Shirley Chisholm delegate campaign.

I never dreamed when my friends and I in the women's movement were fighting all our battles that my grown-up daughters and all their friends would fight the same battles. People used to pat me on the head and say, "These things take a long time," and I'd rail, "My daughters and I don't have a long time, we need these changes now!" Well, a long time has passed. We're still the only industrialized nation not to have government child care; most employers haven't changed to accommodate their workers; and though fathers are doing more parenting, for the most part the bulk still falls on the mothers, employed outside the home or not.

Countless things *have* improved for women in the past thirty-five years, but mothers today struggle with the same child-care issues I did, let's not even get into who's cooking the meals. The big difference today is that women have a language now in which to ask the questions, voice the expectations, make the demands. Before the late 1960s, the word *sexism* didn't exist.

Late at night when my family was sleeping, I used to write long letters to famous writers asking them for counsel, undeterred by never getting any responses. Once I wrote Tillie Olsen asking her if it was inexcusably selfish for me to write when I had children. Years later, I understood that I was really asking her to give me permission to write, and she knew I had to give that to myself.

Of course, you can give yourself all the permission in the world to do anything and a fat lot of good it does if you don't have child care. In the '70s we called that, "The personal is political," and you could still call it that today.

21

Before we started on our trip, I bought seven journals. At nooning stops
Tamsen Donner might have sat on a wagon tongue, a rock, an overturned
bucket, with her journal balanced on a cracker box, a board, her knees
if she was crouching close to a wildflower to sketch it, probably most
often on her lap. She probably wrote in pencil, intending to recopy it
later in ink. In my novel, with trepidation, I was writing her lost journal.
At the front of each of my children's journals, I had written:

> There are moments, when I look out onto this land . . . that . . . I
> yearn to capture my feelings . . .
> —TAMSEN DONNER in *Nearly Time*

> This book is for those moments.

> Love,
> Momma

The audacious act of quoting Tamsen Donner speaking words I had
given her was not done lightly. I had thought about the inscription a

long time, nervous even as I wrote it, but the loss of Tamsen's words had led to my novel, *Nearly Time*, to my imagining her words as honestly as I could, and her words, even once removed, belonged in the beginning of journals that would capture my children's words.

Maria constantly had her nose in her journal. In between writing reams in tiny, nearly illegible script, she wrote tinier notes on scraps of paper to later incorporate and expand upon in her journal. Not unlike me and my novel, she wrote down *everything*, saying that she couldn't trust she'd remember it years from now; she knew that from having been a baby. If she had been able to write things down then, she said, those experiences wouldn't be lost to her now. Jennifer and Ursula wrote in sporadic bursts, often—like the pioneers—catching up two or three days at a time. "What'd we do after we left Chimney Rock?" one or the other might ask, and in any dispute over sequence or detail, Maria was the final authority. Whoever sat next to Gabriella and Charity kept them making fairly regular entries, often drawings of places we were passing. The children also asked people we met to sign their names in their journals. The whole summer, Roger and I barely cracked ours. Whatever diary entries I was making were in my head. Initially, there was just too much to do, the sheer mechanics of the trip taking our time and energy, then I grew too overwhelmed to write. Journal keeping wasn't Roger's inclination, and he remained too busy with the mechanics.

Although the dry dusty Nebraska soil that the emigrants saw had been transformed by irrigation and was now lush and green, the heat they all commented on in their diaries was still fierce. The wheat was golden, the corn high, and the heat shimmered in the air. I didn't mind the heat; the closer we could get to re-creating the pioneers' experience, the better I liked it. I wanted to know what it was like for Tamsen Donner, and to know that I could take it too. Although the air conditioner was fixed, we only used it when reading aloud to cut the wind noise down. I wanted to feel the waves of thick heat, to hear the dry rattle of the grasshoppers, the swarms of mosquitoes. The pioneers' skins broke out in rashes; so did ours. Maria, already fighting her own skin problems, had no interest in re-creating the pioneers'. She hated the casual hygiene and inadequate facilities associated with camping and hiking, but she tried to participate fully in the great outdoors while simultaneously trying to keep the dirt from jumping into her pores. After meeting several sulking teens at campgrounds whose families' entire trips had been reduced to finding their next shampoo, I was proud of her efforts—but not as proud as I'd be of her today. Then I scorned such teens and expected her to be tough and uncomplaining.

I had grown up "offering it up for the souls in purgatory," a peculiar Catholic practice of enduring discomforts so that souls not quite ready for heaven, purifying in the flames of a way station called purgatory, could shorten their agony and get to heaven quicker. I had gotten a lot of souls out of purgatory before I wondered why God would keep track of a little kid lying in bed on a hot summer's night, going through torments to not scratch an itch, then allot her sacrifice to this or that burning soul. The book work alone would be boggling—perhaps that was what required a divine intelligence. Although as a mother I saw the considerable advantages of "offering it up"—it eliminated whining, for starters—I couldn't impose it on my kids. But I never doubted that putting up with small discomforts was good for the character.

A little heat and hives? Come on. I had extravagantly admired the little Spartan boy who stood at attention while a fox inside his tunic gnawed his vitals. Knelt ramrod straight on Good Fridays from 12:00 to 3:00, the hours Jesus hung on the cross. Prided myself on my Marine posture in academic processions in college, luckily the nun's directive—if a body crashes behind you, don't look or break your step—never having to be tested.

Martyrs were my developmental role models. One gory heroic story after another. I thrilled to St. Laurence's spunk, who, put on the spit for his faith, said, "Turn me over, I'm done on this side." Or maybe it was a vat of boiling oil, but he looked them straight in the eye and thumbed his nose.

I had left the Church and would never have expected my children to emulate martyrs, and I now thought that little Spartan boy should have torn his tunic off and yelled his lungs out, but I had been steeped in sacrifice and spiritual discipline. Where I once wondered, "Could I wisecrack while being roasted alive?" I now wondered, "Could I have endured all those months in the snow?"

I told none of this directly to my children, but children find out quickly enough how to please their parents. They knew I valued hardiness; knew—without being told of my experience with hypochondriacs either—that we didn't do minor aches and pains in our family. Maria didn't complain and hardiness was its own reward.

The good part of being on our own surfaced: the variables were lessened. We had only ourselves to consider. It didn't matter when or where we stopped or how long we stayed. We had no deadlines, no schedules. If we wanted to spend hours climbing on rocks or hunting for a grave, we did.

Before Fort Kearny, Nebraska, we reached a dirt road by a series of turns: .9 mile here, .3 mile there. I navigated with Gregory Franzwa's book, the kids craning around Roger's shoulders to keep track of tenths of miles on the odometer, "Start looking out to the right for a sandhill." "There it is!" a trio of voices shouted. We walked out into the fields through tall grass, and in the middle of nowhere iron railings formed a rectangle around a lonely grave.

Susan O. Hail
34 years old
Died June 2, 1852

Six years after the Donner Party passed through here. Died suddenly, probably cholera from drinking polluted water. The disease killers of the trail were typhoid, measles, dysentery, and, from 1849 on, cholera. The other killers were buffalo stampedes, Indian attacks, drownings, falls out of wagons, and mishandled firearms. The emigrants were not careful campers; they used streams for toilets, tossed dead cows down wells without thought for who was coming after. Susan O. Hail came after.

We skipped Kearny Historical Park, which is what's left of Fort Kearny, a military outpost set up to protect pioneers from Indians two years after Tamsen Donner passed by. I felt I could process only so much, had to conserve my energy and attention.

At Ogallala, Nebraska, for a treat, we took the children to a "Wild West" vaudeville show. The age cutoff for children's tickets set at 12, economy trumped honesty: we bought five children's tickets. All the children were put in the front rows and, near the end of the show, the young, enthusiastic, singing actors came down to tap various children to join them for the grand finale. One man—what was his deal?—made a beeline for Maria, just turned 14, but tall: "Oh, right, you're 12," he said sarcastically. "Look here, everybody, at this great big 12 year old." Beet red, Maria sank further and further in her seat. Two rows back, Roger and I were sick for her and ashamed of ourselves, and we promised her we'd never put her in that position again.

Meanwhile, unknown to us, Gabriella, 7, who was painfully shy, was having her own epiphany. While her sisters were outgoing future performers, she couldn't even stand people singing "Happy Birthday" to her, and when an actor extended his hand to her, she shook her head and looked down. "No, no, I couldn't," she said to her lap. He tried to cajole her, but she just kept saying "No, no," so finally he extended his hand to Ursula next to her, who quickly jumped up to join him on the stage. "I watched Ursula up on that stage, doing do-si-do and chorus line kicks, having such a ball," Gabriella said much later, "and I thought, being shy isn't doing me any good. I'd better cut it out. And that was that. I struggled with attention for a long time, but I had changed." In the years to come, we all noticed that Gabriella gradually discovered a new freedom in her skin until it was hard to believe she had ever been so shy. We had assumed it was maturation, until she said, "No. It was something I discovered when we went West."

22

At Ogallala, Nebraska, we turned off U.S. Route 30 to U.S. Route 26 to a series of Oregon Trail landmarks that were famous to the emigrants—Ash Hollow, Windlass Hill, Courthouse Rock, Jail Rock, Chimney Rock, Castle Rock, and Scottsbluff. Everybody knew about these landmarks from those who had gone before and eagerly awaited them.

Ash Hollow State Park was the first. At the head of Ash Hollow, a canyon, was Windlass Hill; we parked in the parking lot and climbed to the top.

The day was hot, the sky bright blue with white puffy clouds. A breeze moved the prairie grasses, easy to see why pioneers spoke of it as waves. Did it look like waves to Tamsen? Make her nostalgic for her birthplace, Newburyport? Or did she think, amused, They've never seen *real* waves.

Newburyport, Massachusetts, Tamsen's birthplace, is a seaside town and, although her father's occupation is not known for certain, she grew up in a world that revolved around the sea. Lucretia Mott, often credited as the first American feminist, was born in the seafaring community of Nantucket, Massachusetts, eight years before Tamsen. Dorothy Sterling in *Lucretia Mott: Gentle Warrior* evocatively describes Mott's childhood, which may have been similar to Tamsen's. Men were often at sea for a year or two at a time, Sterling says, so children would have routinely seen strong capable women in charge of home, money, and business. If the money at home ran low, some women made the long difficult trip to Boston to sell candles and whale oil used to light lamps or exchange them for dry goods they couldn't make at home. And oh, the excitement, the relief, the whispered thanks when a ship was spotted, bringing home the fathers and husbands and the sights and sounds and smells of the world beyond their small island. Men striding down the gangplank, even the small ones tall, leather sea chests filled with exotic goods. Coconuts. Aromatic teas. An opalescent shell cupped to a little girl's ear: hear the trade winds. Maybe those warm blowing winds planted the seed for Tamsen's adventurous spirit and wanderlust.

Will my wandering feet rest this side of the grave? Tamsen asked her stay-at-home sister Betsey in one of the letters I read years later.

What would have been a long difficult trip for the Newburyport women was for our family two years after the Oregon Trail trip an easy drive from Boston, a straight shot up the coast.

Newburyport, the birthplace of the U.S. Coast Guard, is a picturesque town, the harbor crowded with weekend sailors. It's easy to feel the power of the ocean and imagine the excitement of schooners coming in: "All alive and well!"

When Tamsen was six, her mother died. A little over a year later, her father married Hannah Cogswell. She was educated in Newburyport, most likely by her parents and her brothers' tutors. Tamsen's maternal grandfather, Jeremiah Wheelwright, had been a schoolmaster in the 1700s. Education would have been highly valued. (In a historical irony, that grandfather, serving in the Revolutionary War under Colonel Benedict Arnold—not yet a traitor—died at 46 of exposure to cold.)

Tamsen's early life is a mystery, though we know she was bright, a quick learner and avid student. "Your mother started teaching when she was 15," her niece, Frances, wrote Eliza, Tamsen's daughter, in 1879. "She taught Mathematics, Surveying, Geometry. She was one of the best teachers." Frances would know. After Frances's mother, William's wife, died in 1836, Tamsen emigrated from North Carolina to Illinois to take care of and teach her and her siblings.

One of the letters would tell me that when she was 18 or 19, she traveled to Maine for a teaching job. *There are nine families here & I shall have about 20 scholars. I think I shall enjoy myself highly.*

In another of those letters, written after Tamsen was widowed in North Carolina and Betsey implored her to come back to Newburyport, Tamsen reminded her sister how hard she (Tamsen) had scrabbled in those early years in Massachusetts, barely earning enough for one. *But you know . . . that the north is crowded with schools that my utmost exertions when there before were only sufficient to maintain one. That I was compelled to be separated from you, if not at so great a distance.*

At the time of our trip to Newburyport, it was known that in 1824, when she had just turned 23, Tamsen went to North Carolina for a teaching job, sailing alone on a great ship at a time when respectable women didn't travel alone. A letter that she wrote Betsey in the middle of that trip fleshes out the sketchy details and contains a remarkable manifesto. Although supposedly only four feet, eleven inches tall, Tamsen knew her worth.

> And I leave it on record for the benefit of those who may wish to follow my example—that so far from considering me an <u>outlaw</u> people of all stamps from the Senator, Author, & Southern planter downward have treated me with attention & respect, though they have sometimes <u>wondered</u> at my conduct they have never <u>despised</u> me. And I never shall be <u>despised</u>.

We tend to read *despise* more harshly as *hate* or *loathe*, but another sense means to look down upon, to regard with contempt or scorn or as one unworthy of notice. Tamsen Donner was defying convention with boldness and assurance and practically daring anyone to criticize her for it. In modern slang, she was not going to be disrespected.

We walked slowly through the oldest parts of Newburyport, past the Victorians and the widow walks. Some houses had historical nameplates, but none referred to her family. In the early 1990s historian Betsy Woodman said that Tamsen grew up at 50 Milk Street, and in 1996 the mayor of Newburyport issued a proclamation in Tamsen's honor for the Sesquicentennial; but everyone I asked at the time drew a blank. I stared out at the sea as Tamsen must have done often as a girl, but no matter how I strained to listen, the only whisper of her I found in Newburyport was a page I photocopied from the New England Historical and Genealogical Register, Volume 32, page 211: "Tamesin, daughter of William and Tamesin Eustis, born November 1, 1801. Died enroute to California."

Her body and journal lost in the West, her memory in the East seemed erased too. I was glad I had come to Newburyport, but it didn't make me feel any closer to Tamsen Donner.

Roger and the children were hungry, so we asked a fisherman who directed us to the freshest lobster in town. The children weren't as hungry as they had thought, so I alternated watching Roger unbelievably polish off four lobster dinners and looking out at the unfathomable ocean.

The long wavelike grasses on Windlass Hill at Ash Hollow, Nebraska, were scratchy against my legs, and I huffed and puffed during the climb, not in good physical shape at 38. I smoked too much, though I was smoking far less on this trip than I wanted to. I wasn't the only big boss in the family; the children had put their collective foot down: No smoking in the car *or we won't go*. Maria, Jennifer, and Ursula were ferociously against smoking and had indoctrinated Gabriella and Charity as vigorously as any school antismoking program. "Really," I said sarcastically. "You'll give up this wonderful adventure if I smoke in the car?" Five sets of stony eyes called my bluff. I was secretly outraged by the stricture—I WAS THE GROWNUP, they *knew* I would quit smoking when I finished the book, what more did they want?—but I had no reasonable grounds to protest it.

I found grounds. I was tape recording, trying to put down thoughts, simply get some thoughts up to the surface, the wave of bickers in the backseat rolling, rising, crashing like buffalo crossing the Platte into the front seat and my attention. I turned off the tape recorder—never leave evidence that you're a bad mother—hissed, "I am *going to smoke*." "Oh no, Momma, don't, we'll be good." When everybody, especially me, though I didn't tell them, felt suitably rotten, I turned the recorder back on.

When we stopped the car and I lit up outside, they coughed, glowered, and stalked away. Jennifer was the worst. Once at a party at home, I lit up and she burst into loud gulping sobs, running from the room, much to the consternation of our guests. Another time, she staged a pretend asthma attack. **She doesn't have asthma**, I assured our worried guests between clenched teeth. Although the children tried to respect the rule not to go into my work space without permission unless it was an emergency, Demon Cigarette drove them to sneak in in the dead of night and put notes in my typewriter. Every last mitten found, lunches made, schoolbus drawn away, I'd sit down for a few precious hours and there, in huge scrawled letters, was "PLEASE DON'T DIE, MOMMY," a plaintive message that shot my focus, my morning, and convinced me anew: if they didn't drive me to it, I wouldn't *have* to smoke. Now outside the car I glowered back at them but found myself slinking behind trees, sneaking quick puffs, just as I increasingly found myself at home behind the locked bathroom door, blowing smoke out an open window. Sometimes behind the tree, I also found my cigarettes snapped in half inside the pack, which enraged me and made me feel like a damn fool. I never commented on it. I wouldn't give them the satisfaction. Before the summer was out, Ursula, filled with guilt, confessed. I stared slit-eyed at her, the addict's righteous, resentful stare: if I weren't a mother, I'd do everything to excess! The other culprit, Jennifer, continued to glower, not confessing for years.

6. Parking lot of Windlass Hill. We hardly ever saw people.

A lone couple was on another part of Windlass Hill. Although it was high vacation time, we hardly ever saw people at these pioneer spots, which I thought puzzling and our good luck. The children ran off, ran back, zigzagging the hill. At the top, together, we looked down the three-hundred-yard drop to Ash Hollow, talked about how the covered wagons didn't have any brakes; they lowered them with ropes and chains and trees lashed together, hard to imagine. We didn't know, nor did they, that this hill was a mound compared to what waited ahead.

In the old Ash Hollow cemetery, still in use, the first grave was Rachel Pattison's. "Rachel taken sick in the morning, died that night," her husband, Nathan, wrote. Cholera. The original marker was recessed into a monument, preserved behind glass. You could read the name, age, and date of death.

Rachel Pattison, 18, died June 18, 1849. Married 3 months.

23 Trail Landmarks
Courthouse Rock, Jail Rock, and Chimney Rock

A little jog east of Bridgeport, Nebraska, on State Road 92 took us to Courthouse Rock and its companion, Jail Rock, and then, a little south, to Chimney Rock: enormous rocks that, depending on a pioneer's imagination and desire, resembled the old courthouse and jail back home. Even if you were a person to whom rocks didn't mean much, how exciting it would have been, five hundred miles out on the trail from Independence, Missouri, when everything had settled down into an almost monotonous routine, to suddenly squint the anticipated landmarks out there on the horizon. Two days' travel away in that clear air, they'd start sighting them: "Where?" "I don't see it." "I see it!" "There!"

A big event, almost all the pioneer diaries mentioned it; it's likely Tamsen Donner's did too, although we'll never know for sure. People argued about whether the rocks really did look like their namesakes, but imagine the relief, the reassurance that sighting them brought. We are really on the trail. Yes. Yes. This is exactly as the books said.

I felt the same way myself.

7. Chimney Rock. Two days away, in that clear air, they would start sighting the anticipated landmarks.

I wasn't an outdoor person, or a generalist like Roger, interested in things just for themselves. Had I passed this way before I'd heard of the Donner Party, I'm sure I would have sped by with only a glance at the large, oddly shaped rocks, momentarily grateful for a visual distraction in a countryside I would've thought aptly named plain. As it was, I loved the countryside, couldn't get enough of the rocks. I wanted to see and do everything that Tamsen Donner had, as if the careful retracing of her actions would reveal what she had felt and known, ultimately yielding answers to the questions that haunted me: How and why did some pioneers cope heroically while others just gave up and died? Had I been there, would I have acted as Tamsen Donner had, brushing her children's hair, bathing her husband's wound, writing who knows what in her journal, while death piled up around her?

The emigrants climbed Courthouse and Chimney Rocks and we did too. We put on our hiking boots, hitched up our wool socks high—higher, after we got out the snakebite kit and the Swiss army knife in case we had to make the x cut to suck out the venom—and hiked the half mile to Chimney Rock's base, going through barbed wire twice, cactus and yucca and great clumps of grasshoppers, but not seeing any of the rattlesnakes everyone had warned us about. I read about the rocks' composition, Brule clay and Gering sandstone, searching them as if they were runes with answers to mysteries.

Although their surfaces were once so crammed with names that one emigrant complained he could find no space to put his, the names were all eroded now, the carving of the names exacerbating the erosion process. Maria, Jennifer, and Ursula competed over who could climb highest, having more fun going up than coming down, Maria going highest once and Jennifer another time, both having to be talked down when they suddenly froze with fear. Coming down Chimney Rock, shaped like an upside-down funnel, the pebbles started sliding, Ursula flying along with them, scraping her legs, scared too. Like countless parents before us and after us, Roger and I held our breaths ten thousand times while our birds lept from the nest. I gave Ursula and her sisters a hug and a cheer, we hitched up our socks again, and it was time to hit the road.

All across Nebraska, there were traces of the Oregon Trail, and even on Route 26, it wasn't so hard to block out silos and signs and imagine something quite close to what the pioneers saw. But there were some wonders that would never be seen or heard again.

"I have seen the plain, black with them [buffalo] for several days' journey, as far as the eye could reach," John Bidwell wrote in 1841. Thousands upon thousands of buffalo, plunging into the Platte River and swimming across, the water changing texture and form, become brown heaving movement, waves of shiny dark mass, rolling rolling.

A buffalo stampede. William Case in 1844 was only one of many pioneers who described a herd of great shaggy beasts weighing from eight hundred to two thousand pounds each, "the front of the line a half mile long, and several columns deep, coming like a tornado." The ground rumbled like thunder, the earth shook: days off the pioneers heard them, listened carefully for the direction. James Reed, and perhaps George Donner with him, plunged on horseback into those buffalo herds, wildly exhilarated, bringing back buffalo humps for the Reeds' cook and Tamsen to cook over fires made with buffalo chips. George might shoot buffalo for fresh meat, and probably have a great time doing it, but he was a farmer who valued animals, not one of those hunters, I was sure, who before and after him, slaughtered buffalo by the score, leaving them on the ground to rot to the Indians' dismay and anger.

In 1851, five years after the Donners passed, ten thousand Indians assembled on these plains. Arapaho, Cheyenne, Sioux, twelve nations in all, the largest Indian council ever held, gathered at Horse Creek Treaty Grounds, about thirty-five miles east of Fort Laramie, to sign a peace agreement with the U.S. government. The Indians promised good behavior along the emigrant trail, and the U.S. government promised to respect tribal boundaries and pay fifty thousand dollars of merchandise per year for fifty years.

It's hard to picture ten thousand Indians, hundreds of thousands of buffalo, to feel the power, the force of such masses. It was chilling to me to think that they just disappeared. But why? All through history, large seemingly powerful groups have been extinguished by the will of others more dominating.

The power and force of the group: I related to that profoundly after joining the women's movement. Groups, united in vision and goal, could make change an individual couldn't dream of. It was exhilarating and empowering to be a part of that, especially in the beginning. The women's movement had changed my life, or put another way, gave my life to me. But I came to it with a large family, and I wanted them to have their lives too. The kind of family I wanted mine to be, a feminist family, one that thrived together without one of its members sacrificing herself, wasn't possible without a powerful group making radical changes in expectations, roles, jobs, education, society. Would the women's movement prevail, splinter into self-interest, or just mysteriously disappear the way the first wave of feminists during the nineteenth and early twentieth century had, after women won the right to vote in 1919? Could I be my own person and everybody else in my family be their own person, especially in Buffalo where it sometimes seemed to me the women's movement hadn't yet happened?

These were particularly American problems; it was our blessing and our curse that we valued individualism and independence so highly it often clashed with communal values. We were the only culture that almost immediately put its newborns into a separate bedroom, made a mythology of the cowboy, or had a sizable nutty subculture that believed that riding a motorcycle without a helmet was self-reliance and liberty.

The rugged individualist versus the good of the group: the pioneers ran into this problem too. Individualism and independence spurred them West; they formed parties for safety and sociability, but when the going got rough in the Wasatch Mountains and the great Salt Lake Desert, when the food ran low, the Donner Party was rent into individual family groups—every family for itself—and individuals on their own. Those traveling alone were twice as likely to die as those in family groups.

Just east of Scottsbluff, near today's Gering, Nebraska, a Mormon pioneer, Rebecca Winters, mother of five, died on the trail on August 15, 1852. Cholera. To mark her grave, a friend took an iron rim from a wagon wheel and engraved her name and age on it: Rebecca Winters, Age 50. We pulled off SR 26 to visit it.

In *The Oregon Trail Revisited*, Gregory Franzwa describes emigrant burial:

At the end of the day, a shallow grave would be opened at the head of the trail, the body wrapped in an old comforter and lowered to rest. The earth was packed back into the hole. After breakfast the wagons would roll over the grave, one after another, to obliterate the scent of the grave. Too many times, the emigrants had seen trailside graves torn up, covered with wolf tracks, and parts of a human body strewn around. . . . Thus the trains were showing kindness when they rolled over a fresh grave. This is why, of the 30,000 to 45,000 graves along the [Oregon] trail, only 200 have been located today, and almost all of those are unidentified. Those are the few who were not buried in the trail itself, but whose graves somehow escaped violation.

Of the hundreds of photos we took, Rebecca Winters's grave was the one I wanted an enlargement of to hang in my writing room. The weight of the image, a simple iron tire placed into the ground, hit my heart immediately. A wagon wheel placed into prairie grass. Movement and movement stopped. From one angle, it was a ring and one thought of promises. Thought of particular circles that would not complete while the large circle continued unbroken.

Rebecca Winters, Age 50 One of the handful whose names we know. A name etched as permanently as tools would permit on material integral to the trip. How much that friend must have loved her. In the shocking suddenness of sickness, death, and burial all happening in one day, a friend shaped an image that, like a poem, stripped, distilled to the core, contained everything: migration and its cost.

In 1902, fifty years after Rebecca Winters was left behind, surveyors for the Burlington Railroad found the iron rim embedded in the ground and petitioned for the railroad to be moved ten feet over at that spot. A stone marker and a protective fence were added.

At the turn of the twentieth century, they moved a railroad for a pioneer's grave. In the bicentennial year they moved a highway for a proposed golf course, but not for Tamsen and George Donner's farm site.

You could poke around for weeks in Nebraska, zigzagging from one small road to another, hunting down graves and landmarks of the

8. Charity and Gabriella at Rebecca Winters's grave.

Oregon and California Trail. One mile south of Gering on Highway 71, then eight miles west on Robidoux Road, a boulder marked the site of the Robidoux blacksmith shop, the forerunner of the Robidoux Fur Trading Post, which flourished in the 1850s. Nearby, down a dusty road, we found a half a dozen nameless graves. The grass was overgrown, the gravestones crumbling and lonely. Since so few graves were left or known, it had begun to seem important to visit those that were known, to pay our respects.

Three miles west of Gering was the last great trail landmark in Nebraska, Scotts Bluff, a rock formation that reminded the pioneers of an ancient fortified castle. An Oregon Trail museum set up by the National Park Service had many of the original William H. Jackson sketches of trail scenes and landmarks that he made in 1866. Outside the museum was a fully equipped covered wagon, a wooden churn attached to its interior—filled with cream in the morning that churned all day from the wagon's motion, some lucky pioneers had butter at night. *Our milch [milk] cows have been of great service—indeed, they have been of more advantage than our meat. We have plenty of butter and milk,* Tamsen wrote from the trail in June, when they would have been just about at this spot. A cheerful ranger, dressed in period clothes, cooked over an open fire—a living museum of the pioneer period. The children put on their poke bonnets and ate salt pork and spoon bread, ground coffee by hand, cracked a whip, and got a piece of homemade soap for their scrapbooks. After, we walked the summit trail of Scotts Bluff; high, high, high among wildflowers and jet-propelled grasshoppers, we looked east as the pioneers probably did to see how far they had come, and picked out Chimney Rock on the horizon twenty miles behind us.

We met Sandra Harris near here. A young woman in her 20s I guessed, she was walking to Donner Pass. She had left Independence, Missouri, April 19 and planned to arrive in November. Her six and a half months projected time was slower than the pioneers' time, which averaged four months from Independence. Sandra Harris was there because of the social changes of the '60s and '70s that encouraged women to be adventurous and autonomous, and so was I, but I was afraid for her. Walking the Donner Trail was not like hiking the Appalachian Trail. Most of it was unmarked, a great deal desolate. She was young, a woman, alone. At night, she asked farmers if she could sleep on their land. That I had lost my own courage to make the trip alone certainly contributed to my being scared for her; but there was more, having to do with the steady accumulation of nameless graves we were seeing. How easily one dies and is lost. Who would know if something happened to this young woman walking alone; who would mark her existence? "Write me when you get there," I said, "you promise?" She promised, and walked away down the center of a dusty road, heading west. "Take care," I called, and she turned and waved. I watched until she turned a bend.

I've promised to write lots of people I never did. The simplest explanation is that she lost my address or never got around to writing.

24

The Donners on the trail just about where we were now, Tamsen wrote a friend in Springfield, Illinois, possibly Allen Francis, the coeditor of the *Sangamo Journal*. Her letter was published in the newspaper on July 23, 1846, about five weeks after she wrote it—pretty good travel time since emigrants "mailed" letters by giving them to someone they passed who was traveling eastward. As she and George had read letters from earlier emigrants, now future emigrants would read hers to aid in their preparations. Years later, when Tamsen's daughter, Eliza, inquired about the letters, Allen Francis wrote that all his files, including Tamsen's earlier contributions in verse and prose, had been practically destroyed by rodents.

This is the second widely reprinted letter I knew about at the time of our trip, and the last of the seventeen letters that are known to exist.

Near the Junction Of the North and South Platte, June 16, 1846

My Old Friend:

We are now on the Platte, 200 miles from Fort Larimee. Our journey, so far, has been pleasant. The roads have been good, and food plentiful. The water for a part of the way has been indifferent—but at no time have our cattle suffered for it. Wood is now very scarce, but "Buffalo chips" are excellent—they kindle quick and retain heat surprisingly. We had this evening Buffalo steaks broiled upon them that had the same flavor they would have had upon hickory coals.

We feel no fear of Indians. Our cattle graze quietly around our encampment unmolested. Two or three men will go hunting twenty miles from camp—and last night, two of our men lay out in the wilderness rather than ride their horses after a hard chase. Indeed if I do not experience something far worse than I have yet done, I shall say the trouble is all in getting started.

Our wagons have not needed much repair, but I cannot yet tell in what respects they may be improved. Certain it is they cannot be too strong. Our preparations for the journey, in some respects, might have been bettered. Bread has been the principal article of food in our camp. We laid in 150 lbs. of flour and 75 lbs. of meat for each individual, and I fear bread will be scarce. Meat is abundant. Rice and beans are good articles on the road—cornmeal, too, is very acceptable. Linsey dresses are the most suitable for children. Indeed if I had one it would be comfortable. There is so cool a breeze at all times in the prairie that the sun does not feel so hot as one would suppose.

We are now 450 miles from Independence. Our route at first was rough and through a timbered country which appeared to be fertile. After striking the prairie we found a first rate road, and the only difficulty we had has been crossing creeks. In that, however, there has been no danger. I never could have believed we could have traveled so far with so little difficulty. The prairie between the Blue and the Platte rivers is beautiful beyond description. Never have I seen so varied a country—so suitable for cultivation. Every thing was new and pleasing. The Indians frequently come to see us, and the chiefs of a tribe breakfasted at our tent this morning. All are so friendly that I cannot help feeling sympathy and friendship for them. But on one sheet, what can I say?

Since we have been on the Platte we have had the river on one side, and the ever varying mounds on the other—and have traveled through the Bottom lands from one to ten miles wide with little or no timber. The soil is sandy, and last year, on account of the dry season, the emigrants found grass here scarce. Our cattle are in good order, and where proper care has been taken none has been lost. Our milch cows have been of great service—indeed, they have been of more advantage than our meat. We have plenty of butter and milk.

We are commanded by Capt Russel—an amiable man. George Donner is himself yet. He crows in the morning, and shouts out, "Chain up, boys! chain up!" with as much authority as though he was "something in particular." John Denton is still with us—we find him a useful man in camp. Hiram Miller and Noah James are in good health and doing well. We have of the best of people in our company, and some, too, that are not so good.

Buffalo show themselves frequently. We have found the wild tulip, the primrose, the lupine, the ear-drop, the larkspur, and creeping hollyhock, and a beautiful flower resembling the bloom of the beech tree, but in bunches large as a small sugar-loaf, and of every variety of shade, to red and green. I botanize and read some, but cook a "heap" more.

There are 420 wagons, as far as we have heard, on the road between here and Oregon and California.

Give our love to all enquiring friends—God bless them.

Yours truly,
Mrs George Donner

George Donner is himself yet. He crows in the morning, and shouts out, "Chain up, boys! chain up!" with as much authority as though he was "something in particular."

That loving tease suggests the flavor of Tamsen and George's relationship, the ease they had with each other. I bet she read it aloud to him and they had a good laugh. In earlier letters to her sister, rarely completed in one sitting, it's clear that she wrote them amidst bustling family life with various members chiming in.

Mr. Dozier [her first husband] just told me to ask you if you could get potatoes from Boston & says he will send you 20 or 30 bushels if you can.

My husband [George Donner] says there are many opportunities for good bargains. That we are well & glad of it & if you are fond of rabbits he wishes you would come & kill them to keep them from barking his apple trees. Come & he will go with you to hear the members speak as the Legislature meets at Springfield.

Leanna is churning & says, "Mother, write that Frances has white curly hair." Mr. Donner & she think she is quite handsome, but I know she is quite in the way, for I must hold the inkstand in one hand to prevent her spilling the ink & she is pulling my papers & catching hold of my pen.

George Donner is himself yet. Crowing and shouting as though he was something in particular. Tamsen may have been a foot shorter than George, but she doesn't sound like the little woman. She sounds like a woman grinning at her husband who's maybe doing a little posturing but definitely feeling his oats and both of them are enjoying it.

Give our love to all enquiring friends—God bless them. They've only been gone from Springfield two months, and the novelties of the trail are still many, so it seems only a heartfelt complimentary close, not a suggestion of the loss felt by so many pioneer women.

"Oh, I feel so lonesome today," Agnas Stewart wrote on the Oregon Trail in 1853. Only one of a long line of pioneer women, each writing her own version of Agnas's lament, often sharing the same sentence, "Most of all, I miss my friends."

Friends. The pioneer women left behind a world where friends were always plural, a woman's world that no one poked fun at, a support system so strong and deep it gave me a pang to think of it.

"Your novel works best when we don't have the feeling of being trapped in your heroine's lonely head," Leslie Fiedler said after reading a five-hundred-page draft. A cut to the quick, though he didn't know it. Since moving to Buffalo, New York, from Washington DC three years before, I hadn't made any friends. My heroine wasn't the only one trapped in her poor lonely head.

I had experienced that woman's supportive world for the first time in Washington DC with the women in my consciousness-raising group, but the feminists I'd met in Buffalo were hard-line Marxists, an ideology of limited interest to me. They had already circled the wagons. Shortly after arriving in Buffalo, I heard they were sponsoring a small reading by Tillie Olsen, and I called one to see if I could bring my children.

"Are they girls?" she asked.

"All my children are daughters," I said coldly. "My politics are impeccable."

Although my anger at men barely knew bounds, they had to be voting age. To disallow sons from anything, but especially a feminist event, was cruel to both mother and child and revealed a hopelessness that scared me: on some level, they didn't believe the world could change. I took my daughters to the reading, but we skipped the social.

Occasionally a faculty wife or mother at my kids' school asked me to lunch. Were they kidding? I didn't even eat lunch. Roger and I were treading water with both of us trying to carve out careers and raise five children, who were taking piano lessons, violin, bass, in choruses, scholastic clubs, on track teams, field hockey. . . . In the midst of a bustling city, I was as lonely as a pioneer woman on a homestead in the wilderness. I secretly thought my lack of close friends was my fault for not managing my time better—just the thought of having leisurely dinner parties and hanging out was exhausting—not realizing for years that there was no time to manage better.

25 Wyoming

Along with shiny trinkets to distract Indians en route, and bolts of laces and silks to ease the Mexican land negotiations out in California, many of the emigrants of 1846 carried something else from home: a copy of Lansford Hastings's *Emigrant Guide*, which mentioned, almost in passing, an alternative route. With the alchemy of gossip and desire, a single somewhat vague sentence—"The most direct route for the California emigrants would be to leave the Oregon route about two hundred miles east from Fort Hall; thence bearing west southwest to the Salt Lake; and then continuing down to the bay of Francisco"—metamorphosed into a new shortcut said to save three hundred miles and a month of travel. Although Hastings had never been over the route he suggested at the time he wrote his book, modern historians now view him more as an early California booster than the lying scoundrel portrayed by earlier writers. Still, one sentence in a book can be powerful if it strikes a chord. Frequently at campfires, the men debated whether to take Hastings Cutoff. If the women debated, it was not at the campfires, and they did not have a vote.

On the eastern side of Fort Laramie, Wyoming, the Donner Party met up with James Clyman, the mountain man, who was traveling west to east. Fourteen years before, Clyman had served in the Blackhawk War with James Reed—along with another Illinoisan, Abraham Lincoln— and he cautioned his old comrade not to take Hastings Cutoff. He had traveled with Lansford Hastings and thought poorly of both the man and his shortcut. "Take the regular track and never leave it," Clyman warned. "It's barely possible to get through if you follow it and may be impossible if you don't." It's said that James Reed, impetuous and self-confident, was not impressed, that he said, "There is a nigher [nearer] route, and it's of no use to take so much of a roundabout course."

The town of Fort Laramie was just over the Nebraska border on Route 26, Fort Laramie National Historical Site three miles south on Highway 160. The old adobe Fort Laramie was gone, replaced by an extensive garrison that the National Park Service had restored to look as the emigrants from 1852 to 1868 saw it. We sampled typical nineteenth-century foods and explored the buildings, but since Tamsen Donner had never seen this place, it held little interest for me, falling into the educational-for-the-children genre.

That afternoon when we left Fort Laramie, I pointed out a smudge of gray on the edge of a far-off cloud. "Oh, oh," I said, "Looks like rain. We better check into a motel," and the children went crazy with cheers.

Down the street from the motel at Margaret's Cafe, Roger and I got coffee and the kids split a bowl of chili and three hamburgers. The bill was $5.01. Jennifer, the day's accountant, took it to the woman who was cooking, serving, and cashiering, and said it should have been $3.71. The woman said she had to get all the extra utensils, but she'd let it go this time. The children went back to the motel while Roger and I dawdled over coffee, wanting to talk to people, not sure of the etiquette. Everybody knew everybody else. The door continually opened, people sticking their heads in to touch base, sometimes walking over to help themselves to coffee. We were neither hurried nor asked to linger.

We'd seen Western movies. If our timing was off, eyes would narrow:

We don't like nosy strangers round these parts. Or we might give up too soon and walk out to hear behind us an incredulous voice, Who were those masked strangers just passed by? We sat tight and drank coffee, trying to look inviting and nonthreatening, after a while, inconspicuous. We weren't sure how much more coffee our bodies would take.

A man commented on the New York license plates. "Buffalo," I said off-hand, but loudly enough so everybody'd know we weren't people from the New York City sticks who'd never heard animals.

"You had some winter this year," another man said.

"Yep."

A weathered man in a faded plaid Western shirt pulled a chair up to our booth to hear more about the Blizzard of '77. Earnest Garhart. He was married to Margaret, the owner of the cafe. After some blizzard stories, the conversation eased into other areas. We said we were following the Oregon Trail. "I can show you a grave," a man said two booths down. His companions laughed. They looked like they were out of Deliverance. I bet you can, I thought, nodding noncommittally.

A different man, maybe in his 30s, slid in next to Roger. "This is Harold," Earnest said. Harold grinned, and kept on grinning, noticeably retarded. Margaret cooked, served, cleared, bantered with the regulars. She could have been 55, or 65. The traffic thinned. She sat down in our booth. Up and down, she gave out pieces of information between customers. Earnest owned some land. How much or how valuable wasn't clear. Two sons of theirs had had some college education, possibly paid for by their employer.

"My family homesteaded here in 1922," she said. I was thinking about that—that they were pioneers, that in my parents' lifetime, Wyoming had been homesteaded—when Margaret got up and locked the door and closed the blinds. It was still light outside. It seemed an arbitrary closing. She sat back down and continued talking. "We passed Earnest just as his momma had been killed by lightning. He went on with us for a while. He was 12; I was 5. They were really poor. He stayed a while and helped my poppa. Eight, nine, ten years later, we got married."

I was thinking about that lightning bolt striking his mother. Did I hear those ages right? He was 20 to 22, she was 13 to 15?

"I've had a couple of restaurants. I didn't want to leave the last one, but I had to because of Earnest's job." She looked straight at Earnest. "I'm not moving again."

It grew dark. The friends of the man two booths over let themselves out. The man who could show us a grave sat alone. We were the only other people in the cafe. I got up and poured my own coffee like a regular. Tables were still uncleared.

"I remember my mother once going into town to have a baby," Margaret said. "I was 5 or 6. There was a snake in the rafters of our cabin. I was terrified. A townslady took me in. I thought it was a palace. Though I see it now, and it isn't much of anything.

"I had some schooling. If there was a certain number of kids in the family, they'd send a schoolteacher, a young girl; she'd teach us what she knew. There must have been six of us."

She gestured to Harold, still sitting next to Roger. Harold grinned. "Harold is my brother's child. His mother ran off after his birth. My brother was crippled from the war. He got married again and when Harold was 18 months old, his stepmother beat him with a board. He was unconscious for nine days. Every time my brother tried to teach Harold something, something happened to Harold. We took him for two weeks to help out. They kinda lost interest. He's 29. He's been both a burden and a pleasure."

Margaret's face was permanently marked with hard life with an overlay of exhaustion. "It's late," I said. "You have to get up early and you still have a lot of work to do." She shrugged.

"Would you like to see that grave?" the man in the booth asked.

It was a thrilling ride. "It was so late, otherwise we would have come and got you," we told the children the next morning. "You would have loved it, especially the ride . . ."

Charlie Andersen drove an ordinary sedan like a four-wheel drive. We plunged down hills, roared upgrade, in and through and over potholes—every time the belly scraped the bottom of the roller-coaster road, I thought how much fun this was and how glad I was it wasn't our car. And suddenly, the bronco car stopped. Charlie turned off the motor, and we were in silence. The sky was chunked with stars, moonlight spilling down, hitting the irrigation dikes, reflecting off silver ribbons of still water. Everything was in shadow and yet distinct, especially the lonely pioneer grave.

Charlie Andersen had a long, elaborate story to go along with the grave about a rich man, living in Europe because Wyoming memories were too painful, who flew back annually to care for his sister's grave. The story seemed implausible, the dates confusing, but Andersen told it with caring and intensity. How moving it was: the stillness, the sharpness of lines and light, the deep pleasure of standing somewhere in Wyoming with a stranger who shared our passion for lonely graves. We walked slowly and talked. He seemed a placid man, but when he spoke about the vandals who destroyed pioneer graves, and again when he talked about government buying up all the land, his voice trembled in anger. "You can't small ranch anymore," he said, echoing Leonhard Weiland's "You can't small farm anymore" a thousand miles away. Andersen gestured fiercely toward the dikes, "People drown in those dikes!"

The time impressed me most. For months, I puzzled over why people gave us so much time when they had so many claims on it. Maybe they don't have fresh listeners, a friend suggested. It didn't seem as simple as that. It seemed more that maybe they knew some secret of life I didn't know. Andersen had waited in the cafe booth for hours, then drove miles to show us the grave. It was the middle of the night and he was thirty miles from where he lived and worked. He had to get up early, but he was unhurried. He didn't know I was a writer or Roger a professor. All he knew was that we were interested in pioneers. "You take an awful lot of time for strangers," I said. "My father was the same way," he said. "He was police chief and people used to come back twenty years later remembering some kindness he had done."

Twenty years and more from now, I'll remember the kindness of that moonlit grave, Charlie Andersen.

You wouldn't want to think too closely about the fried eggs we ate for breakfast at Margaret's. Harold spread bric-a-brac all over our table: ugly, useless objects he made by pouring plaster into rubber molds. They were for sale. "Thank you for showing them to us," I said. Brain damaged but no dummy, Harold understood immediately. Disappointed, he took them away. I suddenly registered that the walls, shelves, countertops, all the restaurant's surfaces, were covered with Harold's molds. He reappeared and handed me a pink envelope with a piece of pink flowered stationery inside. Written on it was: "Margaret-Earnest Garhart (cafe) & Harold Petersen. Fort Laramie, Wyoming, 1977." He gave us a stone. "A special Wyoming stone," he said. He collected them near Fort Laramie. I wrote down our address and said, "Maybe someday you'll be our way." He grew excited and looked to Margaret for verification. She looked at him like, You birdbrain. All I could think of were those people who say life is what you make it and Harold sitting there grinning at us with his baby brains bashed with a board.

On the trip home to Buffalo, I was sitting with a man in his beautiful house filled with antiques. We were drinking gin and tonics. He was a business executive and I told him about the cafe stuffed with Harold's molds, production up and sales down, tried to describe the Garharts' faces, their hands. "They work so hard," I said. "Those people work harder than any of us will ever work and they have so little to show for it."

"Don't you think they're happier?" he said.

Outraged, but chicken to say so, I said that a priest friend said we shouldn't try to be like the poor, the poor wanted to be like us. I fumbled and said it badly. The man shifted in his velvet chair and talked for some time about the pleasures of the simple things in life.

I use the rock for a paperweight. It's a beautiful rock, browns and yellows, rough and smooth, shiny and chunky. It looks like it came from Wyoming.

About two miles from Fort Laramie, Mary E. Homsley's original grave marker, an old stone, was inserted into a concrete obelisk, preserved under glass. A board fence was around it. The stone was carved by her husband, and we could still read it clearly.

MARY E HOMSLEY
DIED JUNE 10.52
AGE 28

This was six years after the Donner Party, and it's likely Mary Homsley knew the story of the Donners. Most pioneers from 1847 on knew the story; it was the cautionary tale, the horror story.

Mary E. Homsley's stone was discovered in 1925. Her daughter, then 76, was found, and she told the story of seeing her mother buried there when she was 3.

The graves in the middle of nowhere, out in a field, were the ones that touched me most. Farmers cared for those lonely graves, fenced them, plowed around them, remembering the price paid for the land. I thought of the wagons drawing farther and farther away, leaving a child or parent or spouse behind, someone watching the grave get smaller out the oval as Sarah Keyes watched her home and all that was known recede. Then I realized that for the pioneers, all the graves were left in the middle of nowhere.

26

Register Cliff, just before Guernsey, Wyoming, on Highway 26, and farther on, Independence Rock on Highway 220, were where the pioneers signed in on their way by. They were the autograph books of the Oregon Trail.

At the foot of Register Cliff, under a profusion of signatures, were three nameless pioneer graves with an iron fence around them. Nearby, at the base of the cliff, we found the autographs of the Unthanks' clan:

A.H. Unthank 1850
O.N. Unthank 1869
O.B. Unthank 1931

Now there was a family that kept its stories alive. O.N. Unthank was A.H.'s (Alva's) nephew, O.B. was Alva's great-grandson. Searching out Alva's signature to put theirs underneath, the nephew and great-grandson knew what Alva didn't: a week's travel away, Alva would be dead.

Although Alva Unthank and other signatures we noted had nothing to do with the Donner Party, I sought them all out eagerly, because they were some of the rare physical evidence left of the Great Migration. Our trip had grown easily and organically to include pioneers in general, to retracing the California and Oregon Trail as well as the Donner Trail, and to graves over a twenty-thirty-year span. Although every pioneer party, like families, would have its own stories, they all shared many similarities. One could extrapolate, never with certainty, but at least make an educated guess about parts of the Donners' experience.

Outside of Guernsey, a hundred yards up, was Deep Rut Hill. Wagon ruts were eroded, cut, etched six feet deep in the sandstone. Walking in the ruts on a dusty, burning day, in the very tracks of countless wagons, I felt on holy ground. I saw Roger and Charity climbing, disappearing around rocks behind Maria and Ursula, Jennifer and Gabriella ahead of me in the ruts; if they were talking, I couldn't hear them; I blocked out some noisy tourists clambering up a small hill, wished them gone. I wanted to be alone. Tamsen Donner's farm back in Springfield had seemed hallowed ground to me, but just a couple of weeks away, I realized a difference. There I had felt incredulous; I could hardly believe that the Donner farm, the Donners, had been real and I was really there. Here it was as if the swale traces across Kansas, Nebraska, Wyoming had been preparing me for these dramatic marks: stigmata of the Oregon Trail. Here I walked in the proof, and my only incredulity was that this has been here for over a hundred years, how could I have not known this?

A short walk from Deep Rut Hill was the grave site of Lucindy Rollins, who died in 1849. For a long time, the original gravestone was preserved from the elements behind glass like Mary Homsley's, but vandals had recently destroyed both the glass and the stone. A small concrete obelisk marked the grave.

In 1961 a few miles south and east of Glenrock off Interstate 25, a rancher, collecting rocks for a dam, turned one over. Chiseled on the flat side of the boulder was:

1843. J. Hembree

The 4 was reversed.

Paul Henderson, the eminent trail scholar who lived in Bridgeport, Nebraska, came and identified Joel Hembree, a 6-year-old boy who was the first death of the Applegate Party of 1843 on their way to Oregon. William Newby, a member of that party, wrote in his diary:

[July 18] A very bad road. Joel J Hembree's son Joel fel off the waggon & both wheels run over him.

[July 19] Lay buy. Joel Hembree departed this life about 2 o'clock.

[July 20] We buried the youth & in graved his name on the head stone.

Anyone who has ever traveled with children can appreciate the restlessness of children in a covered wagon rolling all day. Children's accidents, in and out of the wagon, were not infrequent. "Little Agnas B. fell in the fire today. Poorly," said one diary.

Word of little Joel Hembree's death might have gotten back East in a letter for Tamsen Donner to read before she left. On the trail, three years later, his grave might still have been visible.

Paul Henderson excavated and moved Joel Hembree's grave. An old oak dresser drawer covered the top part of the body, branches the lower part. The skeleton was intact, and a skull fracture evident, Henderson said, although Marcus Whitman, a doctor traveling with the Applegate Party, wrote that the "small boy . . . died from a waggon having passed over the abdomen." The bones were moved to higher ground, put in a new pine box, and reburied.

Before we got a crib, Maria, our firstborn, slept in an oak dresser drawer in our bedroom to make night breastfeeding easier and because I was afraid she might stop breathing and I wouldn't hear. I used to joke with my heart in my mouth about sleepwalking and closing the drawer, black Irish joking to ward off terrors of doing harm to one's own. I thought about Joel Hembree's parents spreading branches on their little boy like a blanket, tucking him in, carefully placing the dresser drawer over his crushed body to keep him from further violation. I thought about that dresser with one drawer gone, that gaping dark hole, continuing along with them. To bury your child: you couldn't bear it and you'd have to.

Well before the journey, Tamsen knew that pain.

I have lost that little boy I loved so well, she wrote. . . . *O my sister weep with me if you have tears to spare.*

Near Glenrock, there was a lonely grave out in a field of scruffy grass, cactus, and stones. Alva Unthank, who a week earlier had signed in on Register Cliff, now had his name carved on another stone:

A H Unthank
Wayne Co. Ind.
Died July 2 1850

There was a footstone too, the only grave on the Oregon Trail that had one, with initials chiseled:

A H U

Ada Magill got dysentery at Fort Laramie and died five miles west of Glenrock. Somebody had put a little bunch of plastic flowers on her grave.

ADA
THE DAUGHTER OF
G.W. & N.C. MAGILL
DIED JULY 3, 1864

Ada was 6 years old. Charity, a month from 6, and Gabriella, 7, were sober. They walked off by themselves, picked wildflowers, and put them on Ada's grave.

At Casper, we took Highway 220 to Independence Rock and climbed it, about a ten-minute climb, to examine the numerous names still visible. I loved the old names; anything over fifty years seemed history; the new names irritated me, seemed vandalism. By my own standards, a person coming along in 2025 would find our names history, but I wouldn't let the children sign, though they wanted to. It seemed to me that the pioneers earned the right to stake claim; we, tooling along in our red Chevy, hadn't. But that was romantic, I conceded. Maybe it was because it was already so hard to find the old names, I felt we'd just be cluttering the surface up, making the search more difficult. Or maybe it was as simple as there being so many of us—I didn't mean so many Burtons, though we were a lot; I meant now there were billions of us—we no longer could go around leaving our marks wherever we pleased. And what was the difference between people scrawling their names on these historic sites or on the Lincoln Memorial? Wasn't it all a kind of vandalism? The children had seen plenty of vandalism on this trip and didn't like it. If not convinced by my arguments, they deferred to my strong feeling.

We had the huge turtle-shaped Independence Rock to ourselves to go north, go south. If Tamsen Donner signed her name here, I knew I wouldn't find it. Every old name left had already been noted many times. Still I looked, with some kind of childish, magical hope that it would suddenly pop up, Excalibur out of the stone, **T.E. Donner** out of the rock, waiting there all those years for my eyes only to discover, to prove I was chosen to write her story. The black rock held the heat. The grades were steep. I was nervous that the children would fall, got mad at Roger for not watching them more closely, tried to keep an eye on them while trying to imagine myself on this rock 130 years earlier.

27

Where Highway 220 forked into 287, we swung right. Exactly 9.4 miles west of Jeffrey City was a historical marker telling about the Ice Slough, a peat bog that in pioneer times yielded chunks of ice in the middle of summer. "We gathered several buckets of ice, from which we had mint juleps in abundance," Dr. T. wrote in 1848. All who passed dug up as much as they could carry to enjoy the luxury of ice water all day. Our shallow pokings with fingers and sticks revealed cold ground but no ice. Gabriella slipped, her sneaker stuck in the gray foul-smelling muck that only washed off with soap—I pulled her out like a little suction cup. While we worked on the gucky sneaker with sticks and leaves to get it dry enough to carry in the car until we could find a gas station, Charity stuck her foot in up to her ankle—"She did that on purpose!" Maria, Jennifer, and Ursula insisted, leveling the charge Charity hated most: "SHE JUST WANTS ATTENTION." A somewhat humorous charge leveled by three top bananas in a family of six top bananas—the lone exception, Gabriella—it wasn't motivated by jealousy but by fear for Charity's character. Her older sisters were convinced that, without their close monitoring and admonitions, tiny, sprightly, darling Charity would fall victim to the easy, lavish attention heaped on her by family and strangers alike, growing up shallow rather than what they thought of as a proper Burton. Charity, tiny in frame but powerful in personality and force, denied the charge heatedly. Her hiking boot was totally encased in the thick guck. Accident or intentional, she got attention all right.

When Tamsen Donner sent her three youngest daughters, Frances, 6, Georgia, 5, and Eliza, 3, (ages at rescue), out with the Third Relief, she told them again as she had told them many times in the mountains, "Remember. You are the children of Mr. and Mrs. George Donner."

Pioneer journals record the scene of the three little ragged girls wandering around Sutter's Fort, always looking to the mountains for their mother to come, saying by rote to any stranger who would listen, "We are the children of Mr. and Mrs. George Donner."

How do you build a sense of family? Deliberately, I felt at the beginning. Later on: by the seat of our pants.

I don't know at what point we became The Burtons and knew the criteria for "a proper Burton." Long before I'd heard of Tamsen Donner, when Maria, Jennifer, and Ursula were younger than Frances, Georgia, and Eliza, I frequently said, "Never go against your sister. Your friends come and go, but your sister is your sister always. You're family." Roll of drums. Even while saying it, I knew it had its weak spots, but I wanted it to be so. In those years, beginning marriage and motherhood in the Kennedy Camelot time, in the managed news time, I think I aspired to some vague Kennedy compound in my head.

"You're family" proceeded to "Remember, you're the Burtons." And of course, "Burtons don't do that." Surely it was a short step to "Burtons do this," and a mere shift of weight before the children said, "We're the Burtons."

And what did it mean to be "the Burtons"? The list was endless and ever-growing, started by Roger and me, but quickly amplified and extended by the children themselves. Burtons spend Sundays cleaning the house, Burtons don't sass their parents, Burtons don't wear halter tops—that came from her four younger appalled sisters when Maria appeared in a friend's green halter top—of course Burtons don't smoke, Burtons have good table manners, Burtons treat others as they would like to be treated, Burtons pick up trash at pioneer sites, Burtons roll their windows down when it's raining to feel like pioneers . . .

And families have been doing this since the begats. Only God or a good shrink or tears in the night could count all the parental expectations—unspoken, unintended, even unconscious—that pour down through the generations to shape children like Bonsai trees, maybe beautifully, but not necessarily their true natures. When you're older, the tears dry and you accept that this is the way humans parent, and the best you can hope for is an advance of the generations.

After I got into the women's movement, we all struggled together to create a feminist family, trying to maintain an environment that supported both love and work. While sailing alone from Massachusetts to North Carolina in 1824, Tamsen wrote Betsey, *I do not regret nor shall I the fatigue nor embarrassment to which I have subjected myself. My heart is big with hope and impatient with desire.* So was my heart most of the time, though the impatience was often greater than the hope. As far as I was concerned, we were pioneers with few models, leaving the known nuclear family in the dust, traveling our own Oregon Trail to a new, better way of living with and loving one another. The trick was to keep on mile after mile.

We tried always to pull for each other, and when jealousy and competition showed up, the family motto was, "Clap loudly for your sister; next time, she'll be in your audience." We alternated wonderful successes with terrible failures, dissecting both endlessly around our dining room table, making up the plan as we went along, revising when it failed, making something else up. I vacillated between thinking that we were re-creating a bizarre Victorian relic that would eventually swallow or enfeeble us all, and thinking that we were on the eighth day and God had gotten up well rested in good humor and was off to a terrific start.

There were times in later years when one or another Burton filled with teenage hubris leapt up on a dining room chair, the better to claim attention, and stopped discussion of some outlandish proposal with the clincher, "Of course we can go to China. We're the Burtons!"

"This Burton stuff is getting pathological," I said, quite seriously more than once, and everybody laughed and then one of my daughters would say gently, wryly, "Face it, Mom, we are the Burtons."

Although I wondered sometimes, most of the time I loved it.

When does identification become identity? How deep, how permanent are these things? How deep and permanent should they be? I had no idea. I think now that we grew too insular, too self-contained, too tribal for everybody's individual good, but as to the depth and permanency of the Burton identity, I'd say it's akin to the indelible mark on the soul little Catholic babies get at baptism.

28

A marker by the side of a Wyoming road:

> Survivors of Captain Edward Martin's Handcart Company of Mormon Emigrants from England to Utah were rescued here in perishing condition about Nov. 12, 1856. Delayed in starting and hampered by inferior handcarts, it was overtaken by an early winter. Among the company of 376, including aged people and children, the fatalities numbered 145. Insufficient food and clothing and severe weather caused many deaths. Toward the end every camp ground became a graveyard.

An 1856 diarist wrote about one handcart company: "There were old men pulling and tugging their carts, sometimes loaded with a sick wife or children, women pulling along sick husbands, little children six to eight years old struggling through the mud and snow. As night came on the mud would freeze on their clothes and feet."

A second marker tells of another Mormon party and thirteen persons freezing to death in one night, buried in a common grave, two more dying the next day. Of the 404 who started that trip, 77 died.

The emigrants of 1846 feared that the Mormons would kill any Gentiles (what they called non-Mormons) they saw in retaliation for being burned out, shot out, driven out of their towns. The church, founded only sixteen years before, was widely considered an extreme sect, and I, who had grown up cheering the Christians against the lions, never thought once of religious persecution in connection with Mormons. I couldn't get past the polygamy.

One hundred thirty-one years after the Mormons were violently driven West, the Mormon Church was now a multibillion-dollar empire, but for me, the many good characteristics of Mormons—self-reliance, diligence, perseverance, faith—were sullied by the overt unabashed patriarchy of their institution, specifically manifested in its treatment of women and minorities. Of course, women were Mormons too, but in the Mormon Church, as in almost every other organized religion, the men spoke for God and God spoke in bass tones.

In Kansas City, Missouri, we had visited a Mormon Visitors Center to inquire about Levinah Murphy, a member of the Donner Party supposed to be a devout Mormon, though perhaps not in good standing. Because Mormons believed souls could be saved after death through proxy baptism, they had probably the best-kept genealogy records in the country. We never found out anything about Levinah Murphy, but we got a lecture tour by a woman in white, a "sister," who told my daughters a half dozen times that the greatest thing a woman could do was marry and have children. I fumed, smoke started coming out my nose: *Look, Sister, that stuff smells coming from celibate men; it doesn't get sweeter coming from bigamists.* She showed them a two-story-high mural of Jesus: "Watch, children," she whispered piously. "His eyes follow you no matter where you go." My eyes were rolling back into my head; I was frothing when Ursula volunteered eagerly, "We have a poster at home of Uncle Sam that does the same thing." Undaunted, perhaps inspired, by my children's heathenism, she led them from one religious mural, diorama, exhibit to another, spinning Mormon lore about the Angel Moroni showing Joseph Smith the golden plates engraved with hieroglyphics that Smith, with heavenly aid, translated into the Book of Mormon. "And people say Catholicism has loose ends," I hissed to Roger. She let them touch a giant book, six feet tall. "Take a picture, Roger," I said, I was beside myself, "Take a picture." I looked at the woman bubbling about angels and giant books and all I could see were chains, the subjugation of women, her *white* dress, *sister* indeed, I wanted to get it all down, documented, *"Take a picture!"*

At home, we developed numerous slides of Mormon religious exhibits.

But the Mormon tragedies, well documented along the Trail, were deeply moving. At one time these people paid a very high price, and if I didn't like what they got for it, that still didn't negate the price. And for whatever reason, the Mormons also remembered their own. Their eye might be on heaven, but they knew where they came from and who had gone before making their way possible.

This same sense of the past and their own history was shared by the Daughters of the American Revolution, a joke when I was growing up, fussy old ladies who cared only about pedigree, and earlier in 1939, a scandal, preventing opera singer Marian Anderson from singing in Constitution Hall because she was black. Eleanor Roosevelt resigned from the DAR in protest, and on Easter Sunday, Marian Anderson sang for seventy-five thousand people from the steps of the Lincoln Memorial. But if the DAR were afraid of black women's history and afraid to make history, they hadn't let one part of history be lost: many of the markers along the Oregon Trail were put there by the DAR.

From Highway 287 we cut southwest on State Route 28 to South Pass. Actually a valley twenty-nine miles wide, South Pass was the emigrants' access through the Rocky Mountains. Here they crossed the Great Divide. Even though everything had been steadily getting stranger, up until now they had technically been traveling in the East toward the West; now they were in the West, the East, known, behind them.

The Continental Divide. An invisible boundary between East and

West. Were schoolchildren taught the awesomeness of it? It was the kind of boundary children understood and loved, the stuff of fairy tale borders. Here you are in the East. All water flows toward the Atlantic Ocean. Here you are in the West. All water flows toward the Pacific Ocean. Here you straddle nature's dividing line.

If we hadn't had Gregory Franzwa's book, we never would have found it. The roads were so bad you couldn't believe you were on the right one. One impossible road and then a second worse one, only us and a white-tailed antelope bounding, and suddenly, a stone marker that said Old Oregon Trail.

A second marker had the names of Narcissa Whitman and Eliza Spaulding, the first white women to cross the Great Divide in 1836 on their way to Oregon to set up missions to convert the Indians. Narcissa was pregnant with little blonde Alice, first American white child born in the wilderness. Two years after Narcissa stood at this spot, little Alice drowned in the Walla Walla River. In November 1847, seven months after the last survivors of the Donner Party got out of the Sierra Nevadas, Narcissa was slaughtered in an Indian massacre.

29

Twelve hundred miles from Independence, Missouri, the Oregon Trail forked: you swung right, northwest, for Oregon, or left for California. **The Parting of the Ways.** Gregory Franzwa's book said that the official marker was incorrectly placed, but we were definitely in the neighborhood.

Roger drove in the Oregon Trail tracks for a half mile or so, the children alternating walking with me and hopping into the slow-moving car. I was secretly shocked by his driving our Chevy in the ruts. That was the Catholic in me: already the ruts had become relics to be wondered at, revered, not touched. Yet the Oregon Trail was a road and what tracks of it remained were due to ranchers and farmers using it as such.

We backtracked up Route 28 and headed north on U.S. Highway 287 to visit Sacajawea's grave on the Wind River Indian reservation where the Shoshone and Arapaho tribes lived. Although her grave had nothing to do with the Donner Party, cutting up to the reservation didn't seem a detour. Indians, the land theirs at the time, a part of the Donners' experience—*The Indians frequently come to see us, and the chiefs*

9. Roger driving in Oregon Trail tracks.

of a tribe breakfasted at our tent this morning. All are so friendly that I cannot help feeling sympathy and friendship for them.—it seemed almost imperative that in some way they be a part of our retracing. And of course, this whole trip had happened because of searching for a heroine. Had Sacajawea not been female and a minority, my daughters and I might have learned in school about the Sacajawea Expedition.

I felt uneasy when we drove onto the reservation, a little scared. Were whites welcome here? Why should we be? We pulled over, a carful of palefaces, and asked an Indian for directions. He drew us a map.

There were two cemeteries. My guidebook said without elaboration that Sacajawea was buried in the Indian cemetery, Chief Washaki in the government cemetery. The latter was slightly more formal than the former, neither like any cemetery I'd ever seen. The Indian cemetery was particularly wonderful.

Sacajawea guided the Lewis and Clark Expedition from the Missouri River to the Pacific Coast and back during 1805–06. What happened after that is unclear and unresolved. Some say she died in 1812 at age 24. Others say she died in 1884, nearly a hundred years old, and was buried with her two sons on either side of her, one of those sons, Charbonneau, born and raised while on the two-and-a-half-year expedition. Her gravestone here, a tall, rectangular gray stone, could be seen from a long way off, rising out of a field of white crosses, a guide to the cemetery and a reference point within it.

The cemetery, the antithesis of the usual manicured Eastern cemetery, was dusty, dry ground, long wind-tossed desert grasses bending from their own weight, clumps of sage telling you: This is the West, This is harsh land. From a distance, the cemetery appeared to be a mass of white crosses spreading out longitudinally, bounded only by the butte behind and blue sky above, one tall gray stone a sentinel. Close up, it was shocks of color. In between the white crosses, modest commercial headstones and ordinary rocks nestled in overgrown grass and sage; everywhere there were flowers—scattered wildflowers, floral arrangements in varying states of dying and drying with bright satin ribbons, and masses of artificial flowers. Plastic flowers that in Eastern cemeteries often looked tacky in their formal atmosphere, out here against parched earth and brilliant blue sky were riots of vivid color—joyous, celebratory, defiant—dramatic as life and death. So many graves were ingeniously bordered, contained, that it was obviously an Indian custom, but none of my books told the significance. Metal rails that appeared to be delicately curved bedstands ran lengthwise along the sides of one grave, plastic flowers twining in between the rusted bars, the overall effect that of a pretty trellis. Stones, placed in a rectangle, marked out another grave. Little white pickets, a miniature fence, framed another.

A mass of plastic flowers covered a double mound. Two stone hearts overlapped, forever twining.

Mother	Daughter
Sannette	Sonja
1948–1976	1975–76

The commercial marker was raised beyond sentimentality by the tender ages. It used to be diphtheria; what happened last year to this 28-year-old mother and her 1-year-old daughter? There were many premature deaths in this cemetery, and we talked about the high incidence of alcoholism and suicide among despairing Native Americans, their land stolen, culture scorned and debased, no jobs, little hope.

Chief Washaki, the great Shoshone chief, was buried in the government cemetery, a small graveyard enclosed by a stone wall. Many graves there were bordered with wooden rectangles, four pieces of wood making a frame for the grave. More expensive graves with headstones were bordered with commercial stone frames.

Outside the cemetery, which was probably full, there was a Vietnam vet: white cross, red flowers, American flag, his grave bordered on three sides with irregularly shaped stones—the kind you picked up off the ground someplace—the modest headstone at the top completing the rectangular frame. Deep red flowers—making me think more of

Valentines than of blood—on a bone-white cross, the stars and stripes not moving on the hot still day: we talked about the disproportionate number of American minorities who died for our country.

We were the only living people in both these cemeteries and yet there was a strong feeling of presence. These were not neglected or avoided places. Somebody cared that these people lived and died, the expression of that caring so rich in color, ceremony, and spirit that you felt surrounded by life, past and present. What was striking about most of the graves was how personal they were. Even those with commercial stones had unique touches added, making you feel the uniqueness of both the individuals buried and those burying. The real sadness of these cemeteries was the loss of that uniqueness to American society.

We continued northwest on 287 to Yellowstone National Park because it seemed foolish to be this close and not take the children. Almost immediately after we entered the park, we saw money and papers blowing on the road, finding a billfold with $437.00 cash, travelers checks, credit cards. It belonged to John Godley of Montreal, who drove a vw Rabbit, his registration said; for two hours we pursued every vw Rabbit or facsimile. The kids couldn't wait to see the look on his face when we honked him over and handed him the wallet. We eventually turned it and its contents into the rangers, but John Godley came with us the rest of the trip—every one of the scores of lost items we drove by, all those mysterious clothes that probably creep out of motorcyclist's packs, the single shoes that appear in the highway, "Hey look," Gabriella said, "John Godley lost his sneaker." "There's John Godley's T-shirt," Charity said. "Can you believe this guy," Roger said, "there's his khakis."

At Yellowstone, we saw Old Faithful, boiling pools, grizzly bears, moose, wildflowers and algae; we camped, took nature walks, and the kids donned their poke bonnets to board a Yellowstone horse and stagecoach. We made a spate of ranger jokes, based on the rangers' ponderous practice of calling each other Ranger Rick, Ranger Bob, et cetera, and we, Ranger Rog and Ranger Gabe, spoke in dumb accents about obvious things, which broke the children up. We had a good time and it was all educational, but I chafed to get back to Tamsen Donner. Several years before, a child had fallen into one of the boiling pools and had been scalded to death; I was nervous about the children, held Charity's and Gabriella's hands, kept saying to Ursula, Jennifer, and Maria, "This stuff is dangerous, you know."

Inside the tent, Roger and I, our bags zipped together, generally slept in the middle, one or two of the children taking turns sleeping vertically on either side of us, one or two horizontal, head to head, across the bottom. At Yellowstone, Gabriella and Charity, who always slept next to each other—in one bunk at home, alternating top and bottom bunks—zipped their bags together too, because Gabriella was afraid of bears coming in. I'm still not a fan of camping, but I can think of few things sweeter than lying in that canvas cocoon, disembodied voices in the dark telling stories, cracking jokes, asking questions, singing lullabies, one or another of us talking quietly until no one was.

Watching other parents carry babies or toddlers, it dawned on me that this was the first trip that we didn't have a child in arms or in a carrier on our backs. "Do you realize that this is the least physically exhausting trip we've ever taken," I said to Roger. In the middle of the night when Charity threw up in the tent, projectile vomiting, managing to bull's-eye more bags and people than you would've thought possible, five of us running around in the dark, hand-pumping water, grabbing paper towels, cleaning the tent, sleeping bags, and ourselves by a flashlight held by Gabriella next to her wan sister, Roger turned to me and said, "It's great that the days of tiring travel are behind us."

The first day in the park, I encouraged the children to turn in some soft drink cans we saw on a bench, because Wyoming had just enacted a new bottle law, a nickel a can. For the rest of our time in Yellowstone, they proceeded to spend an inordinate amount of time with their heads stuck in trash bins retrieving cans. It drove me crazy. God knew what it cost to show them Yellowstone and they earned $7.40 in four days. Jennifer said they had to fight John Godley for every one of the 148 cans. They blew their entire earnings on a rare treat: junk food for the whole family.

On a drive, we passed a lake where boys were swimming and jumping off a rock ledge, maybe forty feet high. "Can we do it, can we do it?" Maria, just 14, and Jennifer, nearly 13, asked. It looked exciting and dangerous: "Absolutely not," we said. We watched for a while and I asked Roger, demanded really, "If they were sons, would you let them do it?" He nodded. "Then we have to let them do it," I said. We stalled. Asked a boy who had just done it. "It's not dangerous," he said. "Just jump far out." "I want to jump too," Ursula said. Roger and I looked at each other. Well, she's 10.

Maria, Jennifer, and Ursula swam across, climbed up the rock, stood on top, waved to us, we waved back. Maria went to the edge. We died. "JUMP FAR OUT," Roger shouted. Maria jumped, we died, she surfaced. Jennifer stood on top looking down, looking down, looking down. "Jenny was scared and shaking," Ursula said later. "It was very far down there. I said, 'I'll count. One, two, THREE!'" Jennifer jumped, we died, she surfaced. Ursula jumped, we died, she surfaced. Roger, Gabriella, Charity, and I cheered.

Not two years later, Roger and I decided that if we had it to do over again, we wouldn't let daughters or sons jump.

On our way back to the Donners' trail, we stopped at Jenny Lake so we could take Jenny's picture: **Jenny at Jenny Lake**. "We clung to moments where we were the special one," Jennifer said years later. Each child *was* the special one to Roger and me, each a strong distinct personality with her unique gifts, but with five children in eight years, there was little time to spend one on one. Birthdays, recitals, and illnesses belonged to you, but otherwise, we tended to treat them as a monolith. I often spoke of them in the plural—the children did this, the children said that—as if five voices had shouted out the punch line simultaneously. Sometimes I wonder if they had; today, they all lay claim to the funniest jokes.

30 Little Sandy, Wyoming, the Campfire of Decision

Highway 187 south took us to Farson, Wyoming, and a little northeast on Route 28 was Little Sandy, a shallow tributary of the Green River, where the men of the Donner Party voted to take the controversial Hastings Cutoff. This was the shortcut debated at campfires from Independence on and that Jim Clyman had warned James Reed against taking back by Fort Laramie. But now they had reached the campfire of decision, and a month of travel saved in this strange country was a powerful consideration. The Oregon-bound emigrants said good-bye to the California-bound emigrants. Jessy Quinn Thornton, Oregon-bound, noted in his diary: "The Californians were generally much elated and in fine spirits, with the prospect of a better and nearer road to the country of their destination. Mrs. George Donner was however, an exception. She was gloomy, sad, and dispirited, in view of the fact that her husband and others could think for a moment of leaving the old road and confide in the statement of a man of whom they knew nothing but who was probably some selfish adventurer."

Gloomy, sad, and dispirited. Some wonder now if Thornton's

hindsight colored his memory of Tamsen, but if so, why her, why so specific? Maybe Thornton embroidered the mood and the words, but I believed that among the hundreds of people at Little Sandy, the massive confusion of decisions, preparations, and leave takings, he had geared in on an incredulous woman railing against powerlessness. [W]illing to go, she wasn't willing to go this way. Being taken on Hastings Cutoff against her better judgment, she wasn't going silently.

Before Little Sandy, that last campfire of choice, there was no Donner Party. The group of men who voted to take Hastings Cutoff elected George Donner leader a day later, giving the Donner Party its name. An honor in pretty much name only, the captain selected the campsite, gave the start in the morning, and settled minor disputes. Important things were settled by the company as a whole, that is, the men, who had the first and the last say. George Donner was a well-off, good-natured farmer—too amiable to handle crisis, the writers of Donner books usually said. But, except maybe for Tamsen, they weren't expecting crisis at this point. I also doubted that assessment of George Donner as a nice guy, but a bit of a bumbler. He had already emigrated a half dozen times and now to California; he had buried two wives and married a third, fathered eleven children; prospered as a farmer: this was a competent businessman with a great deal of life experience.

Luke Halloran, a twenty-eight-year-old consumptive traveling alone from Missouri to the healing sun of California, got into one of the Donner wagons at Little Sandy. Luke needed all the shortcuts he could get.

Little Sandy, the brick-red creek, was low now. We saw beaver and ducks, an antelope, a rabbit, bees, and flies. There were purple and yellow wildflowers and sage that smelled like turpentine. Ahead were mounds, hills, buttes. The sky was the bluest blue with puffy white clouds. Our time was nearly synchronized with the Donners now; the way the land appeared to us was close to how Tamsen would have seen it that July 20.

In Farson we talked to Marjorie Homan about the Little Sandy, and then drove twenty miles to a campground—a gravel pit where we stumbled around in the dark trying to find a place to put up the tent. "This is ridiculous," Maria and Jennifer said several times until we ended up driving back to Farson and spending the night in Marjorie's hotel.

Marjorie Homan owned the whole town of Farson and it was up for sale: hotel, gas station, grocery store, laundromat, trailer court, cafe. She was asking three hundred thousand dollars. It seemed a buy. You'd get to be postmaster too. "Somebody asked me why I don't call myself postmistress," Marjorie said. "Well, I looked up *master* in the dictionary and it's somebody who controls things. That's what I am—the postmaster. We all know what *mistress* means."

Marjorie's husband had holes in his lungs from Freon gas inhaled while installing refrigerators. That was why the town was up for sale.

Once there was a shooting in her bar, provoked and unavoidable. Marjorie got the body out of the bar, her bartender out of town.

"Robert Redford's a baby," she said. "He romanticizes outlaws. My father knew Butch Cassidy; he was a hoodlum."

The Sierra Club and the conservationists made her sick too. "All those people want to keep this land a scruffy hole so people from the East can come out for two weeks in the summer, see desolate spaces, and say, 'Wow, look at that.'" They couldn't start the mining fast enough for Marjorie. To her, it meant employment, people able to buy themselves some decent things, advancement.

We stood in a corridor of her hotel talking, the light dim, the children sliding down the wall to sit or lie on the carpet runner with its big red faded flowers. Now and then I argued mildly, attempted to put in a good word for Robert Redford, but mostly listened, thinking about Hobson's choice: Was it better to be poor in a beautiful place or doing okay in an ugly place? Without environmental safeguards, you could live anywhere and end up with Freon in your lungs. "Wasn't she brave and pigheaded and wonderful?" I said to the kids when we went into our room. She certainly taught this conservationist something: if you were going to be a conservationist or a writer or a human, you'd better understand the complexity of the argument as well as the complexity of the people you'd cast as adversaries and have a little humility in the face of choices you were never going to have to make.

31

From Little Sandy, the Donner Party swung southwest toward Fort Bridger to meet Lansford Hastings to lead them on his cutoff. We shot directly south to I-80 East so we could take the route used by my modern characters on the motorcycle and I could see country we wouldn't see coming home. At Rock Springs, Wyoming, we spent the night in a Holiday Inn, Children Under 18 Free . . .

These places were a boon for us: we didn't have to lie about our numbers. Otherwise we had a morality test each time. How many children would we say we had, and if we failed it, how did we get the others in?

Our wants were simple: one room with two double beds, one for Roger and me, one for the kids who curled up like puppy dogs—anyone wanting more room could sleep in a sleeping bag on the floor. For security and economy, we wanted to be together in one room; we liked to talk about the day just passed, the day coming. The rare times we had two rooms, everybody ended up in one, nobody wanting to miss the stories or the jokes. We didn't ask for extra towels and took care not to abuse water usage, so it seemed our business if we wanted to stay in one room. Most motels, however, charged per head—I might do the same in their place, but in our place it would mean no motel. Generally, we signed in that we had three children, and then I agonized that there would be a fire, the firefighters would check the register, and after rescuing five people, they would stop.

At one motel, after we had said we had three children, it turned out that the only way to our room was through the main lobby past the desk clerk. Maria, Jennifer, and Ursula went in first, Ursula wearing a red baseball cap. She came back out, the cap in her pocket, and, five minutes later, walked back in with Gabriella wearing a red baseball cap. Gabriella came back out, the cap in her pocket . . . Three times, the red baseball cap on successively smaller heads walked past the desk clerk.

I ate my heart during these petty larcenies. I had the criminal mind to think up the crime but not the temperament to carry it out. It would be infinitely easier to pay whatever was asked, but I couldn't do that either.

At the Rock Spring motel, children under 18 free and a swimming pool besides, the children were ecstatic. Roger took them swimming, and I thought again as I was thinking every day, I could *never* have done this trip without him.

Much later, I thought, that was true, and I was deeply grateful: retracing the Oregon Trail turned out to be a lasting family experience. But the trip I took with my family because I was afraid to take it by myself was rife with paradox and irony. Without the kids, there wouldn't have been a need for Roger to run so much interference. Without Roger, I would have had to ask all the questions myself, make the approaches, read the maps, decide the turns: learn all the skills.

My family was on a vacation, but Tamsen Donner wasn't, and without presuming a parallel, neither was I. I was on a quest, a pilgrimage, a personal odyssey.

"We were your Greek chorus," Roger said once without rancor. "Always downstage. Always in the background."

"Always talking," I said.

I sat in the motel room trying to write something in my nearly blank journal. I'd written Wyoming all wrong in my novel. I'd made it ugly. In my imagination, probably old frames of cowboy movies all mixed up, it was a scruffy hole—I got my modern characters out of there fast and they had an unpleasant trip. Much of Wyoming was stunningly beautiful. Even where it was scruffy or barren, I got the ugly wrong, made it too one-dimensional. The sky was brilliant blue, the bluest sky you ever saw, with big cumulus clouds. Brown land with scraps of green, lots of sage and ponderosa, it was flat, then rolling, suddenly hilly, purple hills on the horizon, now it was red earth, red cliffs, jagged canyons, there were riots of wild flowers, constant rattle of grasshoppers, horses, cattle, sheep, white-tailed antelope grazing: the beauty never quit, just like Wyoming didn't seem to. Mile after mile, everything was distinct, sharply etched against the blue backdrop.

The vastness, appealing at first, slowly, cumulatively, became overwhelming. How did Tamsen Donner day after day keep walking into vastness? For two days I had been feeling sick and sad and aching, but I told myself Tamsen couldn't stop, couldn't quit. As we moved from grave to grave, tears rolled down my cheeks. Tamsen wouldn't have cried, I told myself, and then I thought, maybe I'm weeping for her; she couldn't afford to cry. But that was saccharine as well as unlikely. They were getting worn down by this point, but she still would have been optimistic, Hastings Cutoff not yet taken, thinking the dry drive much less than it turned out to be. Maybe I was crying because I knew the ending to the story and every day we moved closer to it. Or was it the graves? Or the land so ugly, so beautiful that never quit, just went on mile after mile.

I looked out the motel window at scrub land filled with sagebrush—surrounded by mountains. In between me and the mountains were a pair of McDonald's Golden Arches, a Shakey's Pizza sign, a Country Kitchen sign, a Holiday Inn sign, a West Winds Motel sign, a Corral West Ranchwear sign. That was it. How terrifying it must have been when there was nothing.

32

It took the Donners eight days to make the hundred miles from Little Sandy to Fort Bridger, their twelve and a half miles a day good time, the average covered wagon making ten to fifteen miles a day, twenty if they really pushed, but they weren't pushing yet.

They were surprised to find that Lansford Hastings had left Fort Bridger a week earlier to lead another party, but apparently not too concerned. Edwin Bryant, who had traveled with the Donners and Reeds, leaving the party to go faster to California by mule pack train, had left a letter for James Reed at Fort Bridger telling him not to take Hastings Cutoff. Reed never saw it. Reed wrote home that by taking the cutoff, they were only 250 miles from California, they wouldn't have any dust, and Jim Bridger had said that except for one dry stretch it was a fine level road. (Three months later in November, James Reed, banished from the wagon train for murder, had made it to California and was struggling to raise a rescue party to get back to the Party trapped in the Sierra Nevadas. Simultaneously, readers back in Illinois, dreaming of their own leave-taking the next April, were reading and rereading

10. Kids in wagon, Wyoming.

11. Ursula, Gabriella, and Charity (holding giant dandelion) in wagon.

Reed's letter in the *Sangamo Journal*, learning about Hastings's "fine level road," already counting their own miles saved.)

The Donner Party stayed at Fort Bridger four days, repairing the wagons, buying oxen, replacing what supplies they could at any price: Fort Bridger, the last post before the Sacramento Valley, was truly the jumping-off place. To replace a driver who had also gone off with the mule pack train, George Donner hired Jean Baptiste Trudeau (or Trubode or Tribodo or several other variations) from New Mexico. The McCutchens, William, Amanda, and 1-year-old Harriet joined the Donner Party at Fort Bridger also.

At today's Fort Bridger, Wyoming, population 150, the Fort Bridger that the Donners saw was gone. We took the children to the present one, then Roger and I went to the Bucking Horse Cafe and asked for Laura Dahlquist, another name from a Homer Croy footnote: "And here's a chance to thank Mrs. Laura Dahlquist, local historian. Her address: the Bucking Horse, Fort Bridger." I had no idea how Laura Dahlquist had helped Homer Croy, but by now, Croy's trip had become part of ours.

Laura Dahlquist was dead, the waitress said, but her husband, John Dahlquist, the owner of the cafe, would come downstairs to see us. The Bucking Horse was an eyeful of primary colors, Indian portraits, painted plates. The bottom half of each wall was painted bright red, the top white. An animal's rump—an antelope?—was mounted on the wall, its little tail looking at you, kid. The bathroom was red and white checkerboard cinderblocks.

"People come in every once in a while," John Dahlquist said, "and want to know this and that. They've heard different things and I have to set them right."

We sat at a table for several hours and talked about James Bridger and the Donner Party as if the subjects were current and vital.

"Was Bridger in cahoots with Hastings?" I asked.

"No way," Dahlquist said adamantly.

But it was pretty clear that if emigrants started using Hastings Cutoff,

Bridger with his Last Chance Charlie fort stood to make a mint equipping them. Most historians believed that his vested interest clouded his advice to the Donners.

"Jim Bridger tried to tell them not to take that route," Dahlquist insisted. He was unshakeable.

After we went at the topic from several different ways, he shrugged, "Vasquez [Bridger's partner] might be the one who told them to take it." Roger, part Mexican, flicked his eyes to me in a shorthand eye-rolling gesture: blame it on the Mexican.

We drank bottomless cups of coffee. The children checked in and out, sat for a while with us; Dahlquist had the waitress bring them lemonade. He showed us a book on Jim Bridger that he had paid thirty dollars for in 1924. "It's been worth every penny," he said. I hoped that some extravagance I indulged today I'd still think worth every penny in fifty years.

"Wish I had one of those tape recorders when the old guys were alive," he said. "The tales they could tell. The old-timers. There were about eight of them. We'd get 'em in here when we first started in business in '39. Once in a while in the summertime, maybe twice a year. Give 'em a dinner. Have 'em just sit there and tell the tales. People'd come in and listen. Then they'd ask me if that's true. I know they stretched it in places, I know they did that, but who wouldn't when they got an audience, stretch it a little bit. But I didn't tell them any different. I said, 'Those people lived here. Some of 'em born and raised right here.' I said, 'They knew the country. They knew all the different people.'"

He told us about the excavation of the old Fort Bridger presently going on, and we told him about the Illinois Interstate taking the Donner's hill. "Development ruins a lot of history if it's not taken care of," he said.

"Leonhard Weiland's disappointed because other people don't think the Donner Party story is as interesting as he does," Roger said.

"Oh, it's interesting," Dahlquist said. "You bet it is."

His wife, Laura, dead some years, was with us at the table the entire time. I was struck by how much influence she had had on him, how much one person could mark another. He gave us a book she had written in 1948, *Meet Jim Bridger*, now in its eighth printing. Her book, but he was so tied with her and Bridger it seemed perfectly appropriate to ask him to sign our copy. He started, then stopped. "I was struck by lightning, September 20, 1920. So when this kind of weather's on, there's a lot of electricity in the air and I can feel it. I can feel it when the skies are clear, I tell them electricity's building up, something's doing tomorrow, it'll either go around us or go over us. I'm kinda shaky today; this ain't gonna be very good, I'll tell you." He signed his name and stared at it. "When I was going to school, I could write show cards. Look what's happened to me."

It was an arthritis signature. Each of the letters and numbers zigzagged: the signature and date looked exactly like mini lightning bolts.

Dahlquist was 77, and the northern route became the southern route in his telling, but that wasn't important; any facts he mixed up about the Donner Party could be checked in books. What was important was his feeling about James Bridger: a pure and focused passion. I was moved by his springing to defend Bridger, even to the extent of pinning the rap on Vasquez, moved by the depth of his caring. I told him about visiting Jim Bridger's grave in Kansas City, glad I had that to offer him, but for me, visiting John Dahlquist was visiting Bridger's true grave: he carried Bridger just as Tom Hooper carried Homer Croy and Leonhard Weiland carried the Donner's farm, that road leading down away from the farmhouse toward the West.

Leaving the children asleep at the motel in Fort Laramie while Charlie Andersen showed us the moonlit grave, or to wander the small Main Street of Fort Bridger by themselves, would be unthinkable today, probably unconscionable. It never gave us pause. Maria, 14, and Jennifer, almost 13, were experienced babysitters for others' children, but more than that, they had been big sisters as far back as they could remember, routinely in charge of their younger siblings. They knew how to change diapers, whip up a snack, or soothe a cranky child. Ursula at 10, the middle child, could go up or down as she felt: play with "the babies," as we often called them though Gabriella was 7 and Charity nearly 6, or keep up with her big sisters. She and Jennifer, nearly the same height, were occasionally mistaken for twins, which incensed Jennifer: "How could anyone possibly think we were twins? I'm more than *two* years and one month older!" In these tiny towns, everybody knew everybody else, and though they probably harbored their deviates, we simply didn't worry. Maria, Jennifer, and Ursula were smart, savvy, observant caretakers; Gabriella and Charity were easy to take care of. There was also safety in numbers; the kids had been taught always to stick together, and few deviates or child snatchers were going to take on five children. They also all had been taught that if anything seemed scary or peculiar to them, start screaming at the top of your lungs, and if you're mistaken, we'll straighten it out later.

Without romanticizing the good old days of the '60s and early '70s, which had plenty of bad times, the communal spirit present then permitted, even encouraged, impromptu behavior unthinkable today.

At a Women's Equality Day Fair on the National Mall in Washington DC in the midst of all our great monuments to freedom, Charity, almost 1, and Gabriella, 2, played happily inside a portable thirty-five-foot circular play yard we set up on the lush grass, joined by toddlers plunked in by other fairgoers, given balloons by strangers passing by, while Roger and I meandered through the exhibits with Maria, Jennifer, and Ursula who periodically ran back to decorate the play yard with giveaway bumper stickers, posters, and flags until it was practically an exhibit itself.

I carry a vivid image of a summer afternoon in a Washington park where cast members of the Broadway show *Hair* performed selections for an antiwar rally. Maria, 6, and Jennifer, 5, knew the entire score by heart and excitedly made their way to the front of several hundred people to see better. Suddenly the park was wall-to-wall people, thousands of bodies, humming, swaying, smoking pot, separating Roger and me from Maria and Jennifer. Standing, we tried in vain to get their attention, sent a message through the crowd, each person telling those in front: "Maria and Jennifer, come back to your parents now." Like ripples of sound traveling an ocean, it reached them and they waved happily to us, but there was no aisle nor space to make one. We saw them talking and pointing to us, then someone in the front lifted Maria overhead, another lifted Jennifer, and passed them back, hand over hand. Row by row we watched them riding through the air over hundreds of smiling bodies back to us. Everyone cheered, then went back to humming and swaying and puffing. It was one of those spontaneous, nurturant, communal actions of the '60s that seemed both marvelous and unsurprising, as far from a mosh pit as you can get.

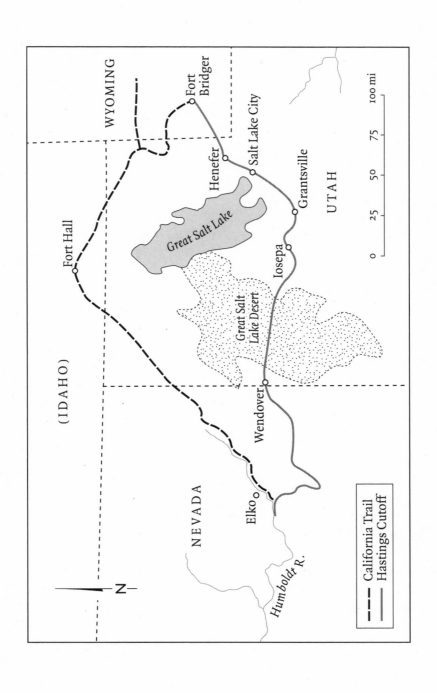

33 Utah

Think of a geographic triangle, I told the children, the regular California trail going around two sides, Hastings Cutoff going across the bottom. On paper and to the mind, the cutoff was the logical route, and if the cutoff had been as logical in reality as it looked on paper, Lansford Hastings, instead of an operator, might have been the first governor of California, and the Donner Party would have been people who bored their grandchildren with reminiscences.

On today's maps, Hastings Cutoff crosses three states, running from the edge of Wyoming through Utah into Nevada. It crosses into Utah at Evanston where there are nearby pioneer graves and wagon ruts, proceeds to the Weber River Crossing at Henefer, to Weber Canyon where the Donner Party found the first note from Hastings, goes through the Wasatch Mountains where the Donners' wandering route could only be guessed at, to Salt Lake City, Grantsville, Tooele, Iosepa, Salt Lake Desert, then crosses into Nevada, joining up around Elko with the old Fort Hall Road on the Humboldt River.

On July 31, 1846, the Donner Party, at that point twenty wagons and seventy-four people, took off from Fort Bridger in Hastings's tracks. At a fork not far beyond Fort Bridger, they passed up their last chance to rejoin the old Fort Hall road, the "regular road," and swung left onto the faint track. Even with gorges, buttes, and a barely discernible trail, they made ten to twelve miles a day.

August 6, at approximately today's Henefer, Utah, they found the first note stuck in the cleft of a stick: Hastings's hand penning a late revision to his book. The Weber Canyon is bad, he wrote. He wasn't sure he could get the wagons of his party through. Any trains coming after should make camp and send a messenger ahead. He'd come back with a better route.

Unlike the regular Oregon and California Trail beaten down by four years of wagon travel, only one train, led by Hastings, had preceded the Donners over Hastings Cutoff. One set of tracks, and now Hastings was saying don't follow them. They might have turned around, cut their losses, rejoined the old Fort Hall road, but that would have meant a certain loss of twelve days, an eternity; they didn't even consider it.

James Reed, Charles Stanton, who had ridden with Tamsen and George since Independence, and either William McCutchen, who had just joined the Party at Fort Bridger, or William Pike rode off to bring Hastings back. The rest made camp, probably in record time, agitation and irritation pumping the adrenaline. Then they waited. Five days by the Weber River, every morning, "Hastings has to come back today," every night, hearts sinking with the sun, "Where are they?"

On the fifth day, a solitary figure appeared in the distance: James Reed. His companions exhausted, their horses broken down, an indication of the terrain they were going to take wagons over, Reed had struggled back alone. Hastings wasn't coming back to lead them. The Weber Canyon was impassable. The party Hastings was leading had gotten through, but barely; they virtually had to lift their wagons over the steep canyons by rope and brute strength.

One look around confirmed the impossibility of the Donner Party's repeating such a feat: a much smaller group, they had too few young men, too many children. Hastings had come back part way with Reed and, on the summit of the Wasatch, indicated an alternative route: a labyrinth of forest, rocky ridges, streams, and ravines that Reed had attempted to blaze.

On August 12, the Donner Party moved out onto trackless country. They had to ax out a road: cut down trees, move giant boulders that had never been moved, hack through timber and brush. At night, they dragged back the pitifully short trail to camp at the previous night's site. On the third day, three wagons appeared from the East.

This was in the Wasatch Range in Utah. "It was the Graves family in those three wagons, remember?" I said to the children. "Thirteen new people. Franklin and Elizabeth Graves, their big family, and their driver, John Snyder, who's going to play a pivotal role in the Donner Party's fate." The Graves family, late arrivals at Fort Bridger, Hastings Cutoff sounding good to them too, would have been relieved to finally catch up, Helloing and Whoaing and Whew; and can you imagine the Donner Party? They would have heard those wagons a long way off. They must have lowered their axes and watched incredulously: those three wagons clattering up out of nowhere meant more hands to hack a road, but more than that, the craziness, hope, and humor of it must have been a shot in the arm for all concerned.

Except for two still to come from the West, the Donner Party had reached its final numbers: twenty-three wagons, eighty-seven men, women, and children:

From Springfield, Illinois, George and Tamsen Donner, and their five children.
Jacob and Elizabeth Donner, and their seven children.
Donner employees from Springfield, Noah James, Samuel Shoe-maker, John Denton; Antonio, a young Mexican herder hired at Laramie and Jean Baptiste Trudeau hired on at Fort Bridger. Also Charles Burger and possibly Augustus Spitzer.
Traveling with the Donners, Charles Stanton and Luke Halloran.

James and Margret Reed, and their four children.

Reed employees from Springfield, Milt Elliott, Walter Herron, James Smith, Baylis Williams, and his half-sister, Eliza Williams, the Reeds' cook.

From Vermont via Indiana and Illinois, Franklin, 57, and Elizabeth Graves, 45; their nine children, Mary, 19; William, 17; Eleanor, 15; Lovina, 12; Nancy, 9; Jonathan, 7; Franklin Jr., 5; Elizabeth, 1; Sarah, 21, and her husband, Jay Fosdick, 23, and their employee, John Snyder, 25.

From Ireland via Keokuk, Iowa, Patrick, 50, and Margaret (Peggy) Breen, 40; their seven children, John, 14; Edward, [13?]; Patrick Jr., 9; Simon, [8?]; James, [5?]; Peter, 3; Isabella, 1. Their Irish friend, Patrick Dolan, [35?].

From Belleville, Illinois, William, 30, and Eleanor Eddy, 25; their two children, James, 3; and Margaret, 1.

From Germany via Ohio, Lewis, 32, and Philippine Keseberg, 23; and their two children, Ada, 3, and Lewis Jr., 1.

Traveling with the Kesebergs: from Belgium via Cincinnati, Ohio, Hardcoop, in his sixties.

Also from Germany, Mr. [name, age?] and Doris Wolfinger, 20, and the former's partner, Joseph Reinhardt, about 30.

From Missouri, William, 30, and Amanda McCutchen, [25?]; their child, Harriet, 1.

From Tennessee, Levinah Murphy, 36; her seven children, Landrum, 16; Mary, 14; Lemuel, 12; William, 10; Simon, 8; Sarah, 19, her husband, William Foster, 30, and their child, George, 1; Harriet, 18, her husband, William Pike, 32, and their children, Naomi, 2, and Catherine, 1.

And still to come, Luis and Salvador, Indians sent by Sutter to rescue the Donner Party, who would be the only ones murdered for their flesh.

Whatever respite the Graveses' arrival provided was momentary. Road-making resumed. One week of bruised and blistered attack on the boulders, the tangle of trees, and the underbrush got them fourteen miles.

We parked our car and left the dirt road, walked a long time and slowly, not slowly to imitate the way they were forced to move—it was nearly impossible to imagine wagons getting through here—but because the country was so inhospitable it weighed the heart as well as the foot. We held branches for each other; I said some things out loud; I sank into my thoughts.

This was where the disintegration began. They hadn't been a company long enough; there weren't deep bonds. Exhausted, they vented their anger and frustration on one another. Fear had already spread throughout when Stanton and his companion, either McCutchen or Pike, finally reappeared with more bad news. They were heading straight down to a nearly impassible canyon. They switched direction. Five more days were spent opening a road six miles.

This country is described often as tortuous: canyons leading into other canyons, the passages narrow and hard to find, twisting and turning. Individuals on foot or on mules, traveling lightly, might have gotten through, but 1846 was the year of the families, and families came in wagons. Many of the history books harped, albeit delicately, that the women and children were a liability. If they mentioned what the women were doing, they usually said they were making coffee, bringing food, and bandaging blisters.

Even under the difficult trail conditions for preparing food, no one made coffee and brought food all day. Most of the historians assigned women a traditional role and then moved on to what interested them: the men. The women were cooking and serving food all right, but I'd stake my life that they, and all but the smallest children, were also dragging brush, lightening and repacking the wagons for the endless fording of streams and swamps, spelling the men on the axes while the food and coffee were being consumed. I was touchy on this point because of historical sexism, my need to have role models for my daughters and myself, and my own physical weakness. Bernard de

Voto, in *The Year of Decision: 1846*, had the women tugging the ropes, but in the main there were no books to prove or disprove me. Virginia Reed said only, "While cutting our way . . ." *Our* way, plural, but you couldn't make a federal case out of that. Tamsen's journal was gone. We didn't know, would never know, what the women were doing. But I knew this: because I didn't have the strength of Roger didn't mean I had no strength. Even I, no pioneer woman, would have been doing a lot more than bringing coffee.

What appeared to be a passage was often a dead-end. They were hacking out a trail by yards, and three times they dead-ended. Three times, they had to drag back down the road they had gouged out, abandon it, and start over in a different direction, which might dead-end on them too.

They came to what is now called Emigration Canyon. A steep hill, seemingly straight up. They couldn't see a pass. They couldn't stand to hack anymore. They hitched nearly every team of oxen to each wagon and, using ropes, chains, rocks, and willed muscle, pulled it up the precipitous hill. One by one by one. It took them most of one day to get all the wagons over.

We stared at Emigration Canyon in wonder, thinking of the desperation that led them to the massive feat: every canyon that opened out closing in again, blind alley, wrong track, dead end, the heat, the bitter fights, the fears, hacking, hacking. There's a historical marker here, called Donner Hill.

The road the Donners hacked out in the Wasatch was the most important road opened in 1846. The Mormons poured through it the next year, and it became the main road into Utah for more than a decade.

34

On August 23, 1846, the Donner Party reached the banks of what is now called the Jordan River. We reached the banks of the river Jordan, Salt Lake City, on July 24, the day the Mormons reached them in 1847: Pioneers Day, a state holiday with a grand parade, a rodeo, and many festivities. "It's our 4th of July," people kept saying, bristling me, sounding a little separatist to my Yankee Doodle ears. Still, it was a festive day to be in Salt Lake City, spirits were high, and I always loved a parade. We got up at the crack of dawn and, although difficult for us to ever make a speedy exit, arrived downtown early enough to get front-row seats on the curb.

We knew a man in Buffalo, a Mormon originally from Salt Lake City, a big, blond, handsome man, healthy and energetic with a golden beard: one of the most striking men I'd ever seen. In Salt Lake City, I was bowled over: everyone in the parade looked like him.

The greatest single attraction in Salt Lake City was Temple Square, two ten-acre blocks of concentrated Mormonism, containing all the central shrines of the Latter-Day Saints of Jesus Christ. I wasn't wildly interested in seeing Temple Square for what might seem a pigheaded reason: non-Mormons couldn't go into the Temple. Say what you want about Catholics, I've said plenty myself, but anybody is welcome in their cathedrals. For me, Temple Square, Salt Lake City, the whole state of Utah, reeked of control. The exclusion of non-Mormons from the Temple where the most sacred rites were performed was of a piece with Mormon treatment of women and minorities: Mormons kept people out of their holiest places.

We took the kids to the places they allowed us. It's one thing to be pigheaded, but you don't have to be ignorant where your children's education is concerned. They had a terrific day: a parade, sightseeing, cotton candy, and that night, a first-rate rodeo. They savored every moment, even recalling "that really nice lady, that sister, in Kansas City, who let us touch the big book." I said to Roger, "They'll probably all grow up and become Mormons."

We took a dip in the Great Salt Lake, an inland sea, a dead sea, 25 percent saline compared to an ocean's 5 percent. It stank. Thousands of tiny black brine flies swirled over the water, thousands of tiny brown brine shrimp wiggled in the water, crawling on the shore, on us. The water made us itch, break out in a rash; the vista was magnificent, mountains surrounding us, blue sky, seagulls darting, people cavorting, laughing, itching, running to the fresh-water showers. It was true that you couldn't drown; you bobbed like a bean in a pot. We had a great time. It's the sort of thing everyone should do once.

On the south side of Salt Lake near today's Grantsville, Luke Halloran, the consumptive who caught a ride with the Donners at Little Sandy, died. It suited the desires and imaginations of some to record that with his head in Tamsen's lap, Luke coughed out his last. Sometimes his blood came splotchy red upon her apron, sometimes he said, "God bless you, Mrs. Donner, I die happy."

Tamsen was not a woman unaccustomed to death: in 1831, in Elizabeth

City, North Carolina, she buried her entire first family in one three-month period. A year after this trip, all seven of us would go to Elizabeth City and see her first husband Tully Dozier's will made out on December 23, 1831, the day before he died, but no record anywhere showed the names, birthdates, or deathdates of the two children always mentioned.

"Have you considered the possibility they were twins?" Edna Shannonhouse, the local historian the Elizabeth City Library directed my letter to, asked in one of her return letters.

I hadn't till Edna suggested it. Tamsen, Tamesin, Tamzine: all were feminizations of Thomas, which meant "twin." In my novel, I made the children twins, Tamesin and Thomas, and that was how they came to be in my mind. But that was fiction, perhaps guessed accurately, imagined deeply, maybe even true. I thought the history died with Tamsen—until I found her double letter two decades later telling her sister what happened. The first letter is stuffed with happy domestic details, then seven months later, on the same paper, she writes,

Jan 26th, 1832

My sister I send you these pieces of letter that you may know that I often wrote to you if I did not send.

I have lost that little boy I loved so well. He died the 28 Sept. I have lost my husband who made so large a share of my happiness. He died on the 24 December. I prematurely had a daughter which died on the 18th of Nov. I have broken up housekeeping & intend to commence school in February. O my sister weep with me if you have tears to spare.

Your sister

Sixteen years later, on the Oregon Trail, Tamsen was 44, Luke Halloran 25—not that much older than her son Thomas would have been. She was a nurturant and competent person. I was sure Luke Halloran had occasion to bless her many times in the last month of his life, but we didn't know what happened in that wagon, didn't know if Tamsen had written about Luke in her journal.

Sometime on August 29, George Donner supposedly pulled the wagon out of line so that Luke could die without jars and lurches. That night, they came into camp with the body. His trunk was opened and revealed that Luke was a Mason and had money. They gave him a full day, and James Reed officiated at a Masonic funeral.

How fast did the news spread, how many people came around to cast their peepers at that trunk; imagine the intakes of breath, whistles of surprise, at seeing fifteen hundred dollars in coin and full Mason regalia. And then that extraordinary burial happening in wilderness.

What did Tamsen think of it all? We talked about that young man from St. Joseph, Missouri, trying to outrun his sickness, joining the party at Little Sandy, but never becoming part of the disintegrating company in the four weeks he had with them, riding in the Donners' wagons getting sicker day by day, trying to hold on until the famed California sun that could heal all. He was probably an object of pity at first becoming an object of resentment and scorn in the Wasatch—standing there racked with consumption, trying to help as much as he could with the unloading, the pulling of the ropes, anything he did not enough and hastening his own decline. Luke Halloran, deadweight in life, suddenly became in death not only a man of means but also a Mason, a man worthy of ceremony.

To give Luke a full day when they already knew they were behind and still had the "dry drive" ahead seems a bad mistake in hindsight. But, with all their troubles, this was the Party's first death since Sarah Keyes in Alcove Springs. Luke had been with the Donners, and the Donners were well respected. Maybe, inside, some were frightened and were whistling in the dark: a burial similar to one at home would be a proof that they were the same people, values intact, everything okay. They might have just welcomed the rest. I wondered if James Reed spearheaded it, putting on the full Masonic funeral he would want for himself, showing, This is what I believe, who I am. They wrapped Luke in clean sheets, made a coffin of boards, said the prayers, and laid him to rest, so it was told, in a bed of almost pure salt. His grave was near a member of the party that Hastings was leading ahead of them. There was speculation about whether the salty soil would preserve the bodies.

Most likely, Luke Halloran would have wanted exactly that kind of funeral, but I thought of the things we carried along in our trunks when we moved from one place to another, and what they signaled to others when we could no longer say yea or nay. Roger's father had a full Masonic funeral too, much to his sons' surprise and perhaps to his too: he hadn't been an active Mason in twenty-five years. Men, all strangers to us and Roger's father, came from who knows where, clanked around in funny hats, said set prayers that occasionally had a pause to fill in the blank with the deceased's name, **Vernon G. Burton**. Only two personal touches at Vernon Gibson Burton's funeral gave a hint of who *he* was: Roger gave a eulogy about his boyhood with his father, and his brother hired a violinist to play "Thais," the piece his father had loved to play on the violin.

"Don't let them say Our Father and all the rest at my funeral," I said to Roger out of the blue. I said it lightly and he laughed, but I made him promise. That I worried that the church would swell with patriarchal prayer and song over my dead body was really a fear that no one, not even the people closest to me, would have taken my life seriously.

Tamsen and George Donner got the fifteen hundred dollars for taking Luke in at Little Sandy. I bet a lot of people wished their charity had been a little greater.

35

This [Carolina] is indeed a delightful country where everything is produced in
rich abundance.

We went to North Carolina the next year partly to look for Tamsen
Donner, but mostly because my novel had again been rejected. My
agent—my third in a series of enthusiastic but revolving agents—
believed that the novel only needed what she called a V.S.E., a Very
Sensitive Editor.

We had gone through all the V.S.E.s and started on the S.E.s.

"I have a feeling that Ms. Burton could write a fascinating novel on
Tamsen Donner," one S.E. said. I never considered it. I was much more
interested in my modern "'70s" heroine, whose story was nine-tenths
of the novel, and her struggles, a lot of which were mine. As the years
passed, I had to keep making her older to keep pace with her mature
insights.

My agent started on the E.s.

As the years piled up, I secretly feared I was a crazy woman, creating
commotion in family routines to find time to write something that

never ended and no one wanted. Each rejection was a blow, not just a rejection of my manuscript but a rejection of me and my choice to do something other than be a wife and mother. The initial euphoria and hope of Bread Loaf dimmed to a pinpoint. No matter what they had said, clearly I wasn't talented enough; I had started too late, had too many conflicting responsibilities. If I were writing, I thought I should be with the children; if I were with the children, I wanted to be writing. I was guilty over insisting that Roger share the housework, guilt squared because I wasn't bringing in any income. The guiltier I felt the louder I yelled. It took a long time to believe that I had a right to work, and that "his" money was "our" money, although I belligerently continued to "act as if" I did and it was. "The mask becomes the anima," the psychologist Gordon Allport said. He didn't say it might take years.

My pattern with rejection was to take to my bed and, like an Irish warrior, bleed a while, then rise to fight again. We rented a ramshackle cottage on the Outer Banks for a month, driving there the day after Roger, a professor of psychology at the University at Buffalo, finished teaching the first summer-school session in July. Mornings, we walked on the beach and swam with the children. Afternoons they napped or read or played quietly while Roger and I went over every line of 520 pages to once again revise and reshape the novel. Roger would say, "This line is kind of obscure; I don't really get it," and I'd be off and running: "For crying out loud, if it were any clearer it'd be crib notes. I can't spell out every single thing. The reader has to do some work . . ." Then a few minutes later, I'd say, "Well, maybe . . . "

I was rough on him, but he was all I had. If truth be told, I needed more. As generous and supportive as he was, he wasn't a writer. He didn't know how to help me fix it.

In fairness, none of the writers I had asked knew either. As the '70s went on, generous writers tried to help me: J.R. Salamanca, John Williams, Leslie Fiedler, Ann Petrie, Esther Broner, Naomi Weisstein. One famous writer, unnamed in that litany, was genuinely destructive for reasons that remain mysterious, but the rest all struggled mightily with my drafts, one or two finally fading away, no longer answering letters or phone calls, but the others hanging in over the years, applauding each revision and offering new suggestions.

With no experience in writing fiction, I was writing a very complicated book. I had a real historical heroine and a fictional modern one, separated by 131 years. The Tamsen Donner parts were written in first person and my '70s heroine in third person. Three-fourths of the novel took place on a moving motorcycle where speech was impossible, so I wrote long interior monologues, a cast of thousands riding along on the noisy motorcycle in my modern heroine's head. The whole thing was so far beyond my nascent abilities that it drove me to devise ever more complicated solutions. I had flashbacks within flashbacks. I explored every nook and cranny.

"Not everything is equally important," Esther Broner wrote me, probably the best advice I ever got in writing and in life, but hard to follow both places. It *all* seemed important; I didn't know yet what was important: *that* was what we were discovering in the women's movement, everything we had been taught examined anew, blinders of conditioning being wrenched off.

My best friend in Washington read a draft and asked, "Why don't you stick to nonfiction? You're so good at it." *As opposed to writing fiction, which you're so bad at.* I didn't want to continue doing the same thing, repeating myself until I was on autopilot. I wanted to develop, grow, become **a serious writer.**

When the guilt I felt about not earning any money grew intolerable, I hustled articles and book reviews, never enough money to justify the months they sucked away from the novel, but enough to allow myself to pretend I was contributing to the family economy. I was writing for the *Washington Post* and major magazines, and you'd think that would have made me feel like "a real writer," but I couldn't see those achievements because they weren't **the novel.** Oh, the myriad ways we find to feel bad when all we're trying to do is feel good.

At the Outer Banks in North Carolina, we were also on a "regimen." I was much too monklike to ever go anyplace for its own sake, so we always had to do something "worthwhile," improve ourselves in some way. The "rules" were daily exercise and eating only healthy food, one new recipe a day. We bought mounds of fresh produce daily, which all seven of us peeled and chopped and steamed, and after dishes and the sunset I'd read the latest edited chapter to the children. Unlike some of the editors, they begged me to go on.

One day, we drove from the Outer Banks to Elizabeth City, North Carolina, to talk with a local historian. She had heard of Tamsen Donner but was amazed that Tamsen had lived and taught there.

On page 131 of the Camden County, North Carolina, Will Book, we found a copy of Tully Dozier's will. Dozier was Tamsen's first husband.

"In the name of God, being of sound and perfect mind, I make this my last will and testament. After paying all of my just debts, I give to my Beloved wife Tamsan Dozier all of my property also it is my desire that my wife shall settle my estate and dispose of my property either private or publickly if she chooses. Tis given under my name December 23rd 1831. Tully B Dozier."

Two witnesses signed their names.

Tully died December 24th.

Six months before, Tamsen wrote Betsey,

I do not intend to <u>*boast*</u> *of my husband but I find him one of the best of men— affectionate, industrious, & possessed of an upright heart. These are requisite to make life pass on smoothly. We live in a very comfortable way. We have a horse, 3 cows, 2 calves, 24 hogs, hen turkeys & ducks. Last year we made enough corn, pork bacon, &c. to serve us this year & perhaps a little to spare. . . . We have a fine potato patch & if we could send them to you could give you plenty of sweet potatoes as we shall make several hundred bushels. . . . This is indeed a delightful country where everything is produced in rich abundance. . . . Mr.*

Dozier just told me to ask you if you could get potatoes from Boston & says he will send you 20 or 30 bushels if you can. My husband is yet Postmaster you will please to direct us before and frequently while he retains the office.

She didn't mail this letter until the January after Tully's death. By then she had lost her entire first family.

36

We were wandering around, driving down a desolate dirt road in Utah looking for Twenty Wells, a Donner Party campsite with extraordinary symmetrical wells of apparently bottomless, cold, pure water. In the front yard of a weathered wooden house, a man with a broken arm was standing by a panel truck. We asked him if we were on the right road. In the eighteen months he had lived there, the man had read everything he could find on local history but didn't know anything about Twenty Wells. We filled him in on the Donner Party background; he apologized for not knowing more. A cowboy, he'd broken his arm when a horse threw him—a bad break, shattered bones that would require months to heal, might not ever heal properly—for the immediate future, his cowboy days were done. A woman came and went, packing things in the truck. Their children advanced and retreated surreptitiously.

"Are you moving?" I asked the woman.

"We're moving to Oregon," she said.

"Right now?"

"In fifteen minutes."

If she had said they were moving to Tulsa or Roanoke in fifteen minutes, I would have thought, That's rough, would have wished them luck. But when she said "moving to Oregon," a little shadow went over my heart. The language, weighted with all the preceding moves to Oregon, instantly conveyed the reality of the uprooting. We were at once intensely in the present with the past and future banging up against us.

Roger, the man, and I stood in the yard talking, the woman carrying things from the house to the truck, directing their children to get this or pack that, occasionally stopping to join in our conversation. The immediate spur for the move was the drought. "They're predicting it'll last five years," the man said. "We can't hold out that long."

But they were really getting out because of their fears of raising their children in such a place. DUGWAY TEST CENTER, DUGWAY PROVING GROUNDS, (Restricted-no travel): forbidding barren brown spots took up half the top of Utah on maps. He said they discussed the government testing often. "This isn't a place to bring up children," he said.

"The government tests kill the sheep," she said. "At least one man has been killed. The incidence of retarded newborns is off the scale. I wouldn't have a baby in this place."

Many people were concerned, they said; everybody knew that nerve gas had leaked and killed six thousand sheep and that one man for sure, but no one would give them straight information, no one would tell them the truth. We told about West Valley near our home, New York State's chief dumping ground for radioactive and toxic wastes, and the people there who said, "They wouldn't let us live here if it wasn't safe." "*They?*" the man said angrily. "What do they care? They don't care."

Roger and the man by the fence talking, our children milling around or in our car writing in their journals, I moved over to the panel truck where the woman was arranging things inside. She made a last adjustment and flopped down on the mattress spread out in back, I leaning in, she and her kids looking up at me.

Her name was Artha. Picking my words carefully so as not to make her defensive, or embarrass or insult her—oh, this *just a housewife* business eats into our souls—I asked, "Now you take care of the children, what else do you do?" She laughed harshly and spit out the words, "I have no time for my children." Not angry at me, angry at her reality—the disparity between what her life was "supposed to be" and what it was.

For the last eighteen months, she had been employed as a cook on an enormous ranch, her husband as a cowboy. She spoke of the long hours, the hard work, how generally hard Utah had been, of their children's resentments that they had had to work so hard. All the time we were talking, her children stared at me.

"Where will he find work?" I asked.

"There is no work," she said. She gestured to his broken arm. "He can't work."

"What will you do?"

"I don't know. If there's no work there, we'll go some other place. We'd like to get a little piece of land," she said, but almost immediately chalked that off as impossible. "We had a piece of land once. Back South." She didn't say what happened to it or how they'd gotten here.

The man told Roger that she was a devout Mormon—maybe roots had brought them back. "We argue about it a lot," he said, then laughing, corrected himself, "We have discussions about it." He lit up another cigarette, and said, "She's fierce about my smoking." (I wish I'd heard him say that. At the truck, I lit up, feeling free to do so because I saw what an addict he was, and her eyes went to slits, the censure crackling.) He said he was no longer such a strict Mormon since he'd moved to Utah and saw how the Church Elders behaved in private.

From stop to leaving, we talked maybe half an hour. "I was dreading the moving," Artha said, "and your coming along made it better." I think she meant there was no time to dwell, we broke the building up of the fears, our carful of kids coming down that road at just that moment to note their leave-taking, say good luck.

"When your book comes out," Artha said, "I'd appreciate your writing me in care of my folks." She wrote down their Salt Lake City address and said, "I didn't see them for thirteen years, and this eighteen months has been very nice and more than enough."

"It'll be a long time before my book comes out," I said.

"I've got time," she said, again punctuating her words with that harsh laugh, as if time were the only thing in the world she had.

Two women talking—how easy it was. She used no cover-ups, was absolutely forthright. Intensity leapt from her but, intense myself, I was comfortable around intense women. She said she found it easy to talk to people, but she had no close friends. I said, or maybe I just thought, I find it hard to talk to people and I have no close friends either.

After their children found out I had written a book, they stared, if possible, even harder at me. At some prearranged signal I didn't see, they began singing a nonsense song in unison, "I'm a nut . . . " We were all in our car by then preparing to leave; they stood outside in a cluster singing the many verses in a deadly serious way. We sang a lot in our family, so the singing per se didn't strike me as strange; it was the way they performed it, the content childlike, but not the form, like a demonstration and an offering: This is our talent, our gift.

Years later I can still see Artha's strong face, the determined set, the refusal to accept defeat although she expected it. Above all, I can see the unwavering direct eye contact, though I couldn't tell you what color her eyes were—gray, it seemed to me after, but the day and the land were gray; in the novel, I had imagined Tamsen's eyes grayish blue, Artha's strength and pioneering qualities perhaps mixing in all that grayness.

Artha and her husband were educated, articulate, sensitive people. They talked a lot to each other. They were voracious readers. She read books off the library bus. He read all the local history he could find, caring where he was, what had happened there, maybe trying to become a good Mormon, or figure out how he got there. That's what I kept wondering: how did these people get here? She a cook, he a cowboy. How did they get to be migrants? They thought a lot about their lives. They planned. They *cared*. Why didn't they have more choice?

Travel. An accumulation of mysteries, small and large. Glimpses into people's lives that sometimes, like a later family trip we'll take to India, rock your world violently, more often shift it ever so slightly. All the people you meet that you'll never see again, you're left with a phrase they said or didn't say, a way they looked, an action, some new *why* or *how* going into you, becoming part of your questions or answers, and you walk away changed, though you hardly ever know it at the time, maybe never. With Artha, I knew at the moment what I'd remember whenever I thought of her: never discount luck.

"Good luck," we called again. It seemed such a puny thing to say when you thought of all the luck they'd need: rain, bones that healed quickly, jobs opening at the right time, a place to live that didn't have poison in the air.

Some people are luckier than others, I told the children. That's a fact of life and it's arrogant and ungrateful to deny or forget it.

And I told them this: a lot of people, maybe most people, could want to take a cross-country trip, plan it, enjoy it, and learn from it, but no way, no how, *never*, were they going to have the time and money to take it.

And for the thousandth time, I told them, our family has been born under a star; don't forget it, you lucky dogs.

When I wrote Artha about the book, I was going to tell her about giving up smoking. But the book never came out.

We found Twenty Wells, or so we thought until recently. Apparently they were covered over by the town of Grantsville or siphoned off decades ago, except for a few seeps. Someone we asked in 1977 directed us to *some* wells he said were Twenty Wells. We spent quite a bit of time there. Perfectly flat ground with holes six to nine feet in diameter filled to the brim with water.

Twenty Wells provided cold, pure water to the Donner Party: when they withdrew a kegful, the surface receded a moment, then returned to its original level. They took a sounding, put down seventy feet of rope without reaching bottom. The water in the wells we found was flush to the brim and cold. If it was pure seventy feet down, I don't know; debris floated everywhere on top.

37 Great Salt Lake Desert, the "Dry Drive"

The Donner Party found the second note from Hastings tacked to a board in a meadow, but birds, wind, the sun had shredded it. Eliza said that they all scrambled around on the ground gathering scraps, and her mother pieced them together like a puzzle. No matter in what order Tamsen arranged them, the message was the same: "Two days and two nights . . . hard driving . . . next grass and water."

The "dry drive" was upon them.

They prepared the rest of that day and all of the next, gathering grass for the oxen and tying it to the wagons, filling every available container with water, cooking food, there'd be no stopping for campfires. They started in the evening, traveled all that night, and the following day and night. "When the third night fell," Virginia Reed wrote, "we saw the barren waste stretching away apparently as boundless as when we started."

All organization broke down. Those able to move faster pushed on, leaving the more heavily laden wagons to get along as best they could. It was every family for itself now.

Hastings's "two days and two nights" was six. His "forty miles" was eighty.

Six days, they traveled all day and most of every night, pushing on through the heat, the glare, the cracked lips, the thirst, the mirages, themselves and their miseries reflected twenty times. The sun dropped and the temperature plummeted; they pushed on in chill moonlight, desert winds, piercing cold. The alkali chalked their faces like clowns or ghosts; in the moonlight, it glittered like snow. They pulled oxen on. They carried babies and pulled small children. The water ran out. Tamsen gave her daughters tiny lumps of sugar moistened with a drop of peppermint to suck, and later, silver spoons and flattened bullets to keep saliva and life flowing. The oxen flagged, finally fell to the ground from thirst. The drivers unhitched them, driving them ahead for water, intending to bring them back to pull the wagons.

The Reeds waited a full day for the return of their drivers, the other wagons catching up, passing them, disappearing from sight. At night, the Reeds set out on foot to try to reach the other wagons: James, carrying the three-year-old, Margret and the three other children staggering along in the darkness after him. A thirst-crazed ox stampeded them; Reed fired into the darkness; at the last moment, the ox turned aside, the whoosh of it searing their bodies. They walked ten miles, Virginia estimated, and finally reached Jacob Donner's wagon. They didn't wake them up. They lay down on the ground and when the bitter cold became intolerable, their parents placed all five of their dogs around the children, the warmth keeping them alive.

All the people got through. Reed, the richest, was struck lowest. Half of the thirty-six head of working cattle taken by the desert were his. He cached two of his three wagons in the desert. To cache, one dug a hole in the ground for a box or a wagon bed, put heavy or cumbersome items into the box—link chain, kegs of nails, family heirlooms—covered it with boards, then threw sand on top to hide it from the Indians. To think that the Indians wouldn't notice large protuberances or that they themselves might come back later from California for their belongings: surely a testament to the human ability to hope and deny.

We took Highway 80 through the Great Salt Lake Desert, a ruler-straight shot through the middle. We left the windows open to feel the heat, 110 degrees rushing in so thick and unrelenting the children felt enervated, queasy, wanted water. Only a little over an hour's drive for us, we stopped, but there was no inclination to linger. This country was so tangibly powerful you didn't need much of it to spur your imagination of the Donner Party's experience, to spark your fear.

Heat waves rolled and rose off the highway. You'd swear it had just poured and in a second you'd be riding through water, but the pavement was bone-dry. Along the edges of the road, mile after mile, big stones had been arranged to spell out names: LOWELL VIC AL KENNY . . . And beer bottles. Was there anyplace in the world you could go that JIM RUSS CLYDE hadn't been there ahead of you leaving their garbage?

I looked out the window past the names, the bottles, and thought about going out to the Silver Island Mountains, surrounded by salt flats and ancient muds where it was thought remnants of the Pioneer Palace were found in the late 1920s, eighty-one years after the Reeds abandoned it. Although that particular find was later disputed, remnants of some large wagon were found, and there were still things out there in the desert waiting for someone to claim them. The whole desert was a graveyard of things. On some parts where the pioneers walked, gray ooze cleaving to their boots and their hems, their feet broke the salty crust, sank in; the wheels rolled through—it was said that the footprints, the wheel traces, were still preserved. Wooden wagons long ago rotted to remnants, but the dry desert air preserved some things, after all these years the blowing sand maybe covering them deeply over, maybe uncovering them. Rusted nails. Ox bones. A creamer from a Bavarian china tea set, darkened, spider-cracked, might be sitting out there upon the sand, a whisper, "My Great-aunt Sarah brought it from Germany," blown away on the wind. I wasn't interested in salvage for money or souvenirs; I wanted to go out to Silver Island to salvage human experience, to find a trace of Tamsen Donner.

There was a road and hiking trails, I read about them, you'd get there at daybreak and walk around before the real heat hit. The children were too young to go, it was too potentially dangerous, but they could stay in a motel, the older watching the younger; they'd have fun, a rare chance to watch TV all day long, blotting out any worries they might have. Roger and I could go at the crack of dawn. It was odd: I'd never go by myself; I had no desert skills and wasn't strong on directions—I'd be afraid for good reason. Roger wasn't exactly Laurence of Arabia, but he had a keen sense of direction—I'd go with him confidently. I'd feel safe, yes, protected—I'd feel that together we'd be okay, he wouldn't let anything happen.

It *was* possible to go to Silver Island. If I simply stated I had to do it, Roger and I could figure out the mechanics, a motel for the children, food, money left for them, emergency phone numbers, find the right person to tell us the right road, the best time, rent a four-wheel drive, buy sun hats, water containers . . . I didn't mention it. It all seemed too complicated, at least a day's preparation and a day in the doing, seemed an enormous amount of energy for a family to spend for me to look for something probably long gone. And what if we did go and something happened to Roger and me out there, the children waiting in the motel?

Trying to do work and family simultaneously, everything was a constant cost-benefit analysis. Was this important enough for me to ask so much of them? What were the chances this would pan out? Was this too dangerous for a mother to do? The constant paring down to essentials: what toll did that take, what effects, on ideas freely and fully explored, a hunch followed, an intriguing notion pursued. The writer had to explore, act on impulse, take risks, plunge to the core of things; the mother had to constantly weigh and measure, watch out, pull back.

38 Nevada

James Reed's fine herd was reduced to one cow and one ox, two of his wagons left in the desert with two others belonging to George Donner and Lewis Keseberg. The company splintered, morale shattered, they banded together enough to spend nearly a week on the edge of the desert at the base of Pilot Peak, Nevada, recouping, repairing, every day some of the men going back into that burning waste on horses and mules trying to find the stampeded oxen, bring out the wagons and, failing that, the food and provisions from the wagons. When all the shifting (my oxen can draw your wagon), repacking, and ugly bargaining (no one would carry Reed's food without free access to it) was done, the company was down to nineteen tattered, warped wheel wagons on the edge of Nevada, and nothing in front of them except Hastings's tracks.

It was the middle of September, the time they had expected to be in California. The desert still in sight behind them, there was a sudden fierce snowstorm. Eliza Donner, 3 at the time, later wrote a mature description of that snowstorm: "The waste before us was cheerless, cold, and white as the winding sheet that enfolds the dead."

They took inventory and confirmed what they had feared: they didn't have enough food to get them through. That *150 lbs. of flour and 75 lbs. of meat laid in for each individual*, all those provisions that seemed so ample in a snug farmhouse the previous winter gone, the broiled buffalo steaks of the prairie gone too, and the long delays had severely depleted the staples. *Rice and beans . . . are good articles on the road—cornmeal, too, is very acceptable.*

Charles Stanton, who had volunteered in the Wasatch to go after Hastings, set off again for help, this time, the historians are certain, with William McCutchen on a mule and a horse to John Augustus Sutter at Sutter's Fort (Sacramento, California). Stanton was single, and some thought he might not come back; McCutchen left his wife and baby—he'd be back. The others pushed along in Hastings's tracks, following a trail that turned south, arguing down their feelings that they should be going west, at one point going south three full days and for another three days reversing what they had done, never dreaming that Hastings hadn't known the route either.

On September 26, southwest of today's Elko, Nevada, a little over a hundred miles from the Utah border on I-80, they rejoined the established California Trail on the Humboldt River. **Take the regular track and never leave it** : surely Jim Clyman's warning echoed cruelly in their heads, the silence of their surroundings sounding even louder, no wagon trains clattering down that road from Fort Hall; they must be the last train on the road—they were—and would they make it, would Stanton and McCutchen come back in time, come back at all? But still, what a relief to see that beaten-down track.

For all pioneers, Nevada was always the roughest stretch of the trail: the animals were jaded, the wagons beat up, people tired, dispirited, nerves raw and reserves gone, and there were still the heat and dust, the harassment by the Indians who stole horses and shot arrows into the oxen, the swamps and creeks to ford, the endless hills to pull over, another dry drive.

They were traveling in two sections now. The Donners, their five wagons, and some of the Reeds' teamsters, were two days' travel ahead.

In the rear section, they were double-teaming the oxen over one of the never-ending steep sandy hills, when James Reed's teamster, Milt Elliott, and Franklin Graves's teamster, John Snyder, quarreled over something, probably over who was going to go first. Maybe the harness became tangled, maybe Snyder was trying to goad his oxen; for some reason, he began beating his oxen. Reed, riding up, protested, and Snyder exploded. "Hard words followed," Virginia wrote without elaboration. Then Reed said, "We can settle this when we get up the hill." "We'll settle it now," Snyder said, striking Reed with his whip-stock, gashing open his head, striking again, and then perhaps—here the stories differ—Margret Reed ran between the two men to separate them and down came the whip upon her. In a flash, Reed's knife was drawn. Moments later, Snyder lay dead.

Everyone was stunned. John Snyder, 25, dead.

They immediately made camp, Reed's wagon at some distance from the other eleven wagons. We have just glimpses of the dramas that went on inside and outside the dozen wagons. Margret Reed was so distraught James asked 13-year-old Virginia to bandage his wounds instead. "When I finished, I burst out crying," Virginia wrote. "Papa said, 'I should not have asked so much of you.'"

Reed offered boards from his only remaining wagon for a coffin for Snyder, but they were refused. Someone wrapped him in a shroud, a board was placed into the ground and one above his body to keep off coyotes, and John Snyder was laid to rest.

A council was held to decide what to do about Reed. Snyder, although new to the Party, was young and with the Graveses' large clan. From the beginning, Reed had been resented by some for his aristocratic ways, his racing horse; even his daughter had a pony. Others may have also irrationally blamed him for the delay in the Wasatch. We don't know. Some stories say that, at one point, feelings ran so high Lewis Keseberg propped up his wagon tongue to hang Reed, and Reed bared his neck and said, "Come ahead, gentlemen."

A compromise was reached: banishment. Reed was to go out alone without arms—in effect, a death sentence.

He refused to go. Imagine the scene: Reed, already stricken with remorse over Snyder, suddenly plunged into a nightmare kangaroo court, saying, "Are you crazy? I'm not going out there alone."

William Eddy or someone later told Thornton that Reed had two supporters, Eddy and Milt Elliott. Three men against a dozen or more. If the Donners had been there, it's unlikely such folly could have happened, but the Donners were two days ahead. We don't know what the women did, if they cried out to their men how insane this was, stood by their men at all costs, wrung their hands, or egged them on.

Margret Reed, fearing that her husband would be killed if he stayed, pleaded with him to go. No, he said, he had only acted in self-defense. She switched tack. Go and bring back food, she said. What good will it do to stay here and watch your children starve? "It was a fearful struggle," Virginia wrote about the husband-and-wife argument. Margret Reed must have feared deeply for his life, because her own life would be arduous without him. "At last he consented, but not before he had secured a promise from the company to care for his wife and children." It had come to that: if they promised to take care of his family, he would agree to a death sentence. I wonder why he trusted in their honoring the promise.

The company, which needed every strong man it had for survival, sent Reed out, alone, without weapons. That night in the darkness, Virginia and Milt Elliott went out in the darkness and gave Reed his rifle, pistols, ammunition, and some food.

About thirty-five years after this happened, an early writer on the Donner Party, Charles McGlashan, and a few years after that, Virginia Reed in her memoir, wrote that Reed killed Snyder at Gravelly Ford. Although historians later placed the killing two days further west—establishing the location by the chronology of logbooks and diaries: on October 5, the day of the stabbing, the train was already further along—Gravelly

Ford, perhaps because of its evocative name, continued to appear in books and poems as the site. I had read it so many times I wanted to go there—even if it had nothing to do with the Donner Party, it had become part of the legend. It was near Beowawe, Nevada, south of I-80, which pretty much followed the Humboldt River and the original California Trail from Elko on.

We were moving through arid land looking for Gravelly Ford when all of a sudden a grove of green trees appeared ahead. We turned into a place that was, quite simply, an oasis, passed under an arch, drove around a curving road, and passed a little stream—not unlike a movie set—with a beautiful ranch house set back from the road. A great deal of money had been spent on irrigation, bringing water from who knows where to create this lush green cool spot in the middle of desert. Oil money, we thought. Whatever kind, big money.

A thin, elegant woman answered the door, speaking with an upper-class accent cultivated almost to caricature. She was so polite to us she was rude. After some time, she told us to go see her foreman, and said it would be all right for us to eat our lunch under a tree.

Seven strangers and a red Chevy station wagon with New York plates must have been spotted a mile off, but the few people we passed didn't see us. If we said hello, they answered, looking at us with the opaque eyes and bland expressions of good servants who observe everything that's going on without letting on. There was a hint of menace in the air. Perhaps it was simply the tension of power, of people poised to spring into action. The very fact that we were there clearly meant that the woman had given us permission. Or orders would have been given.

We ate bread and cheese tidily under a tree, the children speaking in very quiet voices without being told to. After we picked up every crumb—"Poor ants," Gabriella whispered—we found the foreman, working on a piece of ranch equipment. He answered our questions without looking up or stopping his work, answering exactly what we asked, not volunteering any additional information. When we persisted, he said, "You need a four-wheel drive. You can't get there in that big station wagon." (Aha! So they were looking.) "Well, we're going to try," Roger said. The foreman put down his wrench and stood up. "You have to take water. Be sure you have enough gas." He drew us a crude map, showing the choice points where the dirt roads divided. "Be sure you come back and tell me when you leave or we'll have to go in there and get you."

We passed through stunning country. Almost a prehistoric landscape. Gnarled trees. Sand dunes, the same kind of steep sand hills the Donner Party had to double-team the oxen over. Gradations of browns, beautiful browns. Sage. We plunged up and down dirt roads, the sky bright blue, the sun fierce, behind us the dust flying: Ride 'em, cowhand! At some places, dust went way up over the rims, our car sinking down so that the entire tire was covered by the fine, almost greasy dust. If we stalled, we'd be stuck. But we didn't stall. The children and I raucously cheered our car and Roger's driving, our 350 horsepower and his handling of the team.

From a distance, we saw a wooden white cross about twelve feet tall right next to the road. On the crosspiece, it said

PIONEERS

Plural. Who were they? How did they die? The cross was in front of a large flat grave: four pieces of wood, not unlike the Shoshone Indian graves, demarking an eight-foot square filled in with rocks, a weathered wooden cross placed horizontally on top. There was a road, so you knew that people came and went, but you felt you were all alone out there: you and hills on the horizon and sage and browns and a stark white cross casting a long shadow over a pile of gravestones. Both the thought of the pioneers coming through this wide-open empty expanse and stopping to bury some of their own, and the years of people tending this lonely grave were moving.

It's good we came to Gravelly Ford, if indeed that's where we were. Wherever we were, somebody had remembered and honored pioneers. Nobody knew where John Snyder's grave was; we didn't know who

12. "Dust-covered wagon, Nevada. Rast in Pease."

was in this grave. Standing there, perhaps twenty miles or more in any direction from where Snyder had been buried, thinking about him, I felt I'd visited his grave.

Dust plagued the pioneers; all the diarists mentioned it frequently. An Oregon-bound woman wrote, "It will fly so that you can hardly see the horns of your tongue yoke of oxen. It often seems that the cattle must die from want of breath, and then in our wagons . . . beds, clothes, victuals, and children, all completely covered." In Nevada, especially, the dust, with the consistency of talcum powder, sifted into everything.

It was some miles out of the way, and the day fiercely hot, but we felt honor bound to go back to tell the foreman we'd gotten out safely. The sun burned. The back window totally obscured with dust, dust continued to kick up into the car. We shut the windows to turn on the air conditioning. Roger pushed the lever and everybody started screaming as jets of dust blasted throughout the car. The air-conditioning ducts were packed with dust. It kept pouring out as we groped for the lever to shut it off. Dust covered our faces, our clothes, every inch of the car's interior. After the initial shock, it seemed wildly funny; we laughed till we ached with it. Trying to clean each other up sent us off again. Jennifer wrote on the back window, "The dust has buried here today our fortunes." Ursula added, "Rast in pease." Her wit more than her spelling broke us up too.

We finally got ourselves and the car clean enough to go on. At the ranch, unable to find the foreman, we asked a worker to tell him. He said, "Oh yeh, I'll let him know. He told us we might have to go down there with horses to pull you out."

Months later, we'd lift a mat or shift something in the car and there would be tiny, fine brown talc—Nevada dust.

39

Nobody knew for sure, but the best available estimate placed the site of Hardcoop's abandonment ten miles southwest of present-day Winnemucca, Nevada. Nobody knew Hardcoop's first name nor his exact age either. In his sixties, he was always referred to as an old man. Certainly he was old for the trail, but so was George Donner, and he was always portrayed as a virile patriarch—and often Jacob Donner was too, although he was sickly—maybe because they had wives in their forties and young children. Hardcoop was said to have grown children in Belgium—he would have this last great adventure of seeing California, then return to his native Antwerp to live out the rest of his life.

October 8, 1846, three days after James Reed killed John Snyder and was banished, those in the rear section—the Donners still ahead—were walking to spare the oxen. Everybody walked, even little children. Mothers carried babies. Zipping over a graded rise in a car, you don't think a thing about it, but if you were walking or coaxing oxen to pull a heavy wagon, you'd feel every upward slope in your calves, back, and lungs. Hardcoop begged a ride from Lewis Keseberg, whose wagon he was traveling in. Everyone must walk, Keseberg said. Hardcoop went from wagon to wagon. William Eddy, last in line that day, said he'd give him a lift once he got his wagon over a difficult sandy stretch, but Eddy, like all of them, was preoccupied and burdened.

That evening, somebody noticed Hardcoop wasn't with them. Some boys remembered seeing him along the road. Eddy and Milt Elliott tried to borrow horses from Graves and Breen to go back to get him, but Graves and Breen didn't want to wear out their animals on what was surely a futile gesture.

All night, Eddy, on watch, stoked the fire high, hoping that somewhere in the darkness, an old man with high hopes of Western adventure would see it and take direction and heart.

Hardcoop never came in.

Some of the Party had gone from Sarah Keyes to Hardcoop in five months, had gone from a cottonwood coffin, hand-hewed stone, prayers, and flowers planted in the sod to wagons disappearing in the dust, bones bleaching in the sun. There were eighty-five of them now and an omnipresent ghost crawling along behind never to catch up.

Winnemucca, a poem of a word, was named after the Indian Chief Winnemucca. Julia Cooley Altrocchi, who published a two-hundred-page epic poem, *Snow Covered Wagons*, in 1936, about the Donner Party, said that Winnemucca's father was the Indian who came to the lake camp in the Sierra Nevadas and gave Patrick Breen some roots.

Breen's diary entry for February 28, 1847: "1 solitary Indian passed by yesterday . . . gave me 5 or 6 roots resembleing onions in shape taste some like a sweet potatoe, all full of little tough fibres."

I wrote a letter to Julia Cooley Altrocchi. Was that part about Winnemucca's father and Patrick Breen poetic license? was only one of many questions I wanted to ask her. I read your book aloud to my husband and children, I wanted to tell her. But my letter was returned marked **Deceased.**

The town of Winnemucca on I-80 was a little more than midway through the state heading northwest, 164 miles southeast of Reno. Just a small town with a population of forty-one hundred and a wooden Indian on the sidewalk, but after all the lonely graves, the shock of it hit me like a slap in the face.

The children zipped around town collecting freebie coupon books: GOOD FOR ONE FREE KENO GAME AT . . . GOOD FOR ONE FREE DRINK AT . . . GOOD FOR . . . Excitedly, they fanned them out like a deck of cards, shrieking, "You can get all these drinks." Roger and I didn't want drinks. "But they're *free!*" When we traveled, anything free was practically a personal gift from God.

There are no clocks in casinos. There is only casino time. We pushed open the smoke glass door, leaving heat and glare and morning outside, and stepped into midnight: flashing reds and yellows, coins jangling, levers grinding, rows and rows of shiny slots, nickel slots, dime, quarter, dollar slots. When I was little, there were still slot machines around Lansing, Michigan; my beloved Grampa Joe used to give me coins to feed them; I'd always loved gambling, and my pulse quickened now.

A woman with her hair in curlers, a bag of groceries at her feet, glanced over at us, gave no sign of seeing anything, glanced back. She was playing two slots simultaneously—a half dozen stacks of silver dollars five inches high in front of her—and during the time her head swiveled, her hands continued to pump coins and pull levers as precisely as a mechanical person. I imagined a highly developed ear cocked for the sound of tumblers clicking and frozen foods in the paper bag defrosting and spoiling.

Another woman, nearby but similarly encapsulated, playing a machine as if in a trance, wore a golf glove on her slot lever hand.

We passed a faro table; the faro dealer had a wrinkled shirt and bloodshot eyes. I didn't understand the game and the dealer didn't look like someone you'd ask; we moved on to the keno section. Both keno callers, a man and a woman, wore black string ties and black vests. They didn't look Western; they looked like second-string riverboat gamblers.

Everyone looked hungover. The gray wall-to-wall carpeting was littered with stamped-out cigarette butts. I was revolted by the seediness and the excess of this place. What once struck me, and was now striking my children, as excitement, now struck me as fake and fever and frenzy. I fed my freebie coin into the slot, pulled the lever without joy, faking enthusiasm for my kids and memories of Grampa Joe. The children groaned, but naturally I didn't win; I didn't deserve to win: I had neither belief nor hope.

It was breakfast time; there were a half dozen solitary drinkers in the bar. The kids had to leave the casino; "No Minors Allowed," the signs said. "Listen, kids," I said, "if your Great-grampa Joe were here, you'd be playing those slot machines." Disappointed, they headed off in search of more freebies for us; I immediately lit a cigarette, and Roger and I slid onto the barstools. The bartender—Fred, his nametag said—looked bored. When we took out our coupon books, an infinitesimal shift went over his eyes as if he were rolling them internally: how many thousands of people like us had he seen rushing in to get their freebies? "Irish coffee," I said; he nodded and turned around. "And hold the Irish, will you?" He turned back, interest on his face, and said, "I've never had anyone hold the Irish before." He poured me a cup of coffee.

On our second cup of free coffee, Roger asked, "What's it like to live here?"

Sodom and Gomorrah, I thought.

"If you like a small town, Winnemucca's the place for you," Fred said. He looked directly at me.

"Really," I said, lighting another cigarette.

"It's a good place to raise kids because most everybody knows your kids, so they can't get into too much trouble."

Roger, an ex–professional musician who had played in casinos, asked, "Do you do much gambling?"

A shade went across Fred's eyes. "Too much. That's something you have to learn to live with in Winnemucca."

We went to get breakfast. All around us, people were eating pork chops, Swiss steak, hot dogs. We ordered Danish and scrambled eggs, the only people eating breakfast food. The waitress had dangling rhinestone earrings. I lit a cigarette and asked her how she liked living here.

"I'll tell you," she said. "I used to live in Reno, but I'd never go back there again. Reno's a rough town." Her eyes momentarily went back to Reno and roughness; I was glad she got out. "I'm originally from Indiana," she said, "but I'd never live in the Midwest again." Her voice went soft. "Winnemucca's a wonderful town. The pace is slow and easy."

I said it seemed fast to us coming from those vast, isolated spaces of Wyoming, and she looked at me as if I were speaking Serbo-Croat.

We left Winnemucca, and almost immediately it became illusion as the dust and wind and sage took hold again. Of all the states I'd seen, I liked Nevada the least. I'd always thought no place could be all ugly, you just had to look more closely, but here I peered and squinted and stared and, except for the PIONEERS grave site that might or might not have been Gravelly Ford, it all looked ugly to me. The land seemed frighteningly implacable, as if there were no possibility of marking it.

The current drought wasn't helping Nevada either. Everything was brown or gray, parched colors and scrawny sage: burnt-out land. Turkey buzzards—vultures—swooped down for the highway carrion, brown and black and red animal blobs mashed by speeding cars. From Elko on, dust twisters threw up columns of dust and dirt—minicyclones, Roger said, produced by hot air currents hitting some cooler air. He knew all these kinds of physical details; I tape-recorded what he said. The air was clotted with heat.

October 10, two days after Hardcoop was abandoned, the rear section caught up with the Donners, who had stopped to rebury a pioneer from an earlier train, as I hoped that a wagon of '47 stopped and buried Hardcoop's bones. I imagined the Donners moving along, seeing an object ahead—"What's that?"—getting closer, Tamsen distracting the children till the body, rifled by Indians and coyotes, worked on by vultures and heat, was laid to rest again. "The dead don't know our treatment of them," I told our children. "We do these things for ourselves. The dead matter to us."

The Donners had just finished their gruesome task when the rear wagons came up, the first time the full company had been together since before John Snyder's death and James Reed's banishment. They had most likely already heard Reed's version of the story when he had caught up with them. (One of the Donner girls later said Reed didn't tell them about Snyder, but it's more probable that he didn't tell the children.) I imagine the Donners standing there, watching the wagons grow closer, waiting through the "Whoas" and "Hees" and the dismounting to hear the explanations, the excuses. Were they incredulous, or appalled? Did equable George fire up, say, "What the hell's going on? You sent him out there to die!" Or did he stay silent and later tell Tamsen, "We weren't there. We don't know what we would have done."

Who was the first one to mumble that Reed's banishment was not the worst of it, to tell the Donners about Hardcoop? Then the most optimistic heart must have sunk, the realization come that no longer were they a party, a band, cohorts, these people could not be relied upon, then the interior doors shut, the fear ringing deeply: we are on our own.

No matter how frightening the awareness of the social and moral disintegration, the sense of aloneness, what could anyone do at that point but go on?

The Donners told the Reed family that Reed had set out on horseback for Sutter's Fort with his teamster, Walter Herron, on foot. "Every day, we would search for some sign of Papa, who would leave a letter by the wayside in the top of a bush or in a split stick," Virginia wrote, "and when he succeeded in killing geese or birds would scatter the feathers about so that we might know that he was not suffering for food. When possible, our fire would always be kindled on the spot where his had been. But a time came when we found no letter and no trace of him."

As to why the Donners were two days' travel ahead, Eliza, the child ever protecting the parent, said that in the desert their wagons traveled last so that no one would stray or be left to die alone, but as soon as they reached mountainous country, her father took the lead to open the way. Maybe they had split up to spread out the sparse grazing; maybe they couldn't stand all the bickering. Whatever the reason, it seems likely that James Reed and Hardcoop would still be with the Party if the Donners had been there.

On the morning Hardcoop was left behind, October 8, the Reeds had to give up their last wagon. They had two horses left that the two littlest children rode on while the others walked alongside, taking turns holding their hands.

The Indians ran off Graves's horses, the horses that couldn't be spared to go back for Hardcoop, and the next day ran off eighteen oxen and one milk cow, mostly Wolfinger's and the Donners', who had to yoke up cows. Between the Great Salt Lake Desert and the Indians, the company had lost almost one hundred head of stock.

40 The Second Desert

Crossing Nevada, pioneers followed the Humboldt River and then the Truckee River. As the California Trail paralleled the Humboldt and the Truckee, so later did the railroad track, and then Highway 80, following the rivers as the pioneers, the trappers, the Indians, and the animals had. From earliest times, rivers were the natural highways, but the Humboldt River in Nevada didn't behave naturally: flowing ever inland, never to reach the sea, it disappeared, evaporating in an alkaline sink.

Big Meadows, now Lovelock, Nevada, was a few miles northeast of where the Humboldt reached its sink and the dry stretch before the Truckee River began. Here, where the pioneers cut grass and collected water for the dread Nevada desert stretch—their second desert, the one they had known about—the Nevada Emigrant Trail Marking Committee had placed Humboldt River Route Marker #7:

> This famous desert oasis made possible
> the crossing of the 40 mile desert.

The exact location of the marker was on the front lawn of the Pershing County Library. Nearby, there was a children's pool and playground, and a lovely little park with picnic tables and benches where we picnicked. Children's noises coming from the pool, shrieks and splashes as they played and cooled off on this hot day, a lush green lawn in front of a library, a building full of books: it seemed a perfect place to remember Tamsen Donner.

Humboldt Sink was a white sludge with sinkholes. An often-repeated story said that one of those sinkholes had sucked Patrick Breen's best mare down. "Help me," Breen screamed. "Ask Hardcoop to help you," Eddy said coldly. The mare smothered.

We walked along Humboldt Sink as they had. It was hard walking, and we weren't carrying children and prodding oxen. The alkali sand was crumbled and cracked; every step made a little crunch; our feet sank in.

Between Humboldt Sink and the beginning of the Truckee River was the brutal forty-mile desert.

The Indians shot more cattle. William Eddy had to abandon his wagon; he had only one ox to pull it. No one would take his children into their wagon. Eddy carried his three-year-old son and three pounds of sugar, the last of their provisions; his wife carried the baby. Wolfinger, the German, stayed behind to cache some goods to lighten up his load; Spitzer and Reinhard, his countrymen, stayed to help him. The rest walked on with the jaded oxen.

Eddy told Thornton later that his children were dying of thirst and he went to Pat Breen who had a full cask of water. Breen refused him any. "If you stop me, I'll kill you," Eddy said, filling a ladle of water for his children. The Eddys survived the desert stretch.

Tamsen left her books there in the second desert. Her books, painstakingly chosen all the previous winter, to form the core of her school.

What books do you take to a desert island or a new land? It was a literate age. Tamsen was an Easterner. That year, Longfellow had already composed one canto of a long poem called "Evangeline," and Thoreau was plumbing the depths of Walden Pond. There would have been poetry: it's thought that Tamsen's poems had been published in the Sangamo

Journal. Math and science: she had once taught surveying to a group of surprised young gentlemen, and her botanical sketches were much admired for their precision and delicacy. She spoke French; she might have brought Montaigne. A member of the German Prairie Christian Church, she would have had the Bible. And surely Shakespeare, and Emerson, and McGuffey's Readers, and on and on, each book doubly precious for having been bought at the price of those left behind.

All along they had been shedding things and now they were down to the crates of books. Imagine Tamsen walking alongside the wagon, the oxen weakening daily, George yoking up cows, "Chain up, boys! Chain up," the wagons wrenching along, it becoming crystal clear, *My books have to go*. George would wait for her to say it, knowing she would before he had to.

At earlier places on the trail when pioneers had to lighten their loads, some left grimly humorous signs next to their abandoned or poorly cached goods HELP YOURSELF. Later on many just dumped things, no time for ceremony or irony. This would have been a hasty but not a careless caching. George would have known what a sacrifice this was for Tamsen, how bad she felt. It was mid-October; if they buried the books carefully, they might reserve a small possibility of sending someone back to get them the next spring or summer. Maybe she thought, *We take along what we can carry in ourselves; our futures lie in our lives right now*. She may have said, "There will be other books," or "There are more important things than books," but she never would have said, "They're only books." Nor would she turn around to see what she had left behind. She knew what she had left behind.

At the desert's end was the Truckee River, cottonwood trees and wide river; from now on, they would never be out of reach of water.

Eddy and his family were starving. He asked for food: the Breens and the Graveses turned him down; the Donners gave him a little coffee. Eddy borrowed a gun and shot nine wild geese; he shared them out among the families. Think of Peggy Breen and Elizabeth Graves boldly accepting Eddy's geese; especially Peggy Breen, tough as nails, scrabbling for her family. We expect the lioness to kill for her cubs, but aggressive Peggy Breen was rarely the heroine of anyone's version of the Donner story, even though her whole family of nine survived; we ridicule the housewife who grabs the choicest cut of meat, elbows others for the sale item and coupon refund: behavior that's all on a continuum, revealing an intensity of protection and preservation of one's own.

Wolfinger, Reinhardt, and Spitzer didn't catch up with the Party. Mrs. Wolfinger, who spoke little English, pleaded in the universal language of distress; some of the herders rode back and found the Wolfinger wagon, untouched, but no sign of the men. They brought the wagon in.

The next day, Spitzer and Reinhardt caught up: Indians attacked us, they said. Indians killed Wolfinger. They were unable to explain why the wagon was unharmed, why they were unharmed, why Reinhardt carried Wolfinger's rifle.

Everybody had Reinhardt and Spitzer's number, but along the Truckee River in mid-October, their number wasn't up. What could the company do with their suspicions: accuse them, stare them down, go back into the desert to look for proof? Perhaps some of them felt it was, after all, a matter among foreigners. Reinhardt and Spitzer, carrying their secret and perhaps Wolfinger's money belt, continued on; one of the Donners' teamsters drove Mrs. Wolfinger's wagon; Tamsen and George took Mrs. Wolfinger in.

Reinhardt and Spitzer, each about 30 years old, were walking to their deaths in the Sierra Nevadas. In two months, Reinhardt would reform on the brink of eternity, confessing on his deathbed to George Donner to the murder of Wolfinger. But along the Truckee River in mid-October, two months was an eternity away.

Doris Wolfinger, from Germany, suddenly a 19-year-old widow, her inappropriate silk dresses now stained and tattered, walked along in a foreign country, the man responsible for her being there dead, two of the people who spoke her language his suspected murderers. She might have turned to the other Germans, the Kesebergs, but Lewis was cold and bitter, his wife, Philippine, frightened. Tamsen knew swift, sharp widowhood: surely she offered wordless consolations, eyes meeting, hands touching, a cup of sugared coffee when coffee was scarce. Any of it would help, but Doris Wolfinger would never again be as alone as she was then, walking along mute in a surreal landscape with strangers.

October 19, the Party's provisions gone except for scraps of coffee, tea, and sugar, three men and a mule train appeared in the distance from the West. Their first piece of luck in months: Charles Stanton had come back. Captain John Augustus Sutter, the "universal succorer," had sent two guides with him, Spanish-speaking Indians, *vaqueros*, Luis and Salvador, and seven mules loaded down with flour and beef jerky.

"Hungry as we were, Stanton brought us something better than food: news that my father was alive," Virginia wrote. "Stanton had met him not far from Sutter's Fort; he had been three days without food, and his horse was not able to carry him. Stanton had given him a horse and some provisions and he had gone on."

Besides seeing James Reed, Stanton had other news. William McCutchen was ill and couldn't travel, but he was at Sutter's Fort; Walter Herron was alive; the mountain passes were still open. Sutter said they had nearly a month, mid-November, before the snows would close the passes for the winter.

Stanton put the Reeds on the mules, Margret on one, carrying Tommy in her lap, Patty riding behind Salvador, Jimmy behind Luis, and Virginia behind him. The next day, they reached Truckee Meadows.

The Sierras loomed on the horizon, the worst ascent of all waiting for them, three days of hard traveling if the oxen were fit, but California was just over the other side of the mountains. Truckee Meadows was plentiful green grass for pasture and clean rushing water, Charles Stanton had come back, James Reed and William McCutchen had gotten through and would come back, two hopes traveling toward them only days away, meat in camp again and deer on the hills: the smell of fresh bread baking pervaded the camp along with hope. They rested a few days to recoup the animals for the ascent.

Truckee Meadows. Doesn't it sound lush, a kind of Eden, after the aridity of land and experience behind them? Thick green grass, clean rushing water, bread baking in camp again.

41

Truckee Meadows was now Reno, Nevada. THE BIGGEST LITTLE CITY IN THE WORLD, the sign said as we drove into the city. We passed a motel named Donner Inn, and I was thinking with pleasure, Somebody remembered, when I was bowled over. Motel after motel, each with a shrieking sign; it was a burlesque, a parody, maybe a sacrilege: CHAPEL OF THE BELLS WEDDING CHAPEL, GOLDEN BELL WEDDING CHAPEL, WEE KIRK OF THE HEATHER WEDDING CHAPEL, HITCHING POST: RUSTIC WEDDINGS OUR SPECIALTY, MARRIAGE PARKING, CANDLELIGHT WEDDINGS, FREE MARRIAGE INFO, COMPLETE WEDDING $17.95, FREE CHAMPAGNE, NOTARY, FLORIST AVAILABLE 24 HOURS DAILY...

Suspecting I might be a tiny bit dogmatic, I worked hard at not being rigid about different ways of doing things—it is, after all, a free country—but I couldn't imagine what kind of people would get married in a motel. People on the move? Impulsive people? Drunk people? I couldn't imagine couples saving up their money for a Reno motel wedding, but maybe gamblers saw it as an opportunity to kill two birds. I knew my tolerance for ritual was exceptionally high, but certainly most people, whether they denied it or not, liked a little ceremony and ritual for special occasions, the cake on the birthday, the champagne and horn on New Year's Eve, feeling on some level that ceremony recognized that an event meant something, that ritual accompanied a transition. But this kind of prepackaged ceremony seemed pathetic caricature, akin to a TV game show. I pictured some cynic in a cowboy hat wiping sleep out of his eyes at 3:00 a.m. to demonstrate once again "Yep, Ma'am, rustic weddings are my specialty," or over in Wee Kirk of the Heather a tired notary public pulling on his kilt, luckily no need for the underwear. This was like funeral parlors with drive-through viewing windows for people wanting to see the body, but too busy to change their clothes and go inside.

All of Reno seemed a place sustained by excess and greed. Julia Cooley Altrocchi called it "the city of broken vows." There were probably people here celebrating their golden anniversary who loved Reno like Fred loved Winnemucca, who'd tell me in a second like the waitress that they'd tried other towns that were too rough or too boring; this was the place to be. I didn't meet them nor see them and I thought that waitress in Winnemucca was right. This was a rough town and you sensed it around every corner.

We had a good time, found a wonderful independent bookstore that had out-of-print books on the Donner Party and could get me more, ate pizza, walked around all the glitz, then the children went back to the motel to settle in for some serious TV watching while Roger and I went out on the town. We went from one club to another, their surfaces differing but all sharing an atmosphere of frenzy and desperation. In any other town, those kind of mood swings would land people in the booby hatch; here they had bars set up to tranquilize and perpetuate them. In one club, a waitress set down her tray, climbed up on the bar, and started stripping. She was beautiful and had a knockout body, as did almost all of the waitresses, receptionists, salesgirls, and carhops we'd seen. Her face totally impassive, she took off her black merry widow corset like a woman on drugs or practicing Zen. I thought of my daughters, Tamsen Donner's daughters. This pretty young woman barely into her 20s was somebody's daughter; what were her dreams when she came here? To strike it rich: find a rich husband, make a killing at the tables, star in one of the big extravaganzas, maybe all three? Surely she thought she'd have better luck, that her wares, beauty and a knockout body, would carry her further. "Dear Mom and Dad, I'm waitressing at one of the best nightclubs here, and I'm in the show. It's harder here than I thought—I'm really lucky to have this job." What were her dreams now? Maybe there were no mom and dad, no dreams carrying her to this place; maybe I was all wet with sentimentality and she was just happy to have the job. I doubted it. She got off the bar, fastened her merry widow back on, picked up her tray, and resumed waiting tables; another pretty, well-built waitress climbed up on the bar. No one applauded. It wasn't clear if anyone noticed. From the moment you drove into this town, your senses were so unrelentingly assaulted and abused that quickly it took a lot to get your attention. It didn't take long to get the message that bodies, sex, drugs, sleaze, and kink were only commodities, marriage another product to be packaged and sold, everything marketable, nothing really important except making a killing.

On our return to Buffalo, we stopped at Las Vegas and stayed at a hotel called Circus Circus, where the entire second floor was a circular arcade for children who alternately played games of chance for stuffed animals and gimcrack and looked over the railing to watch their parents at the casino tables on the first floor. High above everyone, acrobats swung, flipped, swung all night long. Circus Circus was shocking pink and built in a circus tent shape, and when I saw it sparkling in the heat, I thought it so delightful that we immediately checked out of the motel we'd just checked into so that we could take the children to this zany place. What excitement!

We gave them two dollars each, which, after having no money at all, seemed prodigious to them, and turned them loose. All around, adults were stuffing bills into their children's hands. We, like them, made a beeline downstairs. Everyone had the glitter in their eyes, the fever, but if you weren't a serious gambler or a vacation gambler with money to lose, it was boring at the casinos; after one night, it was like the confessional: same old stuff over and over.

Once I went up to the second floor, which by that point was getting seedy-looking, with bored carneys and tired children, candy wrappers and soft drink cups littering the carpet. Was this really such a great idea training the next generation to be gamblers, I thought; was this really what we meant by child care? But I didn't think about it deeply because the children were having a wonderful time and I enjoyed the respite.

In a large family, you learned early that if you were able to savor only your own pleasures, your pleasures would be few and far between. It was lucky that each of our kids were on close terms with vicarious pleasure, because an evening that revolved around two dollars in Las Vegas would be over pretty quickly. They saw and enjoyed the free things: the acrobats swinging through the air, the colors and excitement, the being on their own. They made their way from booth to booth, cannily figuring out how the games were played to increase their odds of winning. They didn't fan out or play simultaneously, but watched and coached each other at the games. That way, they enjoyed each two dollars spent five times.

They managed by wit and wile and endurance to increase the money we gave them three times and more, finding unused tickets and silver coins on the floor, finding jaded carneys who were amused or touched by enthusiasm or such deep desire that they said "Go ahead, kid, have one on the house," the acts of carelessness and generosity and skill piling up until every one of the five Burtons had won a minimum of two stuffed animals of her choice, all of which continued the rest of the trip with us.

I was repelled by Nevada. The only reason it seemed to exist was so people could gamble, and that didn't seem enough reason. Then it struck me that that's what the pioneers were doing, gambling everything, high risk for high stakes, and, just a few years, later the goldminers too: all were high-stake gamblers. But they were putting their entire efforts in, not expecting a payoff with no input. They worked hard, didn't just sit glazed in front of a slot machine or a stack of chips. Maybe it was the means I objected to, not the end. And even that wasn't it. All the people who stood at those tables with that fever passing through their eyes wanted to change their life in some way, wanted something they didn't now have. And the waitresses getting up on the bar, the stage, in the cage, were certainly not asking something for nothing. I was a gambler myself, risking my marriage and my friendships with my new feminist demands. But I felt disgusted: Nevada sickened me. As Utah reeked of control, Nevada reeked of excess, no control, except the ulterior control of others by those passing off fake freedoms as the real goods. In the drought, you realized that Nevada, especially Las Vegas, was really desert, that, without irrigation, it would revert to desert, all the neon and gaudy hotels crumbling in the dust like a Maharajah's village in India that we would see a few years later. In the drought, Nevada seemed revealed for what it really was: an arid, thirsting land.

The Donner Party's luck had momentarily turned with Charles Stanton's arrival, but it went bad again in Truckee Meadows. A willow stub pierced Lewis Keseberg's foot, crippling him. William Pike, 32, handed a pepperbox gun to his brother-in-law, William Foster, 30; the gun went off and Pike was dead within an hour, leaving his widow, Harriet, and two daughters, 3 and 1. They lay Pike in the ground without box or boards. The sky stayed leaden, snow on the mountains ahead. Snow fell.

Fifteen decrepit wagons with eighty-one people left Truckee Meadows in three sections. The five wagons of the Breens, Pat Dolan, the Kesebergs, and the Eddys went first; the four wagons of the Graveses and the Murphys with Stanton, the Indians, Sutter's mules, and the Reeds next; and finally, the Donner brothers' five wagons and Mrs. Wolfinger's one.

In the camp of the first section, an Indian shot nineteen oxen, not killing but debilitating them; William Eddy killed him. A day behind in the third section, one of the Donner wagons snapped an axle and turned over, nearly killing 3-year-old Eliza, sleeping inside. They pulled her out from under the avalanche of goods, stunned but safe.

Had Tamsen's books been there, I had once read, her precious books given to the desert, little Eliza would surely have been crushed. Initially reading that, I thought that Tamsen had had an ironic piece of good luck, that gifts were given in strange ways. I don't know when I started to wonder, was that male writer making an unconscious no-win statement about women having work in addition to their children?

In the first years of my writing, when I would finish an article, painstakingly packaging it according to the specifications in *Writer's Market*, I would send Maria and Jennifer to the mailbox to post it, get hope traveling on its way immediately so that I could start the three, four, six months of sweating out the wait—please, God, don't let it be another rejection. To get to the mailbox, a block away, required crossing a street: steps to independence and self-sufficiency for Maria, 8 at the beginning although this went on for years, and Jennifer, 7, as well as a miniadventure. "Don't forget to look both ways," I'd say sternly enough so they'd pay heed, casually enough so they wouldn't be fearful, and they'd merrily set out, while I, on the porch with the three littler kids, my heart tightening, watched them walk to the corner, holding each other's hands, holding the manila envelope with my article, look both ways, run across the street, and every single time, the sickening thought coming unbidden: if they get hit by a car, my writing won't be worth it. Fathers almost never had these kind of painful, irresolvable, guilt-ridden, self-blaming thoughts; no writer wrote, "Had George's valuable keg of nails been there, little Eliza would surely have been crushed." A barrel of flour would also surely have crushed her; would that have made any difference at all?

They righted the wagon, and George and Jacob Donner were hastily repairing the broken axle when Jacob's chisel slipped, gashing George's hand. They made light of it because they were brothers and because they knew how serious any wound in their state was. It was a death blow Jacob had delivered, but by the time the gangrene would kill George, Jacob would be long dead.

42 California

And then just suddenly we were there, climbing the mountain thruway to Donner Pass, up, up the magnificent curving road, 80 West and 80 East running parallel for a while and then one or the other ascending, descending, appearing and disappearing amidst pines and granite, looking down on a perfect pastoral scene, Donner Lake—Truckee Lake it was called in 1846, the new name paid for in lives. High above, rhythmic puffs of white smoke, a cheerful whistle, a train snaked across the Sierras: not twenty years after the Donners, Chinese laborers were looking down on the scene, tragedy in the happening watching tragedy in the past, one of the greatest engineering feats ever, track gashed straight through rock, nobody knows how many lives it cost. I was caught by surprise as if I'd thought we'd just go on forever, as they must have thought; I wasn't ready to stop as they weren't ready, but there was one big difference: we were reaching our destination while they, caught by early snows, were making a forced stop before their journey's end.

Attempting to imagine these awesome mountains covered with snow, and people trying to take covered wagons over them, I experienced total disbelief for the first time: there was no way. It was the covered wagons. Seeing the marks of the Oregon and California Trail was such a powerful experience because although a familiar mythology enveloped and informed them, by and large, its images had not been sated. Unlike seeing the Grand Canyon, Niagara Falls, even the Taj Mahal, you didn't have to plough through thousands of other people's impressions and renditions before you could even attempt to get to the essence of what you were seeing and feeling. Here only a relatively few people had preceded you, only a few layers separated you from the original experience. The one image and symbol connected with the Oregon Trail that was sated was the covered wagon, which in movies, Disneyland, and countless barbecue restaurants, had been folksied, cute-i-fied, trivialized. There was no way that covered wagons, musical comedy props, could scale those granite walls. There was no way people could build a railroad through them. It was sickening to think of it, first comical, then tragic. Yet thousands of wagons did cross, the railroad did go through, and had the Donner Party arrived a week earlier or the snow a week later, the pass would not be named Donner.

Not fifty miles from Truckee Meadows to the pass, the Donners with their late start, overturned wagon, and broken axle only made it to Alder Creek, seven miles east of the pass. The storm stopped them October 31, the day before Tamsen's forty-fifth birthday. Three months before, July 31, they had left Fort Bridger on the shortcut that was to save them three hundred miles and a month of travel.

Some in the first two sections almost made it over the summit. November 3, they abandoned the wagons, packed goods on oxen and mules, and carried the children through waist-deep snow. Charles Stanton and one of the *vaqueros*, Luis or Salvador, pressed ahead to find the road in the drifts, making it to the top. The others halted, made a fire, were half encamped when Stanton came back. Those who wanted to push on couldn't break the others' exhausted inertia: they would cross in the morning. Everyone went to sleep and snow began to fall. It snowed steadily for eight days.

A dozen miles on the other side of the summit heading toward them, James Reed and William McCutchen with pack animals laden with beef, beans, and flour were stopped by the same snow and had to turn back to Sutter's Fort.

The emigrants in the first two sections set up camp in four clusters: The nine Breens and Pat Dolan moved into a log cabin already standing at the foot of Truckee Lake—a shanty, Patrick Breen called it in his diary—built in 1844 by three members of the Stevens Party, one of whom, Moses Schallenberger, 17, had spent the entire winter there. Lewis Keseberg built a lean-to against it for his family. A hundred fifty yards upstream, the Eddys and the Murphys built a new log cabin. Using a huge twelve-foot rock for one wall, they laid green tree poles flat from wall to wall, covering the top with tents and wagon covers. A half mile away, a double log cabin with a shared inner wall was built. The Graveses and Mrs. McCutchen took one side, the Reeds, Stanton, the teamsters, and the *vaqueros* the other. Seven miles east at Alder Creek, the Donners and Mrs. Wolfinger had no time to build a cabin. "The snow came on so suddenly," Leanna Donner wrote Charles McGlashan years later, "that we had barely time to pitch our tent, and put up a brush shed, as it were, one side of which was open." They cleared a space under a large pine tree, setting their tent south of the tree and facing east. Using the tree for the north wall, they built a lean-to of pine branches against the tent. "This brush shed was covered with pine boughs, and then covered with rubber coats, quilts, etc.," Leanna wrote. "My uncle, Jacob Donner, and family also had a tent and camped near us." Nearby, the four teamsters put up a wigwam.

In the three shelters at the Truckee Lake camp, there were sixty people: nineteen men and twelve women eighteen or older, and twenty-nine children, six of them nursing babies.

In the three shelters at Alder Creek where the Donners were, there were twenty-one people: six men, three women, and twelve children.

They made attempts to walk across the mountains.

On November 12, thirteen men and two women set out from the lake camp. Unable to advance through the ten-foot-deep soft snow, they came back the same day.

November 21, sixteen men and six women got over the pass, but when the mules flailed in the deep snow, Stanton refused to go on because he had promised Sutter he'd return them. The group turned back.

By the first of December, the cabins and tents were under snow. You entered a hole and slid down a tunnel to a dank, fetid space.

Franklin W. Graves, who had caught up with the Party in the Wasatch, was originally from Vermont and accustomed to heavy snowfalls, as was Charles Stanton from upstate New York. They took the u-shaped hickory oxbows, sawed them into strips, wove rawhide for the surface, and made snowshoes for a party of five women, nine men, and a boy. This group, first called the "Forlorn Hope" in McGlashan's book, set out December 16, the day of the first death at the lake camp, Baylis Williams, age 24, James Reed's teamster from Springfield. Two months would pass without word of them.

Although seven difficult miles separated the camps, there was some communication and traveling between them.

December 21, Patrick Breen recorded in his diary:

Milt got back last night from Donos [Donners] camp sad news. Jake Donno Sam Shoemaker Rinehart & Smith are dead the rest of them in a low situation

Except for Jacob Donner, who was old for the trail and ailing, the others, James Smith, Samuel Shoemaker, and Joseph Reinhardt, were all young men who just lay down and died.

Christmas Day, Patrick Breen recorded that it had begun to snow about twelve o'clock the day before.

snowd all night & snows yet rapidly Great difficulty in geting wood. offerd. our prayers to God this Cherimass [sic] morning the prospect is apalling but hope in God Amen

We don't know what Tamsen did for Christmas, if anything. Burying her first husband on Christmas Eve on the heels of the death of her son and miscarriage of a daughter, the season had to be bittersweet for her in ordinary times. Years later, Eliza wrote simply, "Snowy Christmas brought us no 'glad tidings.'"

But there were glad tidings at the Reeds' lake camp, and Virginia Reed and her siblings would never forget that Christmas. Weeks back, Margret had planned—burying a bit of tripe, a small piece of bacon, some beans, and a few dried apples deep in a snowmound—and early Christmas morning, she began her surprise.

The Reed children clustered around the kettle, their faces bending close to smell the unexpected feast, the cabin filling with unaccustomed sounds—children's noise—"There's mine," Tommy, age 3, shrieked as each bean surfaced, bobbing in the swirling broth.

Margret Reed ladled deep into the pot and said, "Children, eat slowly, there is plenty for all. This one day you can have all that you wish."

"So bitter was the misery relieved by that one bright day," Virginia wrote forty years later, "that I have never since sat down to a Christmas dinner without my thoughts going back to Donner Lake."

"Eat slowly, children, there is plenty for all."

January 4, when nothing had been heard from the snowshoers who had started out almost three weeks before, Margret and Virginia Reed, their cook Eliza Williams, and teamster Milt Elliott set out. Patrick Breen wrote in his diary,

Mrs. Reid Milt. Virginia, & Eliza started about ½ hour ago with prospect of crossing the mountain may God of Mercy help them left ther children here Tom's with us Pat with Keysburg & Jas with Gravese's folks, it was difficult for Mrs Reid to get away from the children.

On January 6, he wrote,

Eliza came back from the mountain yesterday evening not able to proceed, to day went to Graves, the others kept ahead.

On January 8:

Mrs. Reid & company came back this moring could not find their way on the other side of the mountain they have nothing but hides to live on . . . prospects dull

They had narrowly missed the worst storm of the winter that would surely have killed them.

And that party of fifteen that had left the lake camp on December 16? Two Indians dragged the lone William Eddy the last miles to Johnson's ranch (now Wheatland), the first settlement at the edge of Sacramento Valley. The Californians made their way back to the six still alive by following Eddy's bloody footprints and brought them in. All five women who had started out survived and two of the ten men. It had taken them thirty-three days.

But the privation and suffering of the pioneers in the mountains was now known to the outside world and rescue parties formed.

43

The first instance of cannibalism occurred December 27 on the Forlorn Hope. They had thought it would take them six days to walk to Bear Valley, below the snowline. On the sixth morning out, Charles Stanton, snowblind, stayed by the campfire smoking his pipe when the others left. They never saw him again.

On their twelfth day out, when they had been without food for five days, weeping, they roasted and ate Pat Dolan's dead body. Antonio, the herder George Donner had hired at Fort Bridger, died and was eaten. Franklin Graves, who had made the snowshoes with Stanton, died and was eaten. Lem Murphy, 14, and Jay Fosdick, 22, both died and were eaten. When the food ran out again, Luis and Salvador—the two *vaqueros* who had come back with Stanton from Sutters Fort with mules and food for the party—were killed by William Foster, then eaten.

At the camps, the eating of the dead began in February after the first rescue party had come and gone.

Patrick Breen wrote,

Feb 26th Mrs. Murphy said here yesterday that thought she would commence on Milt. & eat him. I don't [think] that she has done so yet, it is distressing. The Donnos told the California folks [the First Relief] that they commence to eat the dead people 4 days ago, if they did not succeed that day or next in finding their cattle then under ten or twelve feet of snow & did not know the spot or near it, I suppose they have done so ere this time.

Georgia Donner, who turned 5 at Alder Creek, wrote when she was 37,

When I spoke of human flesh being used at both tents [Jacob Donner's and George Donner's], I said it was prepared for the little ones in both tents. I did not mean to include the larger (my half sisters) children or the grown people because I am not positive that they tasted it. Father was crying and did not look at us during the time, and we little ones felt that we could not help it. There was nothing else. Jacob Donner's wife came down the steps one day saying to mother, "What do you think I cooked this morning?" Then answered the question herself, "Shoemaker's arm."

They stripped the flesh from the arms and legs and roasted it, opened the abdomens for liver and lights (lungs), the rib cage for the heart; they sawed open the skulls for brains. Not savages and ghouls, the body craved viscera, suffering from vitamin deficiency, we know now.

Most people eat each other to survive, William Lederer had told me at Bread Loaf, talking about emotional cannibalism before I'd ever heard of the Donner Party. Except for one instance—the crazed William Foster, who murdered the dying Luis and Salvador to eat them— members of the Donner Party ate only dead bodies. Foster valued Luis and Salvador less because they were Indians, but he had also suggested killing nearly everyone else on the Forlorn Hope. All his other ideas, threats, and attempts had been interfered with, except for this one. The others would not join in the killing, and they camped apart from Foster, but they ate the bodies.

Family members tried not to eat their own, although it was not always avoidable.

I read a letter to Roger and the children about Nancy Graves, 9 years old, who survived the Second Relief on which her mother and brother died. Eliza Donner Houghton wrote McGlashan,

> A number of weeks ago, . . . a friend joined me . . . and we were talking of "by gone" days . . . and she said, "I never recall my first days in San Jose, without thinking of poor little Nancy G____ who used to cry so much in school. Why that poor child used to break right out during schooltime and it often seemed to me her heart would break. . . . One day my sister and two or three others gathered around her; we cried with her; and begged her to tell us what troubled her so much; and between sobs and sighs she told us of her being at 'Starved Camp'—how her mother died, how part of the flesh was prepared for food without her knowledge—and how she was told of it after she had partaken of it, and how perfectly heartbroken she had been ever since. We tried to soothe and comfort her but it seemed no use; for she would cry 'How can I forget it; or forgive myself?'"

Many lurid tales circulated then and now, this one about as lurid as you can get. That Eliza, supersensitive to sensationalism, told McGlashan this testifies to its veracity. One wonders what it was like for her to talk about this with her friend, and then to later write it down. Poor little Nancy G would not be the only one who cried.

Nearly out of food when they arrived, many of the Party were trapped more than four months, Tamsen Donner nearly five months. Some lay down and waited for death, which came quickly, but others fought to stay alive with an ingenuity both desperate and heroic. First, they slaughtered all the cattle that had not run off in the storm, butchered the meat, froze it in the snow, and put the hides on the tops of the shelters for roofing. They ate every part of the cattle. The bones were boiled and sucked and the broth drunk, then boiled again or burned brown till they crumbled between the teeth. One by one, the green ox rawhides, their roofs, came down, were cut into strips, held in the fire until the hair was singed off, scraped with a knife, and boiled for hours until soft and pulpy. When cold, the hides and the water they were cooked in became jellied and gluelike. There was no salt. Some of the survivors were revolted by jelly the rest of their lives because it reminded them of the gluey pulp they survived on.

At Alder Creek where the Donners were, Jean Baptiste Trudeau, the 16-year-old teamster, frequently probed the snow with long poles with a nail stuck on the end, trying to find the cattle and mules that had run off and been buried in the snow. He never found one. Little mice that crept into the shelter seeking warmth were caught and eaten. At the lake camp, they tried to fish in Truckee Lake without success. At various times in November soon after they were trapped, William Eddy at the lake camp shot a coyote, an owl, two ducks, and a grizzly bear. Even a bear didn't go far when one half went to Foster, the owner of the gun, and a part to Graves, who helped drag the bear in. Eddy and his family shared the rest with Margret Reed. Peggy Breen slipped a bit of meat to Virginia Reed when she was near death, but Eddy's sharing and hers were rarities at the lake camp where, in the main, it was every family for itself. And wouldn't we do the same if need be? Charity begins at home, Dickens said, and justice begins next door. At Alder Creek, the two families were blood relatives, and Georgia Donner, 4 years old at the time, said later, "The families shared with one another as long as they had anything to share. Each one's portion was very small. We tried to eat a decayed buffalo robe, but it was too tough and there was no nourishment in it."

A day came when they ate their pet dogs.

Three months after her rescue, Virginia Reed wrote her cousin in Springfield: "O Mary I would cry and wish I had what you all wasted . . . we had to kill littel cash the dog & eat him   we ate his head and feet & hide & evrything about him   o my Dear Cousin you dont [k]now what trubel is yet."

Although Eliza doesn't say so, and perhaps she didn't know, we can assume that the Donners also ate their dog, Uno. Tamsen and George Donner were farmers, and farmers respect but don't sentimentalize animals. Still their lead oxen had names, Buck and Bright, and Uno was the children's pet. Although some cultures routinely eat dog, ours doesn't and, surely, that was a taboo crossed. But no parents would watch their child starve if there was something to eat.

The little children chewed on twigs to staunch their hunger. They filled porcelain cups with snow, spooning it out and eating it, pretending it was custard. They cut off small pieces of a fire rug and toasted them upon the coals, eating the entire rug before anyone realized what was happening. Levinah Murphy sprinkled flour into snow water, making a gruel for her baby granddaughter, whose father had died on the trail, her mother gone with the group attempting to walk over the mountains, giving her a few spoonfuls every day until the baby died. There were six nursing babies whose mothers' milk dried up. Four died.

When the relief parties finally came, people stole the buckskin strings from the rescuers' snowshoes and ate them.

And then, after the meat, the hides, the bones, the pet dogs, the shoelaces, the other day came. You'd see it coming. Patrick Breen said in his diary that Tamsen told the First Relief that if rescue didn't come soon, they had to commence on the dead.

Cannibalism was the very last resort.

On our trip, the subject of cannibalism came up often enough that our daughters discussed it without affect. Maria, Jennifer, and Ursula were in accord; that was good enough for Gabriella and Charity. They drew the line at killing anybody, but always concluded that if the need arose, we should eat each other's dead bodies. "It's like communion," Maria said. "Take my body and eat." "It's a gift you'd give to people you loved," Jennifer said. Ursula gave everybody her formal permission. They thought you'd feel terribly sad, and now and then they made little jokes about catsup, but it always seemed obvious to them, as it did to Roger and me, that you'd choose the living over the dead.

44

Four rescue parties came from California. "Are you men from California or do you come from heaven?" Levinah Murphy asked the First Relief. Levinah may not have been sure what she was seeing, but it wouldn't be so far afield to place many of the rescuers in the ranks of angels— men of exceptional courage and strength who, altruistically, put their lives in great danger to help others.

The First Relief party (seven men including two Mormon brothers who had emigrated that year, clearly not looking for Gentiles to slaughter), responding to reports from William Eddy and the Forlorn Hope, reached the cabins February 19, nearly four months after they had been snowed in. Twenty-eight-year-old John Denton, who had started out from Springfield with the Donners and had carved *Sarah Keyes Born in Virginia* on that long-ago April day in Alcove Springs, Kansas, and twenty-two others, including Tamsen's stepdaughters, Leanna and Elitha, started out with the First Relief. Tommy and Patty Reed, unable to keep up, were almost immediately returned to the lake camp after about two miles. Near the end of the second day out, John Denton lay down and went to sleep on the snow. He was found and brought into camp. The next day, Denton gave out again. They built him a fire and went on. The Second Relief found his body. William Hook, 12, Elizabeth Donner's son by a previous marriage, and Ada Keseberg, 3, died on the First Relief too.

Everyone on the First Relief was starving when James Reed, leading the Second Relief party, met them in the mountains on February 27. Reed, seeing his family and the other emigrants for the first time since the Snyder shooting and his banishment almost five months before, described the reunion in his diary entry that day:

> proceeded about four miles, when we met the poor, unfortunate starved people. As I met them scattered along the snowtrail, I distributed some bread I had baked last night. . . . Here I met my wife and two of my little children. Two of my children are still in the mountains. I can not describe the death-like look all these people had. "Bread!" "Bread!" "Bread!" "Bread!" was the begging cry of every child and grown person. I gave all I dared to them and set out for the scene of desolation at the lake.

At the lake and at Alder Creek, there were thirty-one people left. On March 3, James Reed, William McCutchen, Hiram Miller (who had started out from Springfield with the Donners and left the group to go faster with a mule train), and four other men took seventeen out on the Second Relief, fourteen of them children, including Reed's own, Patty and Tommy.

Another rescue party due imminently, Tamsen Donner didn't go with Reed, who wrote in his diary,

> at George Donner tent, there were three Stout harty children. his wife was able to travel but preferred to stay with her husband until provision should arrive which was confidently expected by Woodworth who was at Sutter's the day before I left Johnson's.

Woodworth never came nor did he rendezvous with Reed as Reed had expected; a storm raged for three days; food ran out. Both Patty Reed, 8, and her father nearly died on the Second Relief, which almost became the nightmare rescue in which the rescuers perish. Elizabeth Graves, Franklin Graves Jr., [5?], and Isaac Donner, [5?], died on the Second Relief.

The Third Relief was only four men, two of them, William Eddy and William Foster, coming back for their sons. They arrived at the lake camp on March 13 to find them dead and dismembered, Mrs. Murphy moribund, and Keseberg withdrawn.

Tamsen Donner was also there with her three little daughters. The day after the Second Relief started out, the men Reed had left in charge at Alder Creek decided to flee.

"Mother, fearing that we children might not survive another storm in camp, begged Messrs. Cady and Stone to take us with them, offering them five hundred dollars in coin, to deliver us to Elitha and Leanna at Sutter's Fort," Eliza wrote:

> The agreement was made, and we collected a few keepsakes and other light articles which she wished us to have, and which the men seemed more than willing to carry out of the mountains. Then lovingly, she combed our hair, and helped us to dress quickly for the journey. When we were ready, except cloak and hood, she led us to the bedside and we took leave of father. The men helped us up the steps and stood us up on the snow. She came, put on our cloaks and hoods, saying, as if talking to herself, "I may never see you again, but God will take care of you."
>
> Frances was six years and eight months old and could trudge along quite bravely, but Georgia, who was little more than five, and I, lacking a week of four years, could not do well on the heavy trail, and we were soon taken up and carried. After traveling some distance, the men left us sitting on a blanket upon the snow, and went ahead a short distance where they stopped and talked earnestly with many gesticulations. We watched them, trembling lest they leave us there to freeze. Then Frances said, "Don't feel afraid. If they go off and leave us, I can lead you back to mother by our foot tracks on the snow."

After a seemingly long time, they returned, picked us up and took us on to one of the lake cabins, where without a parting word, they left us.

When Tamsen learned that Cady and Stone had abandoned her daughters at the lake camp, she walked the seven miles there, arriving the same day William Eddy and Foster did (the Third Relief). She asked Eddy to delay starting out until she went back to Alder Creek to see if George was still alive. A fourteen-mile round-trip would mean at best another day's delay; a storm was coming; Eddy said they had to leave now. He took her daughters, and Tamsen returned to Alder Creek alone.

The Fourth Relief in April was a salvage crew, guaranteed twenty dollars in wages a day and half of what they carried out, the other half to be auctioned for the Donner orphans. The only person they found alive was Lewis Keseberg.

In the third week of April, 1847, almost a year to the day after the Donners left Springfield, Lewis Keseberg, the last person out of the mountains, forever the scapegoat of the Donner Party, stumbling after the salvage party toward Sutter's Fort, found his daughter's body in the melting snow. "I discovered a little piece of calico protruding from the snow. Half thoughtlessly, half out of idle curiosity, I caught hold of the cloth, and finding it did not come readily, I gave it a strong pull. I had in my hands the body of my dead child, Ada! . . . I thought I should go frantic. It was the first intimation I had of her death."

How many chances does a person get? On the Forlorn Hope, Charles Stanton, 33, gave out on the sixth day. For two days, he had been going snowblind; on the fifth night, he stumbled into camp two hours after everyone else. The next morning, December 20 or 21, he sat at the fire smoking his pipe as the others prepared to leave. "Are you coming?" Mary Graves asked. "I'll be along soon," he said. They went on.

The next June, Stanton's body was found, devoured by wild animals.

In the Wasatch Mountains, Charles Stanton had volunteered to go after Lansford Hastings. He could have stayed with Hastings, going on to California with him, but although he nearly died, he came back. On the Humboldt, he volunteered to go ahead to Sutter's Fort, could have stayed there, but came back with Indians, mules, and food. In the Sierras, he got to the summit, turned back to help the others; that night the snow trapped them. Later in November, he and twenty-one others got across the pass, but when the mules flailed in the snow and gave out, he refused to go on without them. In December, he made fourteen pairs of snowshoes with Graves, went out with the Forlorn Hope, and died.

Duty ruled Stanton's decisions. A bachelor, his tie to the Donner Party was his code of honor. In hindsight it seems so obvious that he should have abandoned the mules, but mules were valuable in California and Stanton had given his word to Sutter that he'd return them. If years back Stanton had been careless with the equivalent of mules, would he have come back to the Party three times? The keeping of his word that brought him back and saved them ended up dooming him and others. At what point did standards turn from firm to rigid, becoming mindlessly black and white? How much could one bend or sway before subtly, ineluctably, changing the character?

At the lake camps, they felt no such allegiance to Stanton. Some resented that he hadn't abandoned Sutter's mules at the summit, that he had told them at Truckee Meadows they had a month before the pass closed. In general, their ability to feel for others besides self and family quickly eroded. On December 9, the mules long run off, buried who knew where in the snow, Breen wrote in his diary:

Stanton trying to make a raise of some [beef] for his Indians & self not likely to get much.

Tamsen Donner sent her two stepdaughters, Elitha and Leanna, out with the First Relief but didn't go with them. She said no to James Reed on the Second Relief, believing that a larger party would be along soon.

She had second thoughts about her younger daughters staying behind and sent them out with the fleeing rescuers, but didn't go herself. When Eddy (Third Relief) said he couldn't wait for her to go back to Alder Creek to check on George, Tamsen kissed her daughters good-bye and went back to her dying husband.

The third time she said no, she couldn't have been sure another relief party would come. None did. George died, she laid him out, and immediately left. But she had waited too long. Like Charles Stanton, her duty had cost her her life.

It took me years to ask the question I'd never read in any book: why did George let her stay? Both James Reed and Eliza Donner wrote that he told her to go with the Second Relief, but she said she'd wait for the next rescue party. When she came back that last time, when George was the only living person left at Alder Creek and that door opened and Tamsen stood there, did George's love and honor and duty give way to relief and gratitude? Two wives already leaving him in death, was it too painful, too frightening, to encourage a third wife to leave him in life to die alone, the wolves howling at nighttime? Or had he said, "Go, Tamsen," and she said, "Shhh"?

Tamsen and George stayed alone together in that vast solitude, a week, two, possibly almost three weeks before he died. Then she set out alone.

I wanted to walk the seven miles from the Alder Creek campsite to the lake camp as Tamsen walked it at least twice. We seven set out to do it, but the people we asked either didn't know the way or gave us vague directions; we tried to combine their pointing in this direction and that with our maps and photocopies of broad sketches in books. We walked a long time, and strenuously, but never knew where we were or got anyplace we wanted to be.

The sky was blue, the mountainside green and beautiful; there was no feeling of fear or panic, but it was a hard walk and you quickly understood how this area could be a labyrinth. I thought of Tamsen hiking fourteen miles that March day, hurrying the seven miles over, struggling through snow, out of breath, fear in her heart. Clark, the rescuer who had not fled Alder Creek, had been to the lake camp and told her that her three youngest children had been dumped there— still in danger. Tamsen was dazed when she arrived. Simon Murphy, 8, spotted her wandering around: "A little woman," he said. "It looks like Mrs. Donner." How her daughters would have flown out of that dismal hut and clung to her. I thought of her decision to send them on with Eddy and Foster, the farewells, and her seven-mile walk back to Alder Creek, no longer any reason to hurry, knowing she was walking away from her children and walking to her dying husband.

If I sold the book, got some money, I wanted to come back here some day, find out exactly where the seven miles were, and make that walk at least one way, round-trip if I were fit enough. Why? Because Tamsen Donner had done it.

I never sold the book, and the desire to make that walk bowed to other desires over the years, but I'm fit enough and again reserving the possibility. Why? Because Tamsen Donner had done it. Not to emulate her, or test myself as I wanted to do then, just to honor her.

45

Ready to be moved by the massive monument to the Donner Party near the lake camp, four bronze figures atop a twenty-two-foot-high pedestal, I felt let down. The figures—a short woman, carrying a baby, hunched into the armpit of a tall man standing ramrod-straight, shielding his eyes and peering into the distance, a child crouched behind his leg—attempted heroic proportion, but they were so massive and so far up there, they seemed indistinct, somewhat blobby. What exactly is this statue commemorating? I wondered, instead of simply feeling wonder.

VIRILE TO RISK AND FIND . . .
KINDLY WITHAL AND A READY HELP . . .
INDOMITABLE. UNAFRAID . . .

I tried to whomp myself up, reading sonorously to the children the words fixed in bronze, not telling them that the Victorian words seemed inadequate to the visceral experience, seemed lies.

The pedestal itself was the real thing, twenty-two-feet-high, the height of the snow that fell the winter of 1846. *Fell*, not accumulated, as the words led one to think:

> The height of the shaft of the monument indicates the depth of the snow . . . ,

Certainly it was that deep and more up in the pass, but the accumulation at the campsites was ten to twelve feet; we knew that from where the trees were cut off for firewood. Still, the solid pedestal bulk captured the feeling, the mass, of twenty-two feet of snow falling, falling.

> Near this spot, stood the Breen cabin of the party of emigrants who started for California from Springfield, Illinois in April, 1846, under the leadership of Captain George Donner. Delays occurred . . . 42 perished, most of them from starvation and exposure.

Almost where we were standing, the Breens were holed up, saying their prayers nightly, 13-year-old Virginia Reed holding little flaming pieces of pine so Patrick could read the Bible, so impressed by his religiosity she vowed to become a Catholic if she survived, a vow she kept. Here the Breens ate Towser, the family dog, and Patrick made entries daily in his diary.

Patrick Breen, the praying Irishman, kept a diary from November 20, 1846, until he was rescued March 1, 1847. It's eight sheets of paper folded to make a book of thirty-two pages. The paper is yellowed, the ink faded. I had read descriptions of it and excerpts from it in many sources; George Stewart in *Ordeal by Hunger* reprints it in its entirety. I wrote a letter to the Bancroft Library, University of California at Berkeley, asking if I might see it when I came.

"The diary has not been upstairs in years," the librarian said when I arrived. "Every few years, it is exhibited."

"But I wrote a letter," I said again. "I'm writing a book."

Someone remembered having seen my letter, there was a whispered conference, some delay, and then I was taken to a private room, the Breen diary brought up and placed on the table, and I was left alone.

The next day, I came back with Roger and the children and the whole scene repeated. I was a kid who had foxed the principal, a scholar deserving of respect, a priest holding the host in my hands for my children to see—"This is Patrick Breen's *actual* diary, do you understand, children?"—to plunge us into that foul cabin with Breen scribbling the laconic entries six miles west of Tamsen Donner:

> snowd all night
> snow higher than the shanty
> Peggy very uneasy for fear we shall all perrish with hunger
> shot Towser to day and dressed his flesh
> Mrs. Murphy says the wolves are about to dig up the dead bodies at her shanty, we hear them howl
> Mrs. Murphy said here yesterday that she thought she would Commence on Milt. & eat him it is distressing.

At the Donner Pass Museum, there was a twelve-foot tree stump. The spring of 1847 yielded a landscape dotted with such stumps: trees cut down at snowpack level. "For years, people carted them away for souvenirs," the ranger told me later. "Someone donated that one up at the museum; we're not sure if it's an original one." Even the tree stump was in question—one more thing that revealed the unknowability or distrust of many "facts" connected with the Donner Party.

John Denton's worn shoe with a hole in the sole was there in a glass case.

Patty Reed's tiny wooden doll, secretly carried over the mountains on her father's Relief, was there. She had carried the doll, hidden in her dress, all the way from Utah after the Reeds cached their wagon. The doll, about three inches long with a painted face and wooden hinged arms, had a little cloth dress with a red sash. A sign said that the original doll was on display at Sutter's Fort, but the ranger told me privately that over the years and the swapping back and forth, the original and the replica had gotten mixed up; no one knew anymore which museum had the original. I was appalled that even the experts didn't know, even more appalled when I got to Sutter's Fort and saw a shiny wooden copy of the doll that no one could possibly mix up with the weathered doll at Donner Pass. The ranger, trained for his summer job, was passing on a good story, but not a true one.

In a case, there was a comb fragment, pieces of leather, indistinguishable metal objects: bits and pieces of things, parts, that's all that was ever found, I thought at the time, though, in fact, hundreds of items have been found.

The photographs were all of survivors years later; there was nothing of how anyone looked at the time. As far as I knew, there were no pictures anywhere of Tamsen or George. (I hadn't yet read Tamsen's letter to Betsey when she was 32, *I intend to have my portrait painted. Not that I think it will be such a pretty picture but I wish you to have it, as I am so little with you.* If she did, the painting's whereabouts aren't known.) The museum's picture of Eliza Donner grown up was the same one I had in a book at home. Countless times already I had stared at that picture, wondering if Eliza had grown into Tamsen's face the way I'd grown into my mother's, or if she favored her father. (In the late 1990s, Tamsen's great-granddaughter, Ann Smith, gave a picture of Tamsen's daughter, Frances, maybe in her 60s, to Mark McLaughlin, and said family lore said that she favored Tamsen. That likeness, so strong and yet so benign, instantly resonated with me, but it also bore resemblance to my own grandmother, so what can you make of that?)

There was a photograph of Reed's initials carved in Alcove Springs, Kansas, JFR—for us, one layer removed, a verification that we had recognized the authentic carving amidst all the vandals' imitations.

There was an immense wheel hub:

Found in 1927 in the Great Salt Desert, believed to be a remnant of the largest of the Reed wagons

"The mighty Pioneer Palace," according to the caption. In my mind, the Reed's family wagon, built to pleasure and ease an old woman, had become something akin to Cinderella's coach, and the desiccated piece of wood in the glass case startled and disappointed me. I don't know if they've changed the caption, but it's no longer believed that the Pioneer Palace, although eventually abandoned, was left in the Salt Lake Desert.

A picture of Mrs. Graves's silver coins was there with one actual coin mounted. James Reed wrote in his diary that the money, several hundred dollars, had been concealed in auger holes bored in cleats nailed to the bed of the wagon. Mrs. Graves's son, William, elaborated that the cleats were placed in the wagon bed to ostensibly support a table, but on the underside of the cleats, the auger holes were filled with coins. Mrs. Graves took the money with her when she went out with Reed's Second Relief party. At their first night's campsite, near the upper end of Truckee Lake, one of the relief party joked about playing a game of euchre with Mrs. Graves's money the pot. The next morning, a frightened Mrs. Graves stayed behind and hid her money. She died on that relief party. Nearly thirty-five years later when McGlashan wrote his book, the money had not been found. It was discovered in 1891 at Donner Lake, and some of it found its way back to the Graves family. The mounted coin was loaned to the museum by the great-granddaughter of Nancy Graves, that little girl who was inconsolable because she believed she had eaten her mother's flesh.

There was also a chisel found in a tree felled in 1961 at Alder Creek adjacent to the Donner campsite. The sign read:

This may be the chisel that cut George Donner's hand

I doubted it.

Most of the things at the museum were interesting, some were moving, but I didn't find what I was looking for. I didn't know what I was looking for. I yearned to see a picture of Tamsen Donner, but more than that, I yearned for something beyond broken artifacts, something that would have direct meaning for my own life. I knew only that I'd recognize it when I saw it and I had to keep looking.

46

The huge rock that formed part of the Murphy cabin was in the middle
of a pine forest. Sunlight filtered through the pines, played over the
rock, cast shadows. Cathedral pines, shadows, and sun: the solemnity
of the place felt almost tangible. The bronze tablet in the middle of
the rock listed the bodies buried there. Historian Kristin Johnson has
since pointed out that the plaque is "rife with misinformation," which
she corrects on her website.

The mistakes on the plaque notwithstanding, this rock formed the
wall of the Murphy cabin.

Originally, the Eddys and the Murphy clan, including the Fosters
and the Pikes, were here—sixteen people, most of them children. Milt
Elliott came here and died. Lewis Keseberg, too lame to go out with the
First Relief, moved here after they left. Here is where the children ate
the fire rug. Mrs. Murphy commenced on Milt Elliott. James Reed, on
the Second Relief, bathed his enemy, Keseberg, who on the trail may
have propped up his wagon tongue to hang Reed. William Eddy, not
recuperated from his ordeals on the Forlorn Hope, knowing that his

13. Rock that formed the wall of the Murphy cabin.

wife, Eleanor, and his daughter, Margaret, were dead, came back here to find his son, James, also dead.

Frances, Georgia, and Eliza Donner, abandoned by Cady and Stone, cowered here in a corner while Keseberg hung George Foster's dead body on the wall. Years later, Eliza wrote, "The dead child that Keseberg hung on the wall was not eaten by him alone. A part was given to my sisters and myself, and Simon Murphy who I remember so kindly cut a piece, laid it on the coals, cooked and ate it."

In January, Landrum Murphy, 17, died here. In February, Margaret Eddy. Eleanor Eddy. Milt Elliott. Catherine Pike. James Eddy. In March, George Foster. Levinah Murphy.

This is where Lewis Keseberg said Tamsen Donner died in April.

She arrived one midnight, about two weeks after the Third Relief had gone, Keseberg told Tamsen's daughter, Eliza, in 1880. (His perception of time may have been distorted.) "My loneliness was beginning to be unendurable. Her husband had died at nightfall, she had laid him out, and hurried away, traveling over the snow alone to my cabin. She was going, alone, across the mountains without food or guide. She kept saying, 'My children! I must see my children! I am bound to go to my children.' She seemed very cold and her clothes were like ice. I think she had got in the creek in coming. She said she was very hungry but refused the only food I had to offer. She had never eaten the loathsome flesh. She finally lay down and I spread a featherbed and some blankets over her. In the morning she was dead. I think the hunger, the mental suffering, and the icy chill of the preceding night, caused her death."

Keseberg with his Prussian accent and manner was for his whole life and after the pariah of the Donner Party. Eliza Donner Houghton at age 36, in an act of bravery that would have made Tamsen proud, met with the demon of the Donner Party, and hearing his story directly from him, believed he did not kill her mother. Charles McGlashan came to believe Keseberg also, but they were notable exceptions.

William Fallon, commonly called Fallon Le Gros, the leader of the Fourth Relief, wrote in his journal April 19, [1847], that Keseberg told him that "Mrs. Donner had in attempting to cross from one cabin to another, missed the trail, and slept out one night; that she came to his camp the next night very much fatigued, he made her a cup of coffee, placed her in bed and rolled her well in the blankets, but the next morning found her dead; he ate her body and found her flesh the best he ever tasted! He further stated that he obtained from her body at least four pounds of fat! No traces of her person could be found."

Historians, poets, novelists continue to imagine Tamsen Donner's ending. A few years ago, a novelist added a twist by having Keseberg rape Tamsen before he murdered her, apparently ignorant or uncaring of the fact that starving people don't have libido except in junk playboy imaginations. Even in 1847, Fallon Le Gros's story was more in the realm of sensationalism than substance. The men on the Fourth Relief were revolted by the moldering, mutilated bodies: limbs sawed off, heads decapitated, skulls and rib cages opened. They were furious because the expected Donner money was not there, not even the fifteen hundred dollars Luke Halloran had left the Donners.

Who knows what happened? Although Keseberg said Tamsen died at the log cabin by the rock, for a long time I liked to think she started out over the mountains and perished there—in truth, so much mystery and murkiness surrounded her decision to stay with her husband, her last weeks, and the circumstances of her death, I didn't like to think about her death at all; especially I didn't want her to have come to an ignominious end. Not a month before, the Third Relief had said Tamsen was comparatively healthy. After enduring and surviving almost five months in the snows, fulfilling her commitment to her husband, her children waiting for her, it made little sense, was unfair, for her body to suddenly, overnight, give out. Still, the average mortality age for women in 1847 was midforties. Tamsen Donner was in her 46th year. Her mother had died at age 47. But much of women's mortality rate was due to childbirth. . . . Round and round I went, arguing with theories, with my preferences.

Keseberg had no reason to lie. Nor could he be faulted if he had used her body for sustenance. He also had no reason to kill her. If he wanted the Donner money, all he had to do was wait till she had set out over the mountains.

Tamsen Donner died, most likely exactly the way Keseberg described it, almost one year to the day after they had left Springfield. And was it the death I should be concerning myself with, or her nearly five months of survival?

In June General Kearny's soldiers passed through on their way East. "A more revolting and appalling spectacle I never witnessed," wrote one member of Kearny's party. "The remains were collected and buried, interred in a pit dug in the center of one of the cabins for a cache." Then the area was torched.

Kristin Johnson says that Kearny's soldiers torched the Breen cabin, not the Murphy one, and in 1984, Donald Hardesty's archaeological dig found only small bone fragments here, not a mass grave. But at the time of our trip I didn't know that and only thought of how in those roaring flames consuming mutilated torsos and limbs, Tamsen

Donner's journal, waterstained but still legible, would have gone to char in a second. The final cache. I felt so sad looking at the big rock I thought maybe Tamsen was buried there. Or maybe I felt sad because of all the others buried there, their burned bones underneath where we walked, the rock their gravestone.

And if I were not in the exact place where all their bones lay, only in the vicinity, my feelings were appropriate.

About a half mile away from the big rock, a white cross marked the site of the double cabin that housed the Graveses in one side, the Reeds, the teamsters, Stanton, and the *vaqueros*, Luis and Salvador, in the other. "It's not the real site," the ranger told me. "They put a highway through the site and rather than move the highway, they moved the cross."

47

"Donner Camp Picnic Site," the sign at Alder Creek said straightfaced, the macabre joke waiting there to be made. "The Donner brothers and their wives perished here at Alder Creek," the sign said. Not so: Tamsen didn't perish here.

Alder Creek—once good-sized, now siphoned off and reduced to trickles and marsh, its path diverted for a large resort hotel—was frozen during Tamsen's months, spring-thawing that April night when she went to Keseberg's cabin. The area where it was thought in 1977 that the three shelters were, roughly a triangle, was spongy, my feet sinking in when I cut across from Tamsen's shelter to Elizabeth's, her sister-in-law. I walked slowly, shortened my stride, closer to her four-foot, eleven-inch stride, and thought of how often in those months the two women went back and forth over this same ground. "Guess what I cooked today," Elizabeth said, "Shoemaker's arm."

The tree that I thought of as Tamsen's tree was a large pine that formed part of the north wall of their shelter.

They put the tent against it, reinforced it with boughs of pine and

14. "Tamsen's tree."

tamarack, put old quilts, water repellent coats, buffalo robes on the top. Inside the tent, they criss-crossed poles: racks to raise sleepers above the wet earth. Every night for almost five months, Tamsen Donner lay here on her rack, a husband dying by her side, her daughters starving, death piling up all around.

Twenty-two feet of snow fell that winter, but here it was ten to twelve feet of snowpack at any given time. Beyond the pines as far as the eye could see were the mountains from where help would come, the mountains that were the gateway to the new land, the mountains where the snow was four times higher than it was here.

Jacob Donner, George's brother and Elizabeth's husband, was the first to die at Alder Creek. "Jacob was a slight man, of delicate constitution, and was in poor health when we left Springfield," Eliza wrote about her uncle. ("He was a whining complaining man," Cousin Frances wrote Eliza much later.) "The trials of the journey reduced his strength and exhausted his energy," Eliza continued. "When we reached the place of encampment in the mountains he was discouraged and gave up in despair. Not even the needs of his family could rouse him to action. He was utterly dejected and made no effort, but tranquilly awaited death. He died while sitting at the table in the tent with his head bowed upon his hands."

His wife, Elizabeth, and seven children were in that tent where Jacob sat waiting for death, their ages 14, 12, 9, 7, 5, 4, and 3. In the teamsters' tent, Shoemaker and Smith, both 25, lay down and died too. Reinhardt, 30, died in George and Tamsen's shelter.

The snow had to be continually shoveled off the top of the shelters to keep them from caving in; inside was damp most of the time. Sometimes they were in wet clothes for weeks, the children remembered, the water coming through the brush, the tent, the ground; on any sunny day, blankets and clothing had to be taken outside to dry. Firewood had to be constantly searched for, dragged back, the ox hides boiled, the children cared for. George Donner was bedridden, his infected wound from the slipped chisel requiring frequent changing of dressing.

That left Tamsen, Elizabeth, the two remaining teamsters, Noah James, who had started out with them from Springfield, Jean Baptiste Trudeau, and the children to do the work. I was in awe at this place. I couldn't imagine what it would be like to spend more than four months here under such conditions: people lying on racks listlessly, sick, starving, depressed, dying, bodies piling up, bodies opened. Tamsen frequently read the children stories from the Bible. She tried to keep them clean and dry. She taught them to say, "We are the children of Mr. and Mrs. George Donner."

We stayed the first night at the Donner Memorial State Park campground, a beautiful campground a short walk from the museum, the monument, the big rock. Signs warned campers to be careful of squirrels: two days before, a little girl had died of bubonic plague contracted at the park. Bubonic plague? Hadn't that been eradicated long ago in the United States? All night long, lodgepole pines and jeffrey pines, their barks smelling of vanilla, moved in the wind, and train whistles shrieked and moaned in the darkness.

The next day I was standing by Tamsen's tree at Alder Creek, thinking about what items I'd need to spend the night there, and without forethought, it came to me with certainty: this is the place I give up smoking.

I had been looking for the right place ever since I had read what the writer Gabriel Garcia Marquez had told Alastair Reid: "I will tell you how to be free of smoking. First, you must decide that the cigarette, a dear friend who has been close to you for many years, is about to die. Death, as we know, is irremediable. You take a pristine packet of your favorite cigarettes—mine were those short black Celtas—and you bury it, with proper ceremony, in a grave you have prepared in the garden—I made a headstone for mine. Then, every Sunday—not oftener, for the memory is painful—you put flowers on the grave, and give thanks. Time passes. For me now, the cigarette is dead, and I have given up mourning."

Shortly after I read that, I bought a pack of Winstons and, in a favorite spot outside my writing room where lilies of the valley grew, dug a small hole, carefully laid my cigarettes to rest, smoothed dirt, said words.

Two days later I dug up the cigarettes and smoked them. It was Garcia Marquez's ceremony, not mine.

Still, I knew, before my children started tightening the screws by feigning asthma attacks, poking needles through the filters so no smoke could be dragged through, leaving notes in my typewriter, "Dear Santa, All I want for Christmas is Momma to stop smoking," that my time for giving up cigarettes was at hand. Like everyone else over the age of reason, I had long been intellectually convinced of the necessity of quitting; the only question was when? One day, I heard the sound of cigarettes in my breathing and my voice, and I knew my *whens* were running out, my lungs and bronchi and throat on the brink of mutiny. If I didn't quit soon, my body would reach a point of irreversible damage. I had taken smoking as far as I could go.

I still resonated to Garcia Marquez's notion of ceremony, however, and, not surprising for someone steeped in ritual, felt that some ritual was necessary to mark the ending of this other ritual that had been part of me for twenty-five years, starting with Viceroys at the White Spot Grill, age 13 but looking 10, the essence of sophistication, draped in the pink plastic booth, blowing long tunnels of smoke and, with elaborate casualness, passing my thumb and forefinger over the tip of my tongue as experienced smokers did, not quite sophisticated enough to know that experienced smokers did that to remove tobacco flecking into their mouths from unfiltered cigarettes, and I was smoking a filtered cigarette. Thirteen to 38, smoking had been a part of me, and though I had progressed beyond taking delicate swipes at my tongue, I could not imagine myself in situations without a cigarette, particularly could not imagine myself writing without a cigarette to pace each page.

We left Alder Creek, went to the campground several miles away where my family would sleep a second night, and gathered up my things. I bought a pristine pack of Winstons: my last pack, though I kept that to myself. Around dusk, Roger and the children brought me back to sleep at the base of Tamsen's tree. Roger was nervous about my staying there and said so; I was afraid and didn't say so. We all knew it was something I felt I had to do. She had stayed four and a half months in this place; I had to stay one night. I had been too chicken to make the motorcycle trip alone; if I didn't stay here alone, I wouldn't be able to face myself.

From a small grove just beyond where Elizabeth and Jacob Donner's shelter had been, the sound of men's laughter came across the clearing. "I'm going to see who's over there," Roger said. "Don't," I said, but he was insistent. "Don't tell them I'm going to be here," I said. We all seven walked across the clearing between George and Tamsen's shelter and Jacob and Elizabeth's and beyond to where three young men were sitting around a fire, drinking beer. We chit-chatted for a few minutes— "Do you know it's illegal to camp here?" I asked casually; they laughed, we laughed. They seemed innocuous, and I was glad of that, but I still didn't want them to know I was across the clearing.

It was the longest night of my life. I was terrified every second. At dark, I put my sleeping bag at the base of the tree, lay inside it, and shook with fear. Every time there was a rustle on the ground I was afraid it was a squirrel carrying bubonic plague. Every time bass laughter sailed in waves across the clearing, I was afraid of those men swigging beer. I was afraid that vandals might decide to trash this pioneer spot tonight. Up and down, but mostly down, cowering, I was afraid that if trouble came, I wouldn't be able to get my Swiss army knife open fast enough. I was afraid I'd fall asleep and roll on my open knife clutched in my hand. I was afraid to turn on my flashlight and call attention to myself. I thought I'd smoke all night long, going out with a bang, but I smoked two cigarettes, the second one only partially. I was afraid to strike a match; I didn't want cigarettes. Maybe my fear blotted out my addiction, maybe I had already psychologically stopped—I didn't wonder about it. I lay shaking in the pitch black listening to the constant sounds of small creatures rustling through pine needles, things scurrying across my sleeping bag. I bunched myself into the smallest possible ball trying not to move or breathe deeply, as bubonic plague, a medieval disease, moved out there, men moved through the night to trash graves, trash me. Tamsen knew fears in this place, but they didn't include human predators.

As it does, light came. I must have finally dropped off, because suddenly light was there. I wasn't afraid anymore. I walked round and round the small place as Tamsen would have walked many times, and tried to see what she might have seen. Looking to the West from where rescue had to come. Looking over at Elizabeth's tree, smoke rising from a hole in the ground. Thought about her watching Jean Baptiste stick long poles into the snow probing for buried oxen to eat. Burying people in the snow. Seeing James Reed come from the West and return to the West. Bundling up her children, tying the red cloak on Eliza, the blue cloak on Frances, and the shawl snugly around Georgia, taking them to George's bedside to say good-bye, sending them out twice. Over four and a half months she stayed here, her husband rotting with gangrene, eight people dying.

One night, she and her husband were the only ones left. And then he died and she was the only living person here. Among the open skulls and the limb-severed torsos, Tamsen Donner prepared her husband's body for burial, winding the white sheet around, wrapping his body, leaving.

Nine people died here, where I walked. How did she stand it? How did she do it?

All of a sudden, there it was in the grass. A bone. A small white knuckle of a bone. I was walking around the site over ground I had covered before and it was just suddenly there. Slowly, I reached down and carefully picked it up. It was a small ivory bone, old and worn smooth, about an inch long, a half-inch wide at its broadest place tapering to a fourth of an inch at its base, roughly a triangular shape, the Hastings Cutoff triangle, the taper of an ox's head, a skull. Old and pitted and grooved, but the pits and grooves worn smooth, it seemed to me most likely a joint bone. I didn't know if it were a human bone or an ox bone. I didn't want to think too closely about that.

I marked the spot where I found it with a rock, then tried to figure out what to do with the bone. My first thought was that I should give it to the rangers at the Donner Pass Museum. But they were just summer employees; I knew more about the Donner Party than they did; they might not understand its significance, might toss it into a drawer, writing someone a letter of inquiry that wouldn't be answered before they went back to their fall jobs. If it were a human bone, it should be buried here. I decided to take it home and if analysis showed it to be human, I'd fly back and bury it here. It was a vow. I was at a holy place and felt that removing a bone capriciously would be a violation. If it was an ox bone, I would keep it.

I paced out strides from Tamsen's tree to the spot where I'd found the bone, diagrammed the spot in my journal with identifying trees nearby, checked and double-checked so that if it was a human bone, I'd be able to tell the exact spot where I found it. Underneath all the throb, the question I couldn't even verbalize: Who was it? Was it Jacob Donner? Elizabeth Donner? George Donner?

I dug a hole and buried my Winstons by Tamsen's tree. I walked round and round like a crazy woman saying over and over like an incantation, "I choose life. I choose life. July 29, 1977, in this place of death where Tamsen had no choice, I choose life."

It wasn't that I compared, even in the tiniest way, giving up cigarettes to anything Tamsen did. I simply knew that if I didn't give up smoking, I would die, by my own hand; I had tried giving up smoking before and failed each time; I was in a place that had been sanctified by death and if I violated a vow taken at a sacred place, then I would never, could never, be the person I thought I was or thought I could be or wanted to be. If I needed a cigarette to deal with every frustration, irritation, anxiety, and happy time, I could never be the writer or the mother I wanted to be.

I was trying to bury more than cigarettes in that hole; I was trying to bury my fears, crippling doubts, and self-lacerations. I had made it this far with my family, I had spent the long night here alone, and now I needed to do this for my children and for myself, my self as a mother and my self as a writer and just my self as an individual. I didn't consciously think this all out, I just knew it in my soul. I was trying to honor Tamsen's deeds, and I was calling on her to help me. It was like swearing on your mother's grave.

Hours later, my family came. It was only 10:30, so I must have gotten up at first sign of daybreak. I showed them the bone, my hand trembling, and told them of my decision to take it home.

It stayed in my front jeans pocket the rest of the trip, a pulsing presence nearly searing a hole in my pocket. Every time I craved a cigarette, every time I wanted to scream from withdrawal pangs or extreme irritability that no one in my family who had bugged me mercilessly noticed I had quit, I reached in and touched the bone. I choose life.

Six weeks later, an anthropologist from the University at Buffalo called and said, "I'm sorry, Gabrielle. The tests show it's a stone."

A stone. I felt like a fool, a person who made elaborate constructs that weren't so. Nervous that I could be so easily had. The stone seemed an example of my inability to distinguish between fact and fancy, to write the novel as well as it deserved, to be true to Tamsen. I tossed it into the back of a drawer.

Two years later, the children were discussing which treasures of mine they wanted when I died. Ursula, then 12, said, "I want the bone."

"It's just a stone," I said.

"It's more than that," she said. "It made you stop smoking."

I'll tell you the truth: it still looks like a bone. And what if it had been a bone? Whatever power it had I gave it. We invest objects with tremendous power and then do whatever we're capable of doing.

48

Tamsen's books cached in the desert, the old Donner farm buried in Springfield by the expressway, the actual changing of the land, reservoirs and damming and flooding to alter and erase that which once was: after a while, it all became a grave; we were driving and walking on bones our whole way across the United States. The weight of the deaths, the few we saw, the UNKNOWNS, reading about them, thinking about them, got to me, pulled at me; I had a growing sense that they were all over, under, around, the whole thing an open grave, until by Wyoming I was weeping and by Winnemucca I was shocked: they died for <u>this</u>?

I knew the graves were the cost of advance, progress, and quests for a better life, but I wanted to be one of those who made it, not one who died en route, was left behind, alone, in the middle of nowhere, a field, a vast empty prairie. Yet those who made it past that point had to look through the oval at what was left behind, like Virginia Reed watching her beloved pony, Billy, grow smaller and smaller until finally he was only a dot, and then an image in her mind.

Tamsen Donner scared me the most. She endured and survived so much and so long, and then was lost, her body, her journal, her poems, her sketches, her botanical specimens, all lost, to be only images in my mind. Tamsen Donner had no grave. That was the terrible absence that weighted all the other graves, known and unknown.

The weight of life and choices pressed on me. All the places I might have gone, things I might have done, I had made conscious and unconscious choices that had taken me to this road to walk on Tamsen's grave. I was Tamsen's grave, connected in the bone to her because I had chosen her, and although my intentions were honorable, my fear was that my lack of skills and my self-doubts might lead me to not imagine her life truly, burying her even deeper. I had come all the way to Donner Pass and I still knew hardly anything about her except what I wanted her to be. Unlike her, I knew deep down I would have taken the Hastings Cutoff willingly, even eagerly, that I had never valued prudence. I hadn't found any clue or key to my own dilemmas of balancing responsibilities. The only thing I knew for sure was that whatever choice I made, write or not write, I was going to pay a price.

And that's a discovery only a young person has to make. You find out soon enough that everything costs, some things worth the price and some not, the rub being you usually won't know until long after you've paid it. Given the same choices, I'd make most of the same decisions today.

After Donner Pass, we still had another four weeks of traveling ahead. Whatever I had learned about Tamsen Donner in me now to be discovered or not, the trip became a family vacation. Ahead were Disneyland; the children's triumphant auditioning for The Gong Show, **Five singular sensations / every little step we take** . . . , their innocent eager efforts not freaky enough to make the cut; visits to Maria's godfather, to Roger's family; a surprise discovery at San Juan de Bautista that Roger's Mexican great-great-grandfather, General Jose Castro, had taken the Breen family in; visiting James and Margret Reed's graves in San Jose, William Eddy's grave; a morning on the loose in a French bakery, croissants, pain de chocolat, Napoleons on the house, the baker, an old friend, saying we nearly bankrupted him; looking at thousands of turquoise rings until five perfect souvenirs had been found; Grand Canyon; Mesa Verde; Zion and Bryce, terrifying mule rides on the rim of the canyon; celebrating Charity's 6th birthday in Wagon Wheel Restaurant; buying the authentic hundred-pound wagon wheel that was out front from the owner and hoisting it on top of the car for my writing room; driving the roads my modern characters used; many many more places and people and sights in the four weeks ahead; but for me, the most important part of the trip was done after that night at Alder Creek.

But there was one more grave.

We drove around Calwa, California, a little town that's gone now, Fresno having swallowed it up though it was country when Roger grew up there. Much of what he tried to show the children—a boyhood home, school, fields he had run in—was gone also. We drove by a cemetery and he said, "That's where my mother is buried." His mother, after being gravely ill for two years with cancer, had died at 41. The children were flabbergasted when he didn't stop. "Dad," they said. "We've gone across the whole country going to people's graves we don't even know. It would be crazy if we don't go to your own mother's, our own grandmother's."

It was dark, the cemetery closed, but there were no fences or locked gates. In the area Roger took us, there were no headstones, just plaques set flush into the ground. Our flashlight was burned out. We walked up and down rows, striking matches over the plaques. "I know it's right here," Roger said. "I used to ride my bike here every night after school and bring flowers." The children fanned out, little bursts of flame appearing, disappearing in the darkness. "No, you're going too far," Roger called. "I know it's over here." After some time, he said, "Let's go." "Dad," the children said. At a gas station across the street, Roger telephoned his brother in Bakersfield. "I'm in Fresno," he said. "Bill, where's Mother's grave? Well, that's right where I've been looking." He asked the attendant if we could borrow a flashlight battery to go back to the cemetery. The guy looked at us as if we were loonies and made us leave the car keys as collateral.

We went back to the same area as before, a man of 48 telling his children about his mother who had died younger than he was now, telling them about a boy of 13 who had ridden his bicycle here every night after school. He found the grave almost immediately. "There it is. Right where I remembered," he said, shining the flashlight on the small flat stone flush in the scraggly grass.

Eunice Margret Burton
Dearest Mother
1900 1941

Rest in peace, Dearest Mother, Tamsen, and all the others who blazed the way.

PERISHED:

George Donner, [60?]
Tamsen Donner, 45
Jacob Donner, [56?]
Elizabeth Donner, [38?]
William Hook, 12
Isaac Donner, 5
Samuel Donner, 4
Lewis Donner, 3
Samuel Shoemaker, 25
John Denton, 28
Milt Elliott, 28
James Smith, 25
Baylis Williams, 24
Sarah Keyes, 70
Charles Stanton, 35
Luke Halloran, 25
John Snyder, 25

[first name?] Hardcoop, 60
[first name?] Wolfinger, [?]
William Pike, 25
Catherine Pike, 1
Charles Burger, 30
Franklin W. Graves, 57
Elizabeth Graves, 45
Franklin W. Graves Jr., 5
Pat Dolan, [35?]
Jay Fosdick, 23
Antonio [name?], 23
Eleanor Eddy, 25
James Eddy, 3
Margaret Eddy, 1
Lewis Keseberg Jr., 1
Ada Keseberg, 3
Levinah Murphy, 36
John Landrum Murphy, 16
Lemuel Murphy, 12
George Foster, 1
Harriet McCutchen, 1
Joseph Reinhardt, 30
Augustus Spitzer, 30
Luis [name? age?]
Salvador [name? age?]

SURVIVED:

Elitha Donner, 13
Leanna Donner, 11
Frances Donner, 5
Georgia Donner, 4
Eliza Donner, 3
George Donner, 9

Mary Donner, 7
Solomon Hook, 14
Noah James, 16
John Baptiste Trudeau, 16
James F. Reed, 45
Margret Reed, 32
Virginia Reed, 13
Martha "Patty" Reed, 9
James F. Reed Jr., 5
Thomas K. Reed, 3
Patrick Breen, 51
Margaret Breen, 40
John Breen, 14
Edward Breen, 13
Patrick Breen Jr., 9
Simon Breen, 8
James Breen, 5
Peter Breen, 3
Isabelle Breen, 1
Mary Ann Graves, 19
William Graves, 17
Eleanor Graves, 14
Lovina Graves, 12
Nancy Graves, 9
Jonathan Graves, 7
Elizabeth Graves Jr., 1
William McCutchen, 30
Amanda McCutchen, 25
Doris Wolfinger, 20
Lewis Keseberg, 32
Philippine Keseberg, 23
Sarah Graves Fosdick, 21
Harriet Murphy Pike, 18

Naomi Pike, 2
William Foster, 30
Sarah Murphy Foster, 19
Mary Murphy, 14
William Murphy, 10
Simon Murphy, 8
Walter Herron, 27
Eliza Williams, 31
William Eddy, 30

* Some ages at time they started out,
  some at rescue, many approximate.

Epilogue

If we count Sarah Keyes and Luis and Salvador, forty-two members of the Donner Party perished, forty-eight survived. More of the members died within a year of rescue. Some bore physical scars their whole lives from frostbite (crippled feet, amputated toes) and burns (insensate limbs fallen too close to the fire), and in that pre-Freudian time, all bore emotional scars, passing their terrible secret and shame down to their children.

The Donner Party was a tragedy without a tragic flaw, their misfortune caused primarily by random bad luck. They made mistakes and misjudgments, but not through willfulness or poor planning. They had what they thought was expert information about the shortcut. They stopped to bury their dead instead of hurrying on, because they were civilized people, carrying their civilization with them. A day here, a day there, and capricious luck against them. If it had snowed three or four days later, they would have gotten over the Sierra Nevadas, to become more of the nearly anonymous pioneers who opened up this country for the rest of us.

After our trip I had enough new information and hope to revise the novel again and again until one day I couldn't bear it any longer, put it away, and began a new novel. I kept writing one thing or another day after day, until some unnoticed day when I automatically identified myself as "writer" without feeling a poseur about to be unmasked or laughed at. Had I thought of writing as a profession, taking years of study similar to medicine or law, I might have saved myself and my family a lot of grief; instead I flogged myself from paragraph to paragraph, always feeling I should have been further along than I was. I rarely recognized when encouragement accompanied rejections: it was all or nothing for me. It's strange to look back at that earnest, anxious, driven, sad, determined young woman I was. I remember her very well, with both sympathy and pride, but I hardly recognize her. She seems to be somebody else, and of course she is. Unreachable now and unchangeable, I'd like to whisper to her: "Have mercy on yourself."

The year after our trip, and for years after on the anniversary of my quitting smoking, July 29, my family made me a carrot cake—at the time considered the height of nutrition and healthy living. Wherever we were, the carrot cake or a close facsimile would be produced—the ultimate one baked in Kuala Lumpur, Malaysia, the ingredients including a freshly picked pineapple and a coconut brought down from a palm with an ingenious contraption Roger made and cracked open on our sidewalk.

The Oregon Trail trip was the start of many other family trips and grand adventures we'd have, most dramatically a summer spent hitchhiking in Alaska, another summer bicycling in Europe, and a six-month bare-bones backpacking trip around Asia. Long after they were over, I realized that the trips were a reprieve, a respite, an escape from our hectic home lives. They, and many other decisions I made in those years, were also a direct response to people who said I couldn't do something. You can't take children to India, you can't become a Guardian Angel, you can't . . . Oh yeah? It took a long time and therapy to learn that automatic resistance doesn't mean guts and grit; it means that somebody else is still calling the shots, that I was still reacting, not acting. I'm glad I didn't get that therapy before we had those incredible trips.

All our daughters grew up to be hardy intrepid travelers, "A Car Is Not a Bed" deep in their bones. Her first year at Yale, Maria called home from Florida where, almost apoplectic with anticipation, she had gone with friends for spring break. "They won't leave the hotel," she said incredulous and disgusted, "because it's *raining*."

Game to leave immediately for anywhere, they travel together, in pairs, alone, or with us. "Want to go to Peru?" Charity asked Maria last year. "Sure," Maria said. Once a year Jennifer, even when toting a breast pump and two car seats, takes her baby and toddler on a nineteen-hour plane ride to India to see their grandmother.

We'll never have another trip like that, all seven of us together, I marveled after the Oregon Trail trip. I said it again after Alaska. And after the Asian backpacking trip. And after, and after, and after, until I couldn't bring up a possible destination without a chorus mocking, "We gotta go, it'll be the last time we'll ever be together."

On every trip, our kids kept journals as Tamsen had. Sometimes the Donner Party showed up unexpectedly. In Tokyo Roger's Japanese colleague had booked three expensive hotel rooms for us. "Oh, thank you so much, but this is more than we need, a more moderate place . . . " He hushed us, "As professor, my honor cannot permit you to stay any place cheaper." His honor not paying for the rooms, we waited until he left to immediately cancel one room—tried to cancel two, but the management's honor wouldn't permit that. Japan was the first of the Asian countries we were visiting; we had limited money we feared would run out, packages of ramen soup, and a tin of nuts and raisins. At breakfast time in the expensive hotel, everyone sat on the edge of the beds and I parceled out a handful of nuts and raisins to each. Maria said, as Margret Reed had on a desperate Christmas, "Eat slowly, children, there is plenty for all."

Her sisters and Roger rolled and, not for the first or last time, I was a little shocked at their irreverence. As a remnant of my Catholic upbringing, I tended to accord sacred status to many more things than they did.

When they wanted to name our Airedale puppy Tamsen, I was against it. It was disrespectful. "Mom," Jennifer said, "we have spent *years* with Tamsen Donner. What more fitting name to give our dog who is going to be with us every minute. It's an *honor*." It took me quite a long time to get used to it.

In the nearly twenty years I was away from the Donner novel, others continued research, excavation, and writing books, a new spate published in time for the Sesquicentennial, and more since then. I discovered, years after my Charity was named, that Charity was the middle name of Leanna, Tamsen's stepdaughter—a coincidence that pleased both Charity and me. Old theories were challenged, new theories advanced. Among other changes, the tree I had slept under was no longer considered the site of Tamsen and George Donner's shelter. Sure, it initially gave me a pang—and another pang when the 150-year-old tree collapsed in 1996—but like the stone bone, did it really matter? What we think we do is what we've really done.

"How did you ever write with five children?" I've been asked countless times over the years. "I rose above my circumstances," I sometimes answered, which always got a laugh, and me off the hook. Occasionally I said, "With difficulty," which was still light, but closer to the truth. The real answer contained so many parts of urgent need, despair, guilt, endless juggling, and what Tillie Olsen called "the craziness of endurance," that I never knew it with any certitude myself. Historically, writers who were mothers tended to write poetry or fragmented prose; not very many writer/mothers were novelists. Even today, it seems a miracle that I wrote four books during those intense child-rearing years—two published, two not. (It's just my job to write them, I'd say with a hollow laugh, it's somebody else's job to publish them.)

Roger and my daughters allowed me to be a writer. I don't mean that they gave me permission, I mean they didn't consume all my time with their demands.

Sometimes I've looked at my beloved family and wondered if it was really necessary to ask so much of them and myself, but that's sentimental "wouldn't it have been nice if . . . " thinking. If I hadn't, I never would have written, and I know I'd do it over again. The nicest husbands and children will eat you up alive if you offer yourself on the plate, and they'll ask for seconds.

Few have ever asked what seemed to me the obvious corollary question: how did you ever write/parent and be a wife? With five children, that was the weakest part of the triangle, the part that always gave. In retrospect I think Roger and I should have tended more to each other, but for better and for worse, our focus was the family. When the children left home, it felt as if Roger and I were in a second marriage with children in common.

If, as a writer, mother, and wife, I often felt a failure, as a family we were perceived by others as a remarkable success. People said that frequently, and it was as much a burden to me as I once felt being called a saint rather than a sinner. All families have their darker side even if they don't go on *Oprah* to spill it. Once a colleague of Roger's said for the twentieth time, "Isn't it wonderful that you can write and have this great family," and I began yelling, "Do you understand the cost? Do you have any idea at all of the cost?" Of course he didn't, because he devoted himself to his research while his wife took care of their kids and of him—at that very moment she was home cooking supper while he was watching me cook supper marveling at how wonderfully I balanced things.

We knew the cost, and we knew some of the rewards at the time. Roger gave his all to fathering, at a cost to his career, and his reward was being cherished by his daughters. I railed about the cost to my career, but I knew the children gave me ballast, made me less egotistical, less selfish. Our children felt the cost too and it's good that they had a lot of delay of gratification. It wasn't easy for them to carry the feminist banner; even in grade school, defensive male teachers took them on. Having to speak up for what they believed caused discomfort, sometimes fear, but made them strong and eloquent. They were admired by their peers, though too often from afar. They also struggled mightily to separate their own person from the Burton persona, to keep the baby and some of the bathwater too.

Today any of us would do anything for each other, or as has been said more than once: to be a Burton is to be a burden. We wouldn't know the greatest reward for years: we all like each other. You know you'll always love your children, but when they grow up and you *like* them, that's a blessing. When they like you back, you fall on the ground and give thanks.

When you're in the midst of raising a family, it often seems endless. Then one day, you turn around and your kids are all grown up. In the understatement of every parent ever born: you wish you could do a lot of things differently. But the one thing Roger and I never regretted were all the family trips. We're all accustomed to stories where men with knives strapped to their ankles go off to exotic places and have adventures, but we went off to exotic places and had adventures as a family. Tamsen Donner, the woman who lived large and loved well and did it with her family, started us on that road and, just the same way my modern heroine in that long-ago apprentice novel carried all those characters in her head on that noisy motorcycle, Tamsen was always there riding along with us.

Acknowledgments

In the poem "Where Is the West," from Ruth Whitman's book, *Tamsen Donner: A Woman's Journey*, Tamsen imagines her daughters in the future: "they will speak my words thinking they have invented them."

It's all very well for parents to hope that our children will absorb some of our words until they become their own, but it's quite a different matter for writers. This book has been long in the making: more than thirty-five years of reading, writing, thinking, and living. In the bibliography I have tried my best to attribute credit to the many sources I consulted or encountered during that time. I beg understanding of the lapses of time and memory if I inadvertently haven't thanked someone whose work influenced this one. Please write me care of the University of Nebraska Press so that credit can be given in subsequent editions.

One of the sad results of working on a book over three decades is that many of the people who helped me in countless ways must be thanked posthumously. If memory is immortality, they live in all their richness and generosity in my mind and heart.

Retracing the Donner Trail, landmarks, and graves gave a focus to our trip but also gave us a personal California trail made rich and unique by the time spent with Leonhard, Mable, and Cindy Weiland in Springfield, Illinois; Tom and Ruth Hooper in Maryville, Missouri; John Dahlquist in Fort Bridger, Wyoming; Margaret and Earnest Garhart, Harold Petersen, and Charlie Andersen in Fort Laramie, Wyoming; Marjorie A. Homan in Farson, Wyoming; and Artha D. Smith, her husband, and their children in Utah.

Gratitude for those open arms and outsize hearts of old friends and relatives who welcomed us along the trail: Carol and Joe Ryan, June and Larry Onesti, Bob and Melba Dailey, Louise Skinner, Richard Bertine, Jack and Janet Johnston, Nancy Gabriel, Elisabeth, Max, and Tony Gaenslen, Richard Brown, Mary Sue Hutchins, Simone and Don Dietiker, Marge and Bill Burton, Gladys and Earl Hummer, Burt and Sharon Rashbaum, and the Nebraska relatives, Louise and Rodney Shuman and their families, who nurtured us going out and listened to our stories coming back.

Surely in the hierarchy of worthy work, librarians and curators rank next to the angels. I am indebted to the Henry Huntington Library at San Marino, California, for permission to publish Tamsen Donner's letters, particularly to Peter Blodgett, H. Russell Smith Foundation Curator of Western Historical Manuscripts, and Jennifer Martinez, for providing an extraordinary opportunity, invaluable assistance, and unfailing courtesy; the Bancroft Library at the University of California at Berkeley for access to Patrick Breen's diary; Lucy K. Morey of California State Library in Sacramento; Margaret Kelleher, librarian of Newburyport Public Library; Edward J. Russo of the Sangamon Valley Collection at the Lincoln Library in Springfield, Illinois; John C. Broderick, chief of the Manuscript Collection Library of Congress; R. O. Klotz of Blue Rapids, Kansas; Paul and Ruth Henderson of Bridgeport, Nebraska; Edna M. Shannonhouse of Elizabeth City, North Carolina; Al Molder of Murray, Utah, for information about Twenty Wells; Gary Hack, Donner Pass ranger; and Diane Rusnak.

A tip of my Bell helmet to my motorcycle mentors: Mike Dolan, who will forever be "Motorcycle Mike" to my kids; and Tom Lancy, who sat in that parking lot watching me navigate pylons. For cabins in Vermont and/or ready hospitality and support, thank you to Tom Landauer and Lynn Streeter, Jonathan and Barbara Reichert, and Gerrie and Len Pearlin.

Deep gratitude to Betsy Rapoport, who urged me to write/finish/rewrite this book for twenty years and who also, with Ken Weiner, took our whole crew in; Lucy Ferriss and Millie Marmur, who gave notes and support on a draft in the 1980s; Raoul Naroll, who analyzed the bone/stone; Rose Glickman, who answered my S.O.S on the latest draft and gave invaluable suggestions, support, and friendship; my editors Ladette Randolph, Kristen Elias Rowley, and Ann Baker, for their belief, guidance, and care; copyeditor Katherine Hinkebein, for her fine reading; the entire University of Nebraska Press team, for its energy and enthusiasm; Sonya Huber Humes, whose insightful questions made me write a better book; and Kristin Johnson, who was an invaluable help, generously sharing her voluminous knowledge of the Donner Party.

Thank you to Yaddo and to MacDowell Colony for their nurturing space and spirit that keep writers going. Thank you to these people, who were there at critical times: William Lederer, who dreamed the whole thing up; and Miller Williams, J. R. Salamanca, John Williams, Faith Gabelnick, Jill Kneerim, Naomi Weisstein, Esther Broner, Ann Petrie, and Leslie Fiedler.

And, finally, what can I say except Thank You, again, to Roger Burton, Maria Burton, Jennifer Burton, Ursula Burton, Gabrielle Burton, and Charity Burton, who as artists and family read numerous drafts, giving important notes and enthusiastic encouragement every single time.

Letters of Tamsen Donner

There are seventeen extant letters written by Tamsen Donner that range in date from about 1819 to 1846. The Huntington Library acquired seven of them, Nos. 5, 6, 7, 12, 13, 14, and 16, in 1935 and 1937 from Eliza P. Houghton, Tamsen's granddaughter. They are part of the Papers of Sherman Otis Houghton, 1831–1914, HOU 1-152.

In 1995 John S. Houghton and Ann Houghton Smith, Tamsen's great-grandchildren, donated seven more letters, Nos. 1, 3, 8, 9, 10, 11, and 15, to the Huntington Library. They are part of the Papers of Eliza Poor Donner Houghton, 1820–1978, HM 58111-58197.

Two letters, Nos. 2 and 4, were not included in the 1995 donation, perhaps because they are typed transcripts. What happened to the originals is as yet unknown. Ann Houghton Smith shared these transcripts with historian Mark McLaughlin, who in turn shared them with me. Their authenticity is certain.

Tamsen addressed all but the last two letters to Mrs. Jonathan Poor—her sister Elizabeth, called Eliza by most and Betsey by Tamsen—who lived in their hometown, Newburyport, Massachusetts. Tamsen named her youngest daughter, Eliza Poor, after Betsey, and refers to her as "Aunty Poor" in one of the letters.

Note: All spellings, crossouts, parentheses, underlines for emphasis, irregular capitalization, punctuation or lack of, and so forth, are Tamsen's. The notation &c. means "et cetera"; do. means "ditto." Tamsen often left out periods, used carets (not shown here) and insertions, and used dashes frequently—a busy woman grabbing a little time here and there to write letters.

LETTER 1

From Huntington Library, H M 58152. From Boobartown & Wells, Maine to her sister Betsey. Year unknown. Unsigned. The Huntington Library estimates that Tamsen was 20 years old, making the year 1821, but it is likely a few years earlier, 1818 or 1819. Her niece, Frances, wrote that Tamsen started teaching at 15, so she may have gone to teach in Maine anytime from 1817 on.

Boobartown June 23rd

Sister I was so tired last eve that I could not perform my promise (that of writing to you every evening) I set out from Bangor at six yesterday morn & arived here a little past sunset. It being very rainy I was prevented from going to Wells today & I was not sorry for 33 miles over a rough road is a long journey. I think I never felt the importance of performing my duty as I do now. I am with Mrs Boobar now who treats me kindly. She is indeed a kind woman. just came in here & saw me writing on my trunk & offered to assist me in making a writing desk.

24 And now Betsey I am seated in my little room at Wells. I have had a curious journey. There are nine families here & I shall have about 20 scholars. I think I shall enjoy myself highly.

26th Yesterday I removed from Mrs Sargeant's to Mrs Shipley's & therefore could not write to you. I shall begin my school on monday. The family in which I board are *is pleasant & I expect to be content. I shall write to you today.*

LETTER 2

Typed transcript of original (whereabouts unknown) from Mark McLaughlin. The typist may have added commas and capitals because the punctuation seems more exact than most of Tamsen's other letters. The heading says simply "Williamsburg" and "June 7, 182-?" Someone—perhaps a family member—has inked in "Mass?" and 1824?" The letter is most likely written from Williamsburg, Maine, since Tamsen says she is close to Bangor, and also mentions "Mr Greenleaf's information." There were Greenleafs in Williamsburg, Maine, at that time—in fact, Moses Greenleaf published "Statistics of Maine" in 1816. The date is most likely 1820 or early 1821, since she asks why her mother hasn't answered her last letter. Her stepmother, Hannah Cogswell Eustis, died January 1821, so Tamsen wrote this letter before her death or before she received word of it. (If this letter was written in 1820, it most certainly pushes the first letter earlier. It also implies that she had had other teaching posts in Maine.) Note that her brother, John, was still alive. (He died in 1831.)

Williamsburg
June 7 182

Dear sister

I have no paper <u>here</u> *but this and therefore I shall offer no other excuse for sending it. Tis quite cool to-day.*

I am surrounded by my little schollars [sic] who are buzzing as fast as possible until school begins. This is by far the most interesting school I have found in this country. The children have advanced considerably in their studies. I have a convenient school house, pleasantly situated, board in a remarkably agreeable family. Mr Greenleaf is a man of good information and his wife has a sound well cultured mind. She is a sister of Mrs Wilder. The children naturally interesting are rendered still more so by the excellent government which they are kept. They have a large library of books. So much for me. Now let us say something about you.

O you say something about my wants. I have none but those which will this week be supplied. You forget that I am near Bangor. You were kind to offer to send me some clothes but unless I am unfortunate I hope I shall not be a burden to those friends who have a right to expect better things, and it is so much trouble to send home, that I rather give a higher price for goods than be at the pains. I intend to write to my father and both my brothers by this conveyance and will get you to see that they are sent to them. Why was it so few of my friends wrote? and why did not my mother answer my last letter to her? I fear I have not answered all questions and said all about myself that you will want to hear.

Good afternoon
T. Eustis

LETTER 3

From Huntington Library, HM 58153. A later letter suggests that Tamsen had been back to Massachusetts, scrabbling jobs together, but could hardly make enough to support one. She turned 23 two weeks before writing this to her sister, Betsey, from Norfolk, Virginia, on her way to North Carolina for a teaching position. Her mother was a Wheelwright, so Captain Wheelwright may have been an uncle or cousin.

Monday November 15th 1824

My dear sister

You requested me to be particular when I wrote from Norfolk. Many occurrences flit by and received hardly a glance of the mind & those which did interest are so blended with their causes & effects as to form a mass so undigested & confused, ~~that~~ as to render it impossible for me to give you a correct & particular statement. There is one impression, however, which rises above this huge chaos & presses itself upon my notice; it is that the hand of God is remarkably visible in directing my steps: so fully aware am I that he will guide me that I feel not the least hesitation in proceeding. In Boston a gentleman at the boarding house interested himself so far as to find a vessel for me & Capt Wheelwright engaged my passage & waited upon me on board. The captain has been very kind. An unpleasant wind detained us in Hyannis Roads & he politely took me to his house & entertained me two days. In which time the School committee waited on me requested me to set a price & engage to keep six months. We left there on Thursday & now in Norfolk.

Thus my sister one half of my journey is accomplished. And I leave it on record for the benefit of those who may wish to follow my example—that so far from considering me an <u>outlaw</u> people of all stamps, from the Senator, Author, & Southern planter downward have treated me with attention & respect & though they have sometimes <u>wondered</u> at my conduct they have never <u>despised</u> me. And I never shall be <u>despised</u>. I meet not so frequently with the look of indifference among strangers as at my own town.

I am now at what the world terms "a stylish boarding house." To describe it meets not my present feelings. O friends I would not forgo the pleasure of your society for more than all this It is dreary in the midst of splendor if in all that show there is no friend to smile, no being to love you.

My letter to Mr Roberts was of infinite importance. Tell Cousin Jane they had guessed at the news. I leave here tomorrow morning in a gig for Elizabeth City from there I go to Tyrrel in a shingle vessel & there my journey ends. I do not regret nor shall I the fatigue expense nor embarrassment to which I have subjected myself. My heart is big with hope & impatient with desire. And this day needful for rest finds me agitated & restless. The past & present is swallowed up in the future. I believe I am not influenced by the love of novelty for passionately fond as I am of scenery I have learned to look almost with disgust upon that which in other circumstances would have delighted me. Happy am I to be enabled to hide my feelings so successfully as to cause many I meet to wish to be in my situation. I think likely I may return immediately. Unless I can be respectably employed employed [sic] I certainly shall. From the character the country bears I may expect to find a Williamsburgh. I know nothing however, compared to what I shall know.

If experience teaches me as many lessons in life to come as in life past I shall be well versed indeed. How highly she charges for her tuition! How cutting to the soul are some of her reprimands. Pity the instruction she gives could not be transferred. Then all would not smart. But tis the lash that gives it its importance & tis the keenness of the suffering that it occasions that renders it unnecessary for her to repeat it. How often have we said, when we saw the consequences of rashness impending "Be pleased to spare the blow," when after it has fallen we have loved, even loved the agony.

What a complex piece of machinery is the human soul. How interesting & various are its constituents. How many are the situations it requires in order to its full development. And in every situation what a vast quantity of ideas & tones of feeling does she discover to herself which occasions her to exclaim in a kind of ecstasy, Thou ever fruitful source of entertainment, why need I wander? How delicate the touch, how nice the texture, how well finished every part, how perfect the super structure. My God, I I [sic] thank thee, that thou hast given to me this inestimable gift & hast enabled it in every situation to furnish a rich and delightful banquet.

I will leave the remainder until afternoon as this kind of writing is a sort of commodity you can pick up anywhere Excuse me 'twas in my heart & I said it. In the meantime I will go & sit with the ladies.

I have called at Mrs Whiteheads she seemed like Northern people. I could have spent days in hearing her converse. Could cousin Jane have heard half the encomiums she heaped upon her friend she would have loved the woman. We both knew the secret both tried to make the other speak and left it. It is late, I am tired, I go at seven in the morning. When I get to Tyrrel I will again let you hear from me.

T Eustis

LETTER 4

Typed transcript of original (whereabouts unknown) from Mark McLaughlin. From North Carolina to Betsey. Tamsen is 29. There is a six-year gap from the last letter. Edna M. Shannonhouse of Elizabeth City, North Carolina, has written that a Miss Eustis taught the "female department" at the Elizabeth City Academy in 1827. In December 1829 Tamsen married Tully Dozier, and they now have a little boy. They've only been married a little over a year, and twice Tully has been seriously ill.

The typed signature on this letter is "Tamsen Dosier"—one of the two letters where Tamsen apparently signed her first name. This transcript, presumably typed by a family member, spells *Dozier* with an *s*, instead of a *z*. *Tamsen* is typed with an *s* and no *e* on the end. In Tamsen's own hand in the original letters, it's fairly easy to mistake her *z* for an *s*, but with a magnifying glass, it's clear she always closes *s* and never closes *z*. Without seeing the original letter, we can't tell how she actually signed this. This letter is remarkable for her mention of their strong dislike of slavery to the extent that they plan to move west.

Camden Jan 23 1831

My dear Sister

The commencement of a new year & the change of season have failed to draw one character from that pen, which has so often been employed by them; nor have the frequent communications of a well beloved sister been more successful. But as this will be the last day the office will be under my husband's care I feel unwilling to delay writing to you.

March 1831

I wrote thus far and was interrupted by the gentleman who came to receive the Post Office from my husband's hands, and as my letter was unfinished it could not be franked. I almost finished another, but Mr Dosier [sic] accidently tore it & I concluded to send this. I am at a loss how to proceed. I know whether I write to the dead, or to the living.

Are you offended with me? What have I said, or neglected to say? What have I done, or neglected to do? Still I cannot persuade myself that you do not feel interested in my happiness. I would not do it if I could. I will therefore tell you how the world goes with me. My husband who was near the grave when last I wrote is recovered. My son grows finely and resembles Grandmother Wheelwright considerably.

We sunk money by boarding & have given it up—have but one at this time. My school prospers & with my husband's exertions we make a comfortable living.

We find it a great advantage to keep an account of expenses; had it not been for that I could not have been convinced of the unprofitableness of boarders. I advise you to do so. We have removed a few miles from our last home & by that means have lost the Post Office. I had had excellent health since I saw you, but Mr Dosier has twice been reduced very low since we were married. His precarious health and our strong dislike to slavery has caused us to determine upon removing to some western state. But not until next year. Mary will have there a fine chance for her trade & I hope she will come to us. How is father? and all friends, are they well

Your sister,
Tamsen Dosier

LETTERS 5 AND 6

From Huntington Library, HOU 8. I count these as two letters although the second is written on the bottom of the first, they are written seven months apart and are markedly different. From North Carolina to her sister, Betsey. In the first letter, Tamsen is 29, and life is busy and happy. In the second, she's 30, and her life has been devastated. A curiosity: In her letter before this one, dated January 23, 1831, she says her son "resembles Grandmother Wheelwright considerably." Now five months later, she says, "he bears no resemblance to our family, being a true copy of his father." Tully is still postmaster. Apparently his replacement didn't work out.

Camden Co June 28th 1831

My dear sister

This busy world so fully occupies me that with difficulty I find time to write to you though its cares are not so many as to prevent my often thinking & speaking of you. Your letter relieved me of many anxious thoughts & mine I presume will be acceptable as it will tell you of the health of those who I doubt not are dear to you. My child has been very sick for a few days we feared we should loose [sic] him but at this time he is in fine health and sitting upon the table while I write he at one time scolds me for the inkstand, at another knocks my knuckles with a spoon. He bears no resemblance to our family being a true copy of his father. If he lives I shall very much desire he should have a northern education.

I do not intend to <u>boast</u> of my husband but I find him one of the best of men—affectionate, industrious & possessed of an upright heart. These are requisite to make life pass on smoothly. His health is improved very much so that he is able to attend to his business. I know you have a kind husband who furnishes everything to make you comfortable but you did not know of my lot in life. We live in a very comfortable way Mr Doziers trade is tolerably profitable. My school has been less so since the birth of my child & I have been compelled to discharge my boarders on that account. Our family consists of, my husband, child, two, little girls, (boarders) a white girl [hired girl] & myself. We have a horse 3 cows, 2 calves, 24 hogs hen, turkeys & ducks. Last year we made enough corn, pork bacon, &c. to serve us this year & perhaps a little to spare. This year we tend no land as we had no servants of our own Mr Dozier thought it was unprofitable We have a fine potato patch & if we could send them to you could give you plenty of sweet potatoes as we shall make several hundred bushels.

I am anxious to go to Ohio but there are so many inducements for us to stay that I hardly think we shall leave. This is indeed a delightful country where everything is produced in rich abundance that is necessary for the support of man. Mr Dozier just told me to ask you if you could get potatoes from Boston & says he will send you 20 or 30 bushels if you ~~have~~ can. My husband is yet Postmaster you will please to direct us before & ~~yet~~ write frequently while he retains the office.

I am truly sorry for Aunt Davis' death The girls are indeed alone but she has been feeble a long time My love to them & all other faces

Jan 26th, 1832

My sister I send you these pieces of letter that you may know that I often wrote to you if I did not send.

I have lost that little boy I loved so well He died the 28 Sept. I have lost my husband who made so large a share of my happiness. He died on the 24 December I prematurely had a daughter which died on the 18th of Nov. I have broken up housekeeping & intend to commence school in February. O my sister weep with me if you have tears to spare.

Your sister

LETTER 7

From Huntington Library, HOU 9. From North Carolina to her sister. Tamsen had just turned 31. Ten months earlier, she had written Betsey that her husband and children died, and apparently wrote follow-up letters. It appears that she had only recently received Betsey's response to this news, and nothing from her brother, William. She doesn't mince words about her hurt—and her anger, which she says she doesn't feel—but resolves to only express it once, and then she immediately returns to equanimity. She says she had made arrangements and could have visited the north twelve months ago, but didn't because of Betsey's and William's lack of interest in her bereavement, but that time is off. Tully died only eleven months before this letter. Regarding her three-month and six-month attacks of former years, malarial fever would cause periodic attacks.

November 22nd 1832

My dear sister,

I have delayed writing until I had an hour that I could call my own when the labours of the week had ceased & I could think what I pleased & write what I think.

   I could not but notice the prophetic language with which you commenced your letter. It seems that there is in the minds of those closely attached a principle, or feeling, rather, that lets them know how it is with each other. That very night on which your letter was dated I was struggling with a fever & preparing mind & body to part. I thought, and those around me thought that we should soon be separated that a few more such fevers would terminate the career that I had commenced. Sister I could die very easily. One after

one of the bonds that bound me to earth are loosened & now there remains
but few. You are the strongest—& when I realize how little you need me, &
how small is the portion of enjoyment you derive from me, I am satisfied,
that my time is not long. Two, perhaps three letters a year, & all the rest of
our intercourse is fanciful.

I will own the truth. I had made arrangements to visit the north & could
have done it twelve months ago but when I looked back & reflected how
small was the interest my brother & sister took in my affairs. How I had
struggled with sickness, poverty, & bereavement unpittied by them & kept
them in ignorance because they wrote not to inquire I concluded to stay
where I was. I have stayed & I will stay, until you are more at leisure. For
sure if you cannot find time to write, you could not find time to sit down &
talk to me if I were with you. I love you & am not satisfied with <u>thinking</u>
you are well & happy. I must <u>know</u> it—<u>know it every month</u>. I will not
write <u>two</u> letters to get one of yours & I will not go home untill I find you are
glad to see me. & I will not believe you want very much to see me when you
let month after month pass without putting pen to paper. I do not feel angry
but I thought I would write the exact feelings of my heart & leave you to act
upon them. I am heartily tired of this style of writing. Look back to every
letter you have received from me since I have been a widow & see if they are
not all filled with entreaty—this is not. But after this if I do not hear from
you once a year I will not complain. Here I will draw a line & resolve I will
never again say "Sister write oftener" or anything that looks like it.

How often since I received your letter have I visited you in fancy both
sleeping & waking I see you blessed with competence, good health, fine
children & an affectionate husband. I am at ease about you & have only
to wish that the day may be far distant when you shall be separated. I
ardently wish that Mr Poor may live many years to enjoy the fruits of his
labour. I intend to have my portrait painted. Not that I think it will be such
a pretty picture but I wish you to have it, as I am so little with you.

I am still in Plymouth Academy & think I shall stay here. I have enough
for my wants & know not that I could better myself by change. I am more

healthy here than I have been in many years. The water is excellent for low country & I am 50 miles nearer the mountains than formerly. That I think must be an advantage. I have been sick only a fortnight & then I was very sick. But that is nothing to the three months & six months attacks of former years. But enough of this. I ought always to give you the bright side, & do try to—but somehow today I have been unfortunate, & must have got up in a grumbling humor. But I am very happy having a knack of believing that all things are for the best, I soon reconcile myself to the evils of life & please myself with thinking that there will some good result from the greatest misfortunes. I must go & put this in the office. Love to all friends.

Farewell Your own Dear sister

LETTER 8

From Huntington Library, HM 58154. From North Carolina to Betsey. Tamsen is 32. When I first saw this letter, it was ripped, a half page gone, parts stuck to each other with red sealing wax. Fold lines were sewed together with white thread. Somebody in the Poor or Donner family carefully tried to preserve it. The Huntington has done a remarkable job of restoring it, though it's still incomplete.

Camden April 21st 1833

My dear sister

Several weeks ago I was made glad by the receipt of a letter from you & though you are never particular & always write too little I gain much pleasure by hearing from you. The fear that you were dead followed me & came between me & enjoyment during the day & my dreams were but pictures of your wretchedness. At one time I would wade through mud in darkness & never find you at another would see you with a pale face & wretched dress wasting with sickness in a most miserable apartment. I would wake & find it a dream but still a fear that it was portentous would in spite of reason, hover round me. But you are well & happy & knowing that I am not unhappy. Yes, my dearest sister, my enjoyment is blended with yours.

I have stopped & thought & hardly know whether it will be for your happiness or not to know that I calculate upon visiting you this fall. But you must make allowance for the uncertainties of life. If nothing happens to prevent I shall start for the north by the first of August. I am undetermined whether I go by steam or packet & therefore cannot tell you how long it will take me. I shall stay until the middle of November—shall visit Wm & Mr Greenleafs family. Now do not prepare disappointment for yourself, for three months with all its changes has to pass by. But I have engaged a school for that time & have laid by money for my expenses, & I see nothing but a suit against my husbands estate that can prevent me & I think I can suspend that until my return. I long to see you all.

You speak of my return. I should be as happy to live with you as you would be to have me, I assure you. But you know that I cannot be burden-some to my friends & that the north is crowded with schools that my utmost exertions when there before were only sufficient to maintain one. That I was compelled to be separated from you, if not at so great a distance. And now I have an opportunity to supply all my wants & have only the care of 15 scholars. With them I can feed & clothe myself & lay up money enough to visit you once in a while. Then is it not better for me to stay? With you I will leave [hole in paper, the decision?] if you think I can support myself at the [hole] I will bid adieu to Carolina to return no more.

I have written to Wm & made the same proposal. Ask him his mind & let me know immediately for I must return here if I do not bring my affairs to a close before I leave & I shall leave them unsettled if I go home only for a visit.

My health is tolerable—an ague once in a while tells me I am mortal. Be of good cheer, "all the days of my appointed time shall I live until my change comes."

Where are Elizabeth & Susan Wheelwright—Martha Davis Abigail Knox John March Mrs Jane Greenleaf (she promised to write but has not, please to give her my direction & respects.) Mary Poor Harriet & Sarah Ann? My love to all and everybody.

Tell your husband I knit him a mighty pretty pair of thread socks & gave them to Mr Barnard, that I have begun him another pair & have got thread to knit him two pair more. I have a moleskin purse drying for him & some of our fashioned fringe for you. I have laid up some stockings for you.

How is father? Has he obtained a pension? My respects to him. Tell him, life lasting, I shall soon see him. O how soon three months will roll away. But yet be not too certain. Think how often I have thought of going home.

Everything around is in bloom. The white bloom of the dog & a slug-wood tree, the jessamine & mayberry & many others perfume the air & nature seems to exert every power to appear beautiful.

Brush every tear from your eyes wipe [hole]
from your cheek & chas[incomplete]

[Rest of page ripped off, bottom half]

LETTER 9

From Huntington Library, HM 58155. From North Carolina. The envelope says Camden Court House, July the 24th, 1833. This was written three months after her last letter to Betsey. Tamsen is 32. Note that she writes that Betsey addresses her as Tamzene.

Camden Co July 20th

My dear sister

I received the scrap you sent me & read it over again to see if I could not make more of it: but twenty lines it was & with all my ingenuity I could not make myself believe that it was a well filled sheet. But sister, I will do as you like to be done by. See how close my lines are together, how small my hand, & how many words I put in one line: & say does it not please you? & will you not smile to see my name at the last end of the third page? Well so should I like to have you write—so pleased should I be? & so would I smile at seeing no blank space in your letter. But you cannot love me as I do you for there is not so much that is estimable about me; you cannot value a letter as I do for you are not a stranger, you cannot realize the delight I feel at the very sight of "Mrs Tamzene Dozier" with Newburyport postmark. And may you never know, for to feel it must be purchased at too dear a rate.

Betsey I hate to tell you, but I must, that I shall not see you this fall. I thought about it, intended to do it, but dreaded to do it & gave it up. I desire to see you more than words can tell but there are so many unpleasant things connected with it that I have concluded to defer it a little longer. My health is excellent for the season & my spirits remarkably good. I am on the whole very happy.

I have moved about five miles from the Creek Bridge & as I cannot introduce you personally to my new associates I will give you a particular description of them. Mr Sash our lord and master is a middle aged man & in very easy circumstances talkative & to me quite obliging. Mrs Sash is a delightful woman woman [sic] who has long been an intimate favorite with me. She is all heart. She says, she wants to see you, sends her love, & says tell her to come while the damsons, grapes, peaches, apples, and cider are in prime. O you would love her I know. They have six children quite interesting. Mr Shaw a baptist clergyman boards with us. He is a Yankee & a man who for many years has been one of my friends. He is one of the most pleasant men in a family that I ever saw. So on the whole I must be one of the most ungrateful persons living if I were not happy. My school is near & pleasant. So much for myself.

And now for your family How is father is he with you? How is Mr Poor did he settle that Breakwater business to his advantage Where is John & whom did he marry. Have Mary & Harriet no sort of word to send when you write. When does Sarah Ann go to school. And tell me everything & anything. How's little Wm. Has he learned my name. Kiss him & tell him I will come & see him. What do you mean to name your little girl. May they live to be a comfort to you.

John still lives in Tyrrel & is well. I really wish you were all here. We could be so happy in this delightful climate. How my acquaintances at the South diminish. How are Uncle Wheelwright & families Martha Davis Mrs Brockways Abigail Knox Mr Withington. Miss Greenleaf &c. When you write do you take my letter & see if I ask any questions? Sometimes I ask the same thing a time or two, & get no answer at last. The sun is just setting & I promised the ladies I would walk out & meet them I will finish tomorrow morning.

Tis morning & nature is lovely indeed. I rise very early & I cannot
describe my feelings on viewing the level dewy southern landscape. It seems
as if my feelings struggle for vent & rushing to my pen are lost for want of
words in which to clothe them. Why was I made with eye & heart to enjoy
all these delights? Because my maker consulted my happiness. He fills me to
overflow. I gaze at the beauties around me & a mass of reflections pour upon
me that I cannot arrange or embody. O could I make you understand. You
can for you have gazed in speechless ecstasy at the moonlight scene, when to
have spoken would have broken the charm.

Sometimes I think I am very happily constituted. For the beauties of
creation are open to me in a striking degree & I do think that I understand &
relish the countless pleasures of retirement. But then I am so deficient in good
feeling that I am a great loser. Could I possess that mild, angel like temperament how many bitter moments it would save me.

Today commences four days meeting at the Creek; there will be a world
of people & preaching will be in the grove. I shall go tomorrow & next day
perhaps. Mr Shaw says give my love to your sister. I saw Spence Hall & wife
who inquire for you. Caroline Spruil asks for you likewise.

To overcome all unamiable feelings—to participate in the joys & sufferings
of others,—to trace every incident in life to a Supreme power & realize that it
is also the expression of goodness. To have an abiding sense that a being who
knows what is best & loves me guides the most minute concerns of my life. I
say to know & feel & do all this, is the darling wish of my heart. This will
reconcile me to bereavement—to absence from you & to disappointment in
my shortsighted plans. And now I must leave you again, and though I would
cause a feeling of sadness or anxiety to come over you Yet I must say farewell.

T.E. Dozier

LETTER 10

From Huntington Library, HM 58156. Written to Betsey from North Carolina.
Tamsen is 34. The letter is in very poor condition, with a chip of paper missing.

Camden April 14th 1836

My dear sister

I am now visiting in Camden & am at Ann Dozier's (now Mrs Grandy). I saw Mrs Marchant yesterday & several of my Camden friends who inquired for you. Left Tyrrel last week. I rather think you never will have a brother-in-law. Matters have been settled [in?] rather an unexpected way. I hope for the best.

I am in excellent health & expect to take a school the lst of May. I know not exactly where but when I determine I will let you know. Think not I am unhappy. Far from it. I realise that on me heaven has been lavish of its blessings.

Tell Wm when you write to him that I cannot tell where he is as I have lost his direction. Here I must stay 3 months longer & it may be then I will go west.

Love to all. You will excuse my short letter—as I am visiting & do not like to be impolite.

Your sister
T E Dozier

.

LETTER 11

From Huntington Library, HM 58157. To Betsey from Camden, North Carolina. Tamsen is 34. Her reference to Mr Greenleaf's prophecy "fifteen years ago" about her teaching would have been in 1821, another indication that Tamsen went to Maine earlier than has been estimated and that letters 1 and 2 were written earlier. Her anticipated annual salary of $1,000.00 would have been remarkable at the time, especially for a woman..

Camden September 13 1836

Sister

I have delayed writing to you until I could give you some information where I shall be & what I shall do. Last week I received a letter from William dated

April 5th which has been to Tyrrel & Currituck & I know not where. It was by far the most affectionate letter I ever received from him. He says he would be not only very much disappointed but also very much hurt if a new school or a new place of abode kept me from him. Query. Did Wm ever invite me to his house on a visit? Would he now but from <u>self interest</u>. And will he think the favor was conferred by me or by himself when I leave a school worth $500 a year to take care of & educate his children. You say he says "he will take care of me." I am greatly obliged to his lordship & to gratify you both I will allow him to take care of me so long as I am necessary to him. But—I am abundantly able at present to take care of myself & to supply every necessary and unnecessary want. When bereft of husband & children & stripped of what he left behind, by the hand of the auctioneer [hole, bad?] health I had to struggle with my feelings—engage as a private instructor for a mere trifle & teach while I was unable to hold my head from the pillow. I say if <u>then</u> my brother had offered me a home (as Mr Poor did) I might not have accepted it, but I never should have forgotten it.

You may think I do not feel for Wm. Deeply do I feel for him & I know how he suffers. But I have not forgotten the cruel indifference of former days & that indifference was occasioned by a course of conduct praiseworthy in motive & honorable in its tendency & successful in its accomplishment. I never did receive a favor from him yet.

My school never was as good as it is present & I believe were I to stay I might make it worth $1000 a year. This day it is worth $600 & was every week improving until I said I was going away. But I asked my heart, what I ought to do & when the question was settled there & I had communicated my determination all was done & all moves easily. I cannot leave until about the last day of October as my term does not close & I cannot collect until then. O how painful it is to think of leaving forever, friends endeared to me by reciprocal kindnesses, by long acquaintance & similarity of sentiment. I wish Jane had my school. Mr Greenleaf's prophecy has been verified. Fifteen years ago, he said, my plan of instruction would one day be found to be superior to the old one. My school is visited by the strangers that pass & the visitors for miles around and since the people have become convinced of its excellence they are as extravagant in their praises as the multitudes [are apt to be?] If I should only believe what they tell me I should think that since the days of Solomon none like unto me has arisen. But, somehow, I cannot believe they mean all they say. This is a charming season, so calm, so mild & the wood filled with wild flowers. & grape whose rich foliage climbs from branch to branch & from tree to tree & beautifying all with its rich chest

[letter ends without signature]

LETTER 12

From Huntington Library, HOU 10. A fragment. This letter was ripped in half horizontally. It is a double page—four pages—written on three sides with partial address on back side. Tamsen, 35, has moved to Illinois to care for and teach her brother's children, and is asking Betsey to send items she needs to set up housekeeping.

Waverly Morgan Co Feb 24th 1837

My dear sister,

Two months ago brother wrote you & as we have not heard from you I presume you have not received our letter. I know not where to begin or how to write. I am here & well—have a plenty to do & plenty to eat, this ought to satisfy me. I wish you were here. Mr Poor would find it pleasant as he could make excellent bargains. I have expected him all winter.

This country affords every flattering prospect to new beginner & were I young I would get here by some means—as it is I don't care much where I am. I have found the world on my side here
[next page]
1 mahogany bureau a dining table with end tables. Doz chairs finished except putting together a plain straw bonnet & if there is anything left put in unbleached cotton cloth. The bureau & tables I should like entirely plain of mahogany the chairs stool bottomed. Put the bonnet & chairs in the bureau drawers & get some cotton wadding & line the boxes to defend the furniture

it will be useful to me. & if you can spare a bed that will be acceptable to me & put it into the table & the looking glass grandmother gave me into the bed. The boxes I should like of clear pine as there is none in this country & we can use it in finishing I forgot a bedstead till now if you can find some cheap yet neat posts (low) & headboard send them. Mr Poor will please to put them up as dry goods are put up when imported & direct them to William Eustis, Waverly Illinois Care of Joshua Chiever Alt[on?] Ill. George Clark & [illegible] Boston I

[second page ends here]

[third page. Different handwriting. From Frances Eustis, her niece, brother William's oldest daughter.]

Dear Aunt

I have an opportunity of writeing [sic] you. We are all well. Aunt Dozier, and Aunt Hariet are getting ready to recieve [sic] company. We give them stools to sit on.

Frances has written so far & intended to fill the page but company came in & neither she nor I can do it. Miss Winslow says be sure and remember me to your father & sister.

Farewell my sister.

[envelope—fourth page—is addressed Apple Creek, Feb 27th—the rest is ripped]

LETTER 13

From Huntington Library, HOU 11. From Illinois to Betsey. Tamsen is 36. Joseph Dozier was Tully's father, Tamsen's first father-in-law. Note regarding the fever cake in her side: "When persons have fever and ague for a long time a hard cake forms above the edge of the ribs on the left side, as large as a plate, this is commonly called an ague cake, and is known to be the result of the hardening and enlargement of the spleen, situated on that side of the body." W. W. Hall, *Health at Home, or Hall's Family Doctor* (Hartford CT: James Betts, 1876), 115.

Sugar Creek Jan 16th 1838

My dear sister,

I have waited with no little impatience for a letter from you. Every time I
have seen or heard from brother I have to obtain the wished intelligence &
for a month I have sent twice a week to the Sugar Creek post office in vain
I expect to see Wm here tomorrow & shall put in a word or two after his visit.

Since I last wrote you I have heard of the death of Jos. Dozier & many more
of my Southern friends. My desire to return to them weakens as I become interested in this country. Think you that my wandering feet will rest this side the
grave? My health is constantly improving. Fatigue & constant employment
have produced a salutary effect. The fever cake in my side has lost 3/4ths its
size & I sometimes think my constitution will triumph over disease. My school
has been more difficult than I have been accustomed to but I believe I have
given satisfaction. In March I shall return to brother's to continue there until
he finds a wife. His children seem delighted with the thought of my returning
to them. For myself I have no large expectations & therefore shall be in little
danger of being disappointed I was sorry I wrote to you as I did I am glad I
came here. Had I not a narrow house would have been my home. The furniture
you sent I did not see until two weeks ago as I do not go to brothers, you know.
Our children are very interesting & well worthy our love—they speak often
of you & wish much to know more about your babe. Did you think I took
so little interest in it as that you could anticipate no questions. Oh! my sister
how many thousand inquiries would I gladly make about you & yours. I was
much pleased with the furniture bonnet &c. & Mr Poor has my thanks The
overplus I will send by Mr Greenleaf when he goes back. Has Mr Poor given up
the thought of coming to see us? Has Mr Kinny relinquished his plan. If so, I
am sorry. Mr Greenleaf is our neighbor. He left my boarding house this morning in fine health & spirits. He has purchased a delightful place. Is very much
beloved & has a prospect of doing good. Take pains to let his mother hear from
him. I did not think of writing this morning or perhaps he would have sent
some word. He intends to return in the course of the year. If Wm should marry
& I can afford it I shall see you then but do not calculate upon it.

Wm has raised an immense crop hundred bushels wheat do. oats & one thousand bushels corn & hired but 12 days labor. I have learned to spin & have spun the stocking yarn for Wm's family. Also I make vests, pantaloons & short jacket. I have knit 15 pair of stockings & as many pr socks since June & am about to learn to weave. So you see how smart we western folks are. We suckers think we know as much as the Yankees. For you must know I am not called yankee here; but a Southerner. Here many of our Eastern people think they will come & bear rule, setting a pattern of good manners & fine living—they really appear ridiculous & it makes me sorry for them.

Bring up your children with enlarged ideas & teach them better sense than to say "We are the people."

And now my dear sister, I wish I could look into your heart & find out why you are so guarded in your expressions. Instead of that easy free manner that once marked your communications, you are as systematick as though you were giving in evidence. Is it because we are so much separated that you are beginning to feel estranged or do you really feel unwilling to trust your pen for fear it shall go wrong.

On one subject I was silent or nearly so. Twas not want of confidence but delicacy of feeling that kept me silent & not until you suspected Mr [Mc-Clure?] of unhandsome conduct did I speak. I do not feel sorry for the course I pursued & shall always respect the man. He has made another unsuccessful attempt in the matrimonial line. You need not fear having a brother-in-law, for I know not a man old enough for me in the county. Tell Sarah Ann there are many here for her & she may have her choice if she will come out. Where are Mary & Harriet? How are father & Mr Poor? Tell me something about the children.

To say that I have any particular source of anxiety or cause of unhappiness I cannot. To say that I have any particular pleasure I cannot. Life moves on as smoothly & quietly as a summer stream Has Wm recovered of his deafness? Try that salt & water. Is Jane Brockway well? She could get a good school here but nothing like the southern one I offered her. On the prairie grows a fragrant flower shaped like an Indian mockasin & bearing that name. A beautiful white spotted with pink The rich luxuriant foliage of the woodland the abundance of wild fruit & the extended prairie carpeted with verdure & bespotted with an endless number & an immense variety of blossoms feasted my eye during the summer. And now the lofty arch of heaven, dressing itself at sunset in such "glorious apparreling" produces a feeling of amazement & delight. I stop, I gaze & am awestruck. Winter has been mild. Snow has not been an inch deep as yet & I walk to school more than a mile in the open prairie & have lost but two day. I will wait till tomorrow. I may see brother.

[Next sentence is different handwriting] *Sarahan I am candidate for matrimony.*

J. S. [Coulter?]

Feb 3rd

All well. Have not seen Wm yet. Shall return to his house in four weeks. Mr Greenleaf well. First snow day before yesterday about four inches. Miss Winslow gone to Wavelry [sic, Waverly] to live with her brother.

[Address on envelope—folded over paper—says]

Sugar Creek
Illi 5 Feb
Mrs Jonathan E. Poor
Newburyport Mafs.

LETTER 14

From Huntington Library, HOU 12. To Betsy from Springfield, Illinois. Tamsen is 38. Seven months earlier, on May 24, 1839, she married George Donner. She was 37 and he was about 52, with eight children from his two previous marriages. Only Elitha and Leanna, the two daughters of his second marriage, were still at home. At the time of this letter Elitha is 7, Leanna is 5, and Tamsen is three months pregnant (with Frances).

Springfield Sangamo Co Jan 12 1840

My dear sister

Your long expected letter at length came to hand. Shall I tell you I was glad
to hear from you? You seem to be so cheerful that I hardly have room to
wish for you here: yet were Mr Poor here with his capacity to "get & keep"
I should heartily rejoice. Would he but come & see. A man that can keep
from starving in Newburyport cannot help getting rich in Ill. Is not father's
health remarkable. Tell your little girls that mine are sitting, the one of them
cracking wallnuts, & the other marking on a slate & would be glad indeed
to see them. Mary had better marry & come along. Mr Donner would soon
find business for her husband & my house should be a home for her until
she could be better suited. Tell Sarah Ann there is but one single girl in our
neighborhood & lots & lots of men. Jane Maria I should think was out of
her element. Where are Betsy & Abigail. How does Harriet & her family get
along, Enoch, John, where are they.

It may be that you may never visit me & I will endeavor to give you some
idea of my situation. husband & I live two miles from the capital on a farm
containing 80 acres. 60 of which is under fence & in cultivation the remainder fenced & woodland. Our house is story & half, two rooms below a passage through & three above. We have an excellent well of water, an orchard
of young apples peaches pear trees coming on. Have Jackasses, horses, cows,
pigs, geese, turkeys, hens. Mr Donner has another farm of 160 acres 1 1/4
miles distant from the one we live on 80 acres of which is woodland. Cows
sell at 16 to 20 dol the summer feed cost nothing. They graze on the prairie
& corn sells at 25 cts per bushel. We sell our milk at 5 cts per quart at this
time by the quantity at the door. Eggs are 25 cts a doz. Butter brings 20 cts.
lb half the year. My husband hauls two loads of wood a day to town for
which he gets $4.50 cts & gets it cut for .62 1/2 cts. You see there are sources
of income. Bees do well here on the wildflowers. I find my husband a kind
friend who does all in his power to promote my happiness & I have as fair a
prospect for a pleasant old age as anyone. Mr Donner was born at the south,
in N. Carolina, at eighteen he went to Kentucky, thence to Indianna then to

Ill. & a few years ago to Texas. But his movings, he says, are over: he finds no place so much to his mind as this.

Wm was here a few weeks ago & took Frances [Tamsen's niece] home. They are all in good health. One or the other of his girls have been with me ever since I was married. They speak often of Aunt Betsey & her family Wm is building up quite a settlement around him & in a few years he will be finely situated. He lives 22 miles from me. It is very convenient for him to come to Springfield to market & to see his sister. He is as good as the bank, highly respected but an amusing droll sort of man. I should not mind his not writing to me one bit. If it would help you out of trouble or into any improvement he would write if he were hungry before he would eat but he has so much corn, oats, turnips &c. to see to that he unloads his waggon before he comes in to see me when I go to see him. Mr Greenleaf is living very snugly & both are very much respected. But I do not hear often from him.

My husband says there are many opportunities for good bargains. That we are well & are glad of it & if you are fond of rabbits he wishes you would come & kill them to keep them from barking his apple trees. Come & he will go with you to hear the members speak as the Legislature meets at Springfield.

I will close for fear I may have a wish to send to the office but I hope to fill this page. How is little Wms health? I expect you are all but buried in snow as we have more than we have had in many years. Our prospect for wheat on the ensuing years is flattering. We are building an elegant stone state house 180 feet long & 150 feet wide. A railroad is in progress from Meredosia on the Ill to Springfield that will open a ready communication between Springfield & St Louis.

And now my sister what more can I say. The time is short, it looks darkish like the approach of night & I have been in the house all day. I will send my love to my friends, forgiveness to my foes, & my particular regards to your husband & the rest of the family. My respects & kind remembrance to our father.

Your sister

Direct to "Mrs George Donner Springfield Sangamo County Ill"

From Huntington Library, H M 58158. From Springfield, Illinois, to Betsey. Tamsen is 40. Her daughter Frances was born July 8, 1840. Her daughter Georgeann, later known as Georgia Ann, was born December 4, 1841. It appears that she signs this letter Tamzine as the i is firmly dotted. However, there are ink smears nearby, so it's most likely Tamzene.

City of Springfield Sangamo Co April 3rd 1842

My dearest sister,

After so long a silence I hardly know where to begin or what to say. My last letter to you was written after the birth of "Frances Eustis" & to it I received no answer. I know not that it reached you. To give you the outlines of my fortune from that time on is all I can do.

My health is excellent & my spirits good. I am as happy as I can reasonably expect in this changing world. Things have turned round very much to my satisfaction. I have quit keeping school. My husband's brother has removed from the farm, Mother died about three weeks ago & father has gone to spend the summer with one of his sons. My husband is kind to me. The security money that embarrassed us we have nearly paid & we have a plenty around us to make us comfortable. Our neighbors call us rich & we feel that few are better off than we are. Indeed my dear sister was your family near so that I could visit & see you occasionally I should have all my large wishes gratified.

We have another daughter 4 months old today. We call her Georgeann. Both are healthy. Frances begins to talk—has blue eyes, fair skin & red cheeks, light curly hair & is as thick as she is long. Never was sick but two days in her life & lives on bread & milk. Georgeann has black eyes & hair, dark skin, & never knew pain that I know of. She lies in her cradle beside me in a sound sleep.

Everything is cheap here. Butter 8cts, eggs 4cts doz. Hens doll. a doz. Bacon 3 cts. Superfine flour $2 hundred weight. We shall milk 5 cows this summer. They feed on the prairies & come home without trouble to their calves every night. Stock is no expense except in winter.

Last week the place looked like a garden. About 50 peach trees were in bloom besides several pear & cherry trees. The gooseberry bushes & wild plum were crowded with bloom & the sweet briar perfumed the air. Never in March was there such a sight on this farm. The apple trees are now quite covered with blossom. The bees are humming in the flowers & I am writing by an open window.

Tell Wm his Uncle George thinks as much of a horse as he does. He has little horses & big ones & mules & jackasses & if he will come he will let him ride them. Is Mary married? She had better come out here. Mr Donner sold a likely mare last week for $50 & takes labor in pay. This is the country for the industrious poor man. The railroad comes within three miles of us & Springfield improves rapidly notwithstanding the pressure for money. Do you suffer with the rest.

Wm is doing well, improving his place & making things comfortable around him. His wife is a pleasant woman & suits him exactly. Elizabeth is to [hole, be married?] in the fall to John Bargar Frances was [hole, here?] last fall seven weeks. The two boys are serviceable in the field. Charles, his babe, grows finely. He comes to market every five or six weeks & stays all night with us. Mr Greenleaf has a fine garden & lives very snugly, is much respected, & I doubt not will make a good living.

May 2nd

So far I wrote & put off finishing my letter until I came back from Wms. Week before last Mrs & Miss Eastman visited me from the city & told me Mrs Greenleaf has gone east to visit her friends. You no doubt will see her.

I found Wm well & how his eyes sparkled when he saw us. but he did not <u>say</u> he was glad. He has a fine orchard coming on & whereas was an unvaried prairie the peach & the cherry tree blooms. His prospect for making more than a living is greater, he says, than it has been since he has been here. He says he wrote to you last fall. Did you get his letter? On the whole Wm is doing <u>very</u> well. He comes to market about once a month & stays with us all night quite pleasant & convenient. We live so near town that we know exactly when to send to market to get a good price. I wish you could step in. Leanna (my step daughter) is churning & says, "Mother, write that Frances has white curly hair." Mr Donner & she think she is quite handsome, but I know she is quite in the way, for I must hold the inkstand in one hand to prevent her spilling the ink & she is pulling my papers & catching hold of my pen. I just told her to send Aunt a kiss & she kissed the spot where I now write. How does Father get along. I wish Mr Poor would come out here. He would like Mr Donner I know & how quick I would put on the teakettle! My sister I write in excellent spirits. I am as happy as anybody. Give my love to everybody.

[Written on top of third page which folds to make the envelope]
Fare you well, my dearest sister, all the warm feelings of my soul are stirred up as I write that sincere & heartfelt wish. God, Almighty God bless you. Fare you well.

Tamzine [or Tamzene] Donner
Mr Donner sends his love to you also.

[Written upside down on the bottom of third page]
May 11th So my letter is here yet. We have had a cold spell & almost all the peaches are killed.

LETTER 16

From Huntington Library, HOU 13. Tamsen is 44 and on the Oregan and California Trail. She writes Betsey from Independence, Missouri, their "jumping off" place. This letter has been reprinted frequently with minor variations. This is the original. The 7000 wagons Tamsen mentions was an error; probably she meant to write 700.

Independence, Mo, May 11th, 1846

My dear sister

I commenced writing to you some months ago but the letter was laid aside to be finished the next day & was never touched. A nice sheet of pink letter

paper was taken out & has got so much soiled that it cannot be written upon
& now in the midst of preparation for starting across the mountains I am
seated on the grass in the midst of the tent to say a few words to my dearest
only sister. One would suppose that I loved her but little or I should have not
neglected her so long. but I have heard from you by Mr Greenleaf & every
month have intended to write. My three daughters are round me one at my
side trying to sew Georgeanna fixing herself up in an old indiarubber cap
& Eliza Poor knocking on my paper & asking me ever so many questions.
They often talk to me of Aunty Poor. I can give you no idea of the hurry of
this place at this time. It is supposed there will be 7000 wagons start from
this place, this season. We go to California, to the bay of Francisco. It is a
four months trip. We have three waggons furnished with food & clothing
&c. drawn by three yoke of oxen each. We take cows along & milk them &
have some butter though not as much as we would like. I am willing to go
& have no doubt it will be an advantage to our children & to us. I came here
last evening & start tomorrow morning on the long journey. Wm's family
was well when I left Springfield a month ago. He will write to you soon as
he finds another home. He says he has received no answer to his two last letters, is about to start to Wisconsin as he considers Illinois unhealthy

Farewell, my sister, you shall hear
from me as soon as I have an opportun
ity, Love to Mr Poor, the children
& all friends. Farewell

T.E Donner

LETTER 17

The last letter was written along the Oregon and California Trail on June 16, 1846,
and sent back to Springfield, Illinois, where it was published in the *Sangamo Journal*
on July 23, less than five weeks after it was written. The heading read, "From the
California Company." Tamsen's daughter Eliza says that Allen Francis, the coeditor
of the paper, later sent her the original—if still in existence, its whereabouts are now

unknown. The letter has been widely reprinted in books from 1880 on, with minor variations of punctuation, spelling, and the number of wagons, 420 or 470.

Near the Junction of the North and South Platt, June 16, 1846.

My Old Friend:

We are now on the Platte, 200 miles from Fort Larimee. Our journey, so far, has been pleasant. The roads have been good, and food plentiful. The water for part of the way has been indifferent—but at no time have our cattle suffered for it. Wood is now very scarce, but "Buffalo chips" are excellent—they kindle quickly and retain heat surprisingly. We had this morning Buffalo steaks broiled upon them that had the same flavor they would have had upon hickory coals.

We feel no fear of Indians. Our cattle graze quietly around our encampment unmolested. Two or three men will go hunting twenty miles from camp;—and last night two of our men lay out in the wilderness rather than ride their horses after a hard chase. Indeed, if I do not experience something far worse than I have yet done, I shall say the trouble is all in getting started.

Our waggons have not needed much repair, but I cannot yet tell in what respects they could be improved. Certain it is, they can not be too strong. Our preparations for the journey might have been in some respects bettered. Bread has been the principal article of food in our camp. We laid in 150 lbs. of flour and 75 lbs. of meat for each individual, and I fear bread will be scarce. Meat is abundant. Rice and beans are good articles on the road— cornmeal, too, is very acceptable. Linsey dresses are the most suitable for children. Indeed if I had one it would be acceptable. There is so cool a breeze at all times on the plains that the sun does not feel so hot as one would suppose.

We are now 450 miles from Independence. Our route at first was rough and through a timbered country which appeared to be fertile. After striking the prairie we found a first-rate road, and the only difficulty we had has been in crossing the creeks. In that, however, there has been no danger.

I never could have believed we could have travelled so far with so little difficulty. The prairie between the Blue and Platte rivers is beautiful beyond description. Never have I seen so varied a country—so suitable for cultivation. Everything was new and pleasing. The Indians frequently come to see us, and the chiefs of a tribe breakfasted at our tent this morning. All are so friendly that I can not help feeling sympathy and friendship for them. But on one sheet what can I say?

Since we have been on the Platte we have had the river on one side, and the ever varying mounds on the other—and have traveled through the Bottom lands from one to two miles wide with little or no timber. The soil is sandy, and last year, on account of the dry season, the emigrants found grass here scarce. Our cattle are in good order, and when proper care has been taken none have been lost. Our milch cows have been of great service—indeed. they have been of more advantage than our meat. We have plenty of butter and milk.

We are commanded by Capt. Russel—an amiable man. George Donner is himself yet. He crows in the morning, and shouts out "Chain up, boys! chain up!" with as much authority as though he was "something in particular." John Denton is still with us—we find him a useful man in camp. Hiram Miller and Noah James are in good health and doing well. We have of the best people in our company, and some, too, that are not so good.

Buffalo show themselves frequently. We have found the wild tulip, the primrose, the lupine, the ear-drop, the larkspur, and creeping hollyhock, and a beautiful flower resembling the blossom of the beech tree, but in bunches as large as a small sugar loaf, and of every variety of shade, to red and green. I botanize and read some, but cook a "heap" more.

There are 420 [470?] wagons, as far as we have heard, on the road between here and Oregon and California.

Give our love to all inquiring friends—God bless them.

Yours truly
Mrs George Donner

Eide, Ingvard Henry, ed., photographer. *Oregon Trail*. New York: Rand McNally, 1972.

Fisher, Vardis. *The Mothers*. New York: Vanguard, 1943.

Franzwa, Gregory M. *The Oregon Trail Revisited*. St. Louis: Patrice Press, 1972.

Gibbons, Boyd. "The Itch to Move West." *National Geographic*, vol. 170, no. 2 (August 1986): 146–77.

Goodyear, Dana. "What Happened at Alder Creek?" *The New Yorker* (April 24, 2006): 140–51.

Gregg, J. R. *History of the Oregon Trail, Santa Fe Trail, and Other Trails*. Portland: Binfords & Mort, 1955.

Hardesty, Donald L. *The Archaeology of the Donner Party*. Reno: University of Nevada Press, 1997.

Houghton, Eliza P. Donner. *The Expedition of the Donner Party and Its Tragic Fate*. Chicago: A. C. McClurg & Co., 1911; reprint, Los Angeles: Grafton, 1920, and Sacramento: Sierra District of California State Parks, 1996.

Houston, James. *Snow Mountain Passage*. New York: Alfred A. Knopf, 2001.

Johnson, Kristin, ed. *"Unfortunate Emigrants": Narratives of the Donner Party*. Logan: Utah State University Press, 1996. Also see Johnson's web site and blog, listed below.

Keithley, George. *The Donner Party*. New York: George Braziller, 1972.

Kelly, Charles. *Salt Desert Trails*. Salt Lake City: Western, 1930.

King, Joseph A. *Winter of Entrapment*. Revised edition. Walnut Creek CA: K & K, 1994.

Laurgaard, Rachel K. *Patty Reed's Doll: The Story of the Donner Party*. Caldwell ID: Caxton Printers, 1956; reprint, Davis CA: Tomato Enterprises, 1989.

Mattes, Merrill J. *The Great Platte River Road*. Lincoln: Nebraska State Historical Society, 1969.

McGlashan, C. F. *History of the Donner Party*. Stanford CA: Stanford University Press, 1940. Originally published 1880.

McLaughlin, Mark. *The Donner Party: Weathering the Storm.* Carnelian Bay CA: MicMac, 2006.

Morgan, Dale, ed. *Overland in 1846: Diaries and Letters of the Oregon Trail,* vols. 1 & 2. Georgetown CA: Talisman Press, 1963; reprint, Lincoln: University of Nebraska Press, 1999.

Murphy, Virginia Reed. *Across the Plains in the Donner Party.* Olympic Valley CA: Outbooks, 1977.

Nevada Emigrant Trail Marking Committee. *The Overland Emigrant Trail to California: A Guide to Trail Markers Placed in Western Nevada and the Sierra Nevada Mountains in California.* Reno: Nevada Historical Society, 1976.

Parkman, Francis. *The Oregon Trail.* New York: A. L. Burt, 1912. Originally published 1849.

Pigny, Joseph. *For Fear We Shall Perish.* New York: E. P. Dutton, 1961.

Place, Marian T. *Westward on the Oregon Trail.* New York: American Heritage, 1962.

Rarick, Ethan, *Desperate Passage: The Donner Party's Perilous Journey West.* New York: Oxford University Press, 2008.

Read, Piers Paul. *Alive.* New York: Avon Books, 1974.

Ross, Nancy Wilson. *Westward the Women.* New York: Alfred A. Knopf, 1944.

Ruth, Kent. *Touring the Old West.* New York: E. P. Dutton, 1971.

Schlissel, Lillian. *Women's Diaries of the Westward Journey.* New York: Schocken, 1982.

Sterling, Dorothy. *Lucretia Mott: Gentle Warrior.* New York: Doubleday, 1964.

Stewart, George R. *Ordeal by Hunger.* Boston: Houghton Mifflin, 1960.

———. *The California Trail.* New York: McGraw-Hill, 1962; reprint, Lincoln: University of Nebraska Press, 1983.

Teggart, Frederick J., ed. *Diary of Patrick Breen, One of the Donner Party.* Berkeley: University of California Press, 1910.

Thornton, J. Quinn. *Camp of Death: The Donner Party Mountain Camp 1846–47.* Silverthorne CA: Vistabooks, 1995.

Unruh, John D., Jr. *The Plains Across*. Urbana: University of Illinois Press, 1982.

Whitman, Ruth. *Tamsen Donner, a Woman's Journey*. Cambridge MA: Alice James, 1977.

Zauner, Phyllis. *Those Spirited Women of the Early West*. Sonoma CA: Zanel, 1989.

WEB SITES AND BLOGS

www.anthro.umt.edu/donner/team.htm: Donner Party Archaeology Project. Donner family camp archaeology research and a virtual trail hike.

www.donnerpartydiary.com: The Donner Party. Daily diary of the Donner Party's journey from original sources created by Donner Party enthusiast Daniel M. Rosen. Also includes locations, maps, links, and other interesting information.

www.nps.gov/cali: National Park Service, California. The site of the California National Historic Trail. If you're planning to retrace the California Trail, this site has an auto-tour route of each state, with museums, hiking trails, stories, photos, and more.

www.octa-trails.org: Oregon-California Trails Association (OCTA). OCTA preserves overland emigrant trails, provides classroom materials, and offers virtual trails.

www.thestormking.com: Mark McLaughlin's Web site. McLaughlin is a Sierra Nevada historian with a special interest in Sierra Nevada weather, particularly the winter of 1846.

www.utahcrossroads.org/DonnerParty: New Light on the Donner Party. Donner Party Historian Kristin Johnson's exhaustedly researched and frequently updated Web site. Also see Johnson's blog: http://donnerblog.blogspot.com.

In the Shadow of Memory
by Floyd Skloot

Secret Frequencies: A New York
Education
by John Skoyles

Phantom Limb
by Janet Sternburg

Yellowstone Autumn: A Season of
Discovery in a Wondrous Land
by W. D. Wetherell

To order or obtain more information on these or other University
of Nebraska Press titles, visit www.nebraskapress.unl.edu.